# Zebulon Pike, Thomas Jefferson, and the Opening of the American West

# Zebulon Pike, Thomas Jefferson, and the Opening of the American West

Edited by

MATTHEW L. HARRIS and JAY H. BUCKLEY

UNIVERSITY OF OKLAHOMA PRESS : NORMAN

Library of Congress Cataloging-in-Publication Data

Zebulon Pike, Thomas Jefferson, and the opening of the American West / edited by
Matthew L. Harris and Jay H. Buckley.
   p. cm.
 Includes bibliographical references and index.
 ISBN 978-0-8061-4243-2 (hardcover : alk. paper) 1. Pike, Zebulon Montgomery, 1779–
1813. 2. West (U.S.)—Discovery and exploration. 3. Explorers—West (U.S.)—History.
4. Jefferson, Thomas, 1743–1826. I. Harris, Matthew L. II. Buckley, Jay H.
 F592.Z43 2012
 978'.02—dc23

2011031062

Frontispiece: *Zebulon Montgomery Pike,* by Charles Willson Peale, from life, ca. 1808.
Courtesy of Independence National Historical Park.

The paper in this book meets the guidelines for permanence and durability of the
Committee on Production Guidelines for Book Longevity of the Council on Library
Resources, Inc. ∞

1 2 3 4 5 6 7 8 9 10

# Contents

# Illustrations

## FIGURES

## MAPS

# Acknowledgments

Zebulon Montgomery Pike's letters are scattered in collections through-out the United States. We are grateful to the numerous archives, reposi-tories, and libraries for allowing us to examine their rich collection of Pike materials. These include the National Archives and Records Ad-ministration in Washington, D.C.; the New-York Historical Society; the Denver Public Library; the Colorado Historical Society; the Pike Fam-ily Archives in Salisbury, Massachusetts; the Pike National Bicenten-nial Commission; the Colorado College Special Collections Archives; Harvey Hisgen and the Zebulon Pike National Historic Trail Associa-tion; and Roy E. Pike and the Pike Family Association of America. We also thank Matt Mayberry, Leah Davis Witherow, and Kelly Murphy of the Colorado Springs Pioneers Museum for their research assistance; Brian Q. Cannon and the Charles Redd Center for Western Studies at Brigham Young University and the Provost's Office at Colorado State University–Pueblo for research grants; students Julie H. Adams, Loren Smith, and Jeremiah Blaha for research assistance; and cartographers Brandon Plewe and Chris Maderia for crafting the maps.

We also appreciate the professionalism of the contributors of this volume: James P. Ronda, John Logan Allen, Jared Orsi, Leo E. Oliva, and William E. Foley. The Pikes Peak Library District deserves recogni-tion, too, for giving us permission to publish the papers that John Logan Allen and James Ronda gave in the spring of 2006 as part of the Library District's third annual Pikes Peak Regional History Symposium. Like-wise, we acknowledge Virgil Dean, editor of *Kansas History: A Journal of the Central Plains,* for granting permission to republish Leo Oliva's essay "Enemies and Friends: Zebulon Montgomery Pike and Facundo Melgares in the Competition for the Great Plains, 1806–1807," which was originally published in the spring of 2006. Our academic institutions have also been generous and supportive. Mark Gose, chair of the history department at Colorado State University–Pueblo, and Donald Harreld, chair of the history department at Brigham Young University, offered their encouragement.

We wish to thank the staff at the University of Oklahoma Press, especially Editor-in-Chief Charles Rankin and Managing Editor Steven Baker, for their keen judgment and good sense. Copyeditor Sally Bennett and the anonymous reviewers for the Press provided sound advice that made this a better book. Our wives, Courtney Harris and Becky Buckley, have been especially patient and supportive. This book is dedicated to them.

Matthew L. Harris and Jay H. Buckley

ZEBULON PIKE,
THOMAS JEFFERSON, AND THE
OPENING OF THE AMERICAN WEST

# Introduction

## ZEBULON MONTGOMERY PIKE

## IN AMERICAN MEMORY

*Matthew L. Harris*

The bicentennial commemoration of Zebulon Pike's journeys in the American West passed without much fanfare. Unlike the Lewis and Clark Bicentennial in 2004–2006, which overlapped with Pike's, there were no national conferences devoted to him, no movies made about his life, and no books published revisiting his story.[1] Except for a few museum exhibits and some local newspaper coverage in Colorado and New Mexico, the Pike Bicentennial was hardly a blip on anyone's radar. This is unfortunate, because Pike was one of the most significant explorers in the early republic, yet most Americans know little about him today. His accomplishments as an explorer, mapmaker, and soldier during the War of 1812 have been tainted by his connection to a shadowy conspiracy to wrest the Louisiana Territory from American control. Moreover, historians have dismissed him as a lost explorer or a spy, further contributing to his obscurity. But the truth is that Pike was a capable explorer with ambitions of advancing Thomas Jefferson's "empire of liberty" in the American West.[2] His two expeditions mapping and exploring the boundaries of the Louisiana Purchase marked the beginning of a long chain of commercial and political events that helped the United States secure the border with New Spain.

Pike's journals, first published in 1810, gave Americans their initial look at the southwestern borderlands. He wrote about the vast trading

3

opportunities between the Mississippi Valley communities and the New Mexican colonies, thus providing the impetus for the Santa Fe Trail.[3] He wrote about trade goods and trade routes; he discussed Spanish American and American Indian customs and cultures. He noted the climate and the region's abundant natural resources, including gold and silver. In addition, he published maps of the region, which provided Americans with their first glimpse of the geography of the Southwest—what Pike called the "vast plains" of the "sandy deserts." All told, Pike's writings provided an image of the Southwest that would be emblazoned in American memory for years to come.[4]

And yet, despite Pike's significance in promoting the region and his significance in mapping the West, he has, in the words of one historian, "slipped out of the American consciousness."[5] His connection to the Burr-Wilkinson conspiracy cast a cloud over his memory, obscuring his accomplishments as an important Jeffersonian explorer. Pike (the soldier and patriot) aligned himself with General James Wilkinson (the highest-ranking officer in the U.S. Army), who aligned himself with Aaron Burr (the former vice president of the United States). Still bitter over his loss to Thomas Jefferson in the presidential election of 1800 and disillusioned at the fallout from killing his arch nemesis Alexander Hamilton in an 1804 duel, Burr's future lay in the West. He therefore conspired with Wilkinson to detach the southwestern borderlands from the United States and form an independent empire, with him as president and Wilkinson in control of the army.[6]

Some historians believe that Pike's involvement in this shadowy conspiracy began when he was commissioned by Wilkinson to explore the southwestern boundary of the Louisiana Purchase, a territory whose western boundaries remained undefined after the United States purchased it in 1803. In his first expedition in 1805, he was instructed to explore the headwaters of the Mississippi River, gather information about American Indians in the region, and escort Osage captives back to their homelands.[7] In his second expedition in 1806—the one that got him lost and subsequently arrested—Pike's orders were to find the source of the Arkansas and Red rivers, establish peace with Native peoples in the region, and map and spy out the land with the purpose of providing Wilkinson with important military intelligence on Santa Fe and the

Spanish provinces in preparation for an upcoming American invasion of the region.[8]

To enhance the mission, Wilkinson—who was being paid by the Spanish as a double agent—notified Spanish authorities about Pike's plans.[9] For Wilkinson, this was the perfect opportunity to facilitate his young lieutenant's reconnaissance. The Spanish arrested Pike and his men, confiscated his papers, and escorted the group to Santa Fe and on to Chihuahua, where they "got," according to one historian, "a guided tour of the very Spanish territory" they had been "sent to spy out."[10] Although that part of the story remains contested, the aftermath is not. The Burr conspiracy unraveled in the winter of 1807 when Jefferson had Burr arrested and imprisoned. In a dramatic turn of events, Wilkinson turned on Burr by apprising Jefferson of Burr's role in the conspiracy.[11] The plot reached a climax when Wilkinson testified against Burr at trial, thus sparing himself from the humiliation that Burr experienced. In the meantime, the vice president was acquitted for lack of evidence, but the verdict did not repair Wilkinson's tarnished reputation, nor did it spare his young protégé, Lieutenant Pike, from the ire of angry newspaper editors.[12]

The affair had a profound impact on Pike's reputation. Even though government officials assured Pike that he would be exonerated from any wrongdoing (one government official said his "services [were] held in high esteem by the President of the [United States]"),[13] newspaper editors doubted his innocence. Consequently, they assailed him as "the beast of Santa Fe," "a parasite of Wilkinson," and "a second Benedict Arnold."[14] Pike did not help his cause, either. When the Spanish released him from custody in the spring of 1807, Pike continued to defend General Wilkinson. This led one newspaper, the *Natchez Weekly Chronicle*, to publish a scathing article on Pike during the summer of 1809: "A striking coincidence of opinion prevails among all parties in the United States relative to Wilkinson. Here where his atrocities were first ushered into light, and where the effects of them are still palpable and present, there are some who were concerned with—and others who were his dupes, who pretend not to credit the charges which have been exhibited against him. It can only be a pretense—a person might as well deny the light of the sun, as to deny the truths which are well known."[15]

Pike always maintained his innocence, but historians have challenged that assertion. They have vigorously debated whether he was an explorer or a spy—whether he knew about the Burr-Wilkinson conspiracy and was a willing participant or just a loyal foot soldier doing the bidding of a man whose plans were unknown to him.

One of the earliest mini-biographies of Pike, published in 1821, claimed that he was more than just a scientist and explorer—he was also a spy. In John Nile's "Biography of General Pike," General Wilkinson commissioned Pike to reconnoiter the Spanish outposts in the Louisiana interior. With the United States unable to resolve a longstanding boundary dispute with Spain, Nile wrote that war was imminent between the two countries. Pike embarked on a fact-finding mission to gather information about a country expected to wage war against the United States. His spying activities were under the auspices of national defense and not for the sinister motives to which he had become maligned. For Nile, Pike was a heroic explorer and a courageous soldier—a man who "displayed a degree of personal heroism and hardihood" in his adventures, someone who had "done honour" to himself and his country. He was not a traitor.[16]

Henry Whiting, another Pike biographer, agreed. In his 1845 "Life of Zebulon Montgomery Pike," Whiting extolled the virtues of Pike's character and noted that the lieutenant first learned about the "Burr conspiracy" when he read a Spanish newspaper after his arrest. Burr's actions, Whiting affirmed, made the Spanish suspicious of Pike's "movements on the Mexican frontier"; they saw him as a cog in Burr's "revolutionary scheme." Furthermore, they viewed Pike as an unwelcome intruder in their homeland. But he was not spying for Burr or Wilkinson when he was arrested by Spanish authorities, Whiting asserted. Instead, the ambitious young soldier was in the wrong place at the wrong time, a result of having been disoriented with the mountains and streams that had "confuse[d] his calculations." He was not in Spanish territory by any sinister design but rather "by mistake." Once that mistake became known, the Spanish released him and sent him home, where he received a hero's welcome. For Whiting, this not only was a befitting end to two remarkable expeditions but also marked the beginning of America's limitless trade opportunities in the region. With the publication of Pike's journals in 1810, he wrote, Americans now had the knowledge to make these trade opportunities a reality.[17]

Pike's reputation continued to soar throughout the nineteenth century, in part because of his untimely death during the War of 1812. When a mortar exploded in 1813, killing him and a dozen of his men, Pike became an instant hero. In the years following the war, he had some sixteen counties and towns named after him and several poems written about him. Moreover, he was the subject of various books published on the War of 1812. Such books as *The Glory of America* and *The Military Heroes of the War of 1812* praised him for his valor and courage on the battlefield.[18] In 1893, Charles Greely devoted a chapter to him in his book of important American explorers. "It should be recorded of his explorations," the author wrote, "that, taking into consideration [Pike's] small force, and almost inadequate means, no other man ever contributed to the geographical knowledge to that which the world owes to the heroic efforts and indomitable presence of Zebulon Montgomery Pike." Greely never mentioned Burr, Wilkinson, or the conspiracy.[19]

Two years later, in 1895, Pike's papers were published, providing further acclaim to the lieutenant's career. The editor, Elliot Coues, had already published a well-received account of the Lewis and Clark papers, and now he tried his hand with Pike. In the three-volume account titled *The Expeditions of Zebulon Montgomery Pike,* Coues played it safe and ignored the question of whether Pike was an explorer or a spy. Instead, he praised Pike, saying that his "luster is dimmed only in comparison with the incomparable story of Lewis and Clark."[20] The volumes, which were the first accessible accounts of Pike's life, were an immediate success. They became the go-to guide for understanding Pike's expeditions until Donald Jackson published his two-volume account of Pike in 1966.

In the twentieth century, Pike's reputation became a matter of intense debate by scholars. Scholars began to question his motives, his integrity, and most of all his association with General Wilkinson, a known rogue. What intensified the discussion was the discovery of Pike's "lost papers" in 1907—the ones that the Spanish had confiscated a century earlier when they arrested Pike near Santa Fe. For much of the nineteenth century, these papers were believed to hold the clue to Pike's connection to Wilkinson and Burr, but when they were discovered by historian Herbert Bolton in an obscure Mexican archive, they proved to be more of a bust than a blessing. The papers, which contained a series of maps and tables, revealed nothing about the conspiracy, nor did they shed light on Wilkinson's or Burr's motives.[21] But this did not prevent scholars from rendering judgments about Pike's guilt or innocence. They loaded their weapons anyway, taking dead aim at Pike and in the process infuriating some of Pike's most ardent supporters.

The first to strike was Isaac Cox, whose 1906 book, *The Early Exploration of Louisiana,* suggested that Pike's southwestern expedition was "designed to obtain information for the use of those arch conspirators [Wilkinson and Burr] in their invasion of Mexico." Cox argued that because Pike was a close associate of Wilkinson, it was hard to believe "that he was guilty of nothing more than a sincere friendship for the man who had given him his opportunity for advancement" or that "he was the unwitting agent" of Wilkinson's "in a certain filibustering scheme." For Cox, the evidence was overwhelming: Pike was a spy doing the work of a man he admired. "His own letters reveal this only too openly," Cox concluded.[22]

Cox's "guilty verdict" was further pronounced by the journalist Kyle Crichton, whose article entitled "Zeb Pike" was published in 1927 in *Scribner's Magazine.* This popular American magazine had a wide readership, which probably gave most Americans their first glimpse of a man whose only fame they knew lay in the Colorado peak that bore his name. Now they would have a different version of him. In Crichton's breezy account, Pike emerged as a traitor—a "highly unethical and untruthful explorer" who trotted into Spanish territory on purpose with the sole aim of spying on the Spanish. When he was arrested by the Spanish and told that he was in forbidden territory, Pike feigned innocence and told them they were mistaken. Crichton admitted that the evidence linking Pike to the Burr conspiracy may not have been conclusive, but for him the evidence did not get in the way of rendering a verdict. Pike's "own letters," Crichton surmised, "and his reports to General Wilkinson prove it despite the innocent air he adopts when referring to his surprise at finding himself on the Rio Grande when he thought he was on the Red River on American soil." This was ample proof for Crichton that "Pike was simply a cog in the [Burr-Wilkinson] machine."[23]

The Cox and Crichton accounts of Pike touched a raw nerve with Pike's supporters. Stephen Harding Hart and Archer Butler Hulbert, the editors of *The Southwestern Journals of Zebulon Pike, 1806–1807*, published in 1932, did not think he was a spy at all, either innocently or by some sinister design. In their introduction to the Pike journals, they wrote a blistering attack on Pike's critics. They were so indignant, noted one writer in his review of their work, that their vicious attacks on Cox and Crichton made them more of an "advocate than [a] historian."[24] They called Pike's detractors "ignorant critic[s]" and "low grade literary fortune hunters who have exploited sensationally Pike's 'treachery' and 'disloyalty' for gain," making "delightful historical nonsense out of Pike's 'hostile advance' on Santa Fe, or his 'military demonstration against New Mexico.'" They published Pike's journals, they declared, because they wanted to begin anew, to rid the scholarly world of "such rubbish" and set the record straight from that created by "sensational historians."[25]

What infuriated Hart and Hulbert was the evidence Cox and Crichton used to make their case. Critics such as Cox and Crichton imputed motives to Pike that were not borne out by the evidence, nor did they offer any proof that he knew he was part of a conspiratorial design to separate the southwestern borderlands from the United States. "If Pike's adventure in the Southwest," Hart and Hulbert speculated, "was intended to be what his critics claim . . . , Pike certainly would not have been chosen for the mission." There were other men, they opined, who had a better knowledge of New Mexico and the Spanish language that would have been more suitable in "spying out the land for Aaron Burr."[26]

The attacks on Pike and the rejoinder by his critics were advanced in articles and book chapters, but the first full biography of Pike was published in 1949. Reviewed favorably in academic journals, it was praised for being grounded in serious archival research.[27] The author, Eugene Hollon, saw Pike first and foremost as a "lost pathfinder," and that phrase served as the title of Hollon's book. When Spanish troops arrested Pike near the Rio Grande in 1807, his excursion into forbidden territory was a genuine mistake, a result of bad maps and a poor understanding of the region.[28]

It was therefore inconceivable to Hollon that Pike would have committed an act of treason, even despite his intense loyalty to General Wilkinson, a man with whom he was particularly close. Pike's years of public service and his sacrifice to the country furnished enough proof to reject such claims. "His great fault," Hollon averred, "lies in an unflinching faith in Wilkinson."[29] With this statement, Hollon was not deaf to the charges against Pike. He understood why some critics thought Pike was involved in the Wilkinson-Burr affair, but Hollon dismissed their claims when Pike's journeys were put in proper context. When "Wilkinson ordered Pike into the Southwest," Hollon wrote, "war was imminent between the United States and Spain." Pike was therefore "trying to get information about a likely foe. So Pike may have reasoned that the data Wilkinson wanted was to be used for a legitimate purpose, i.e., national defense."[30] This was the same argument that John Nile made in 1821, and it was the safest explanation for Hollon given what he considered to be a dearth of evidence about Pike's true motives.

Another writer, Donald Jackson, echoed similar remarks in 1965 when he wrote a popular article for *American Heritage Magazine* titled "The Question Is: How Lost Was Zebulon Pike?" Like Hollon, Jackson saw Pike as a lost explorer who had blundered into Spanish territory unwittingly. When Pike thought he discovered the headwaters of the Red River, in reality he was at least three hundred miles away, "high up" on the Arkansas River, Jackson noted. While lost in an ice-choked river canyon (today's Royal Gorge in Canyon City, Colorado), Pike and his men suffered hardships and depredations of every kind, from frostbite to hunger and fatigue. It was therefore disingenuous, Jackson postulated, to assert, as other writers had done, that Pike knew where he was going, because he never would have exposed himself or his men to those conditions if he was not lost.[31]

For Jackson, then, the burden of proof rested on Pike's critics. They had to show "that Pike—who travelled with defective maps and no true mental image of western geography—conducted an elaborate campaign to convince the Spanish that he was lost." They had to show that "Pike knew there was no Red River as far west as the Rockies, despite the information he had from [the mapmaker] Baron von Humboldt." They had to show that when Pike "and his men were freezing and starving in the Wet Mountain Valley he was engaging in deliberate subterfuge." And finally, they had to demonstrate that when Pike "was confronted by a Spanish officer and was told he was encamped on the west side of the Rio Grande, his plea of ignorance was a long-planned lie." For Jackson, they could not do it; it was an impossible task.[32]

Jackson advanced these themes again the following year, in 1966, when he edited and published a two-volume account of Pike's journals and papers. These were the fullest, richest, and most expansive set of primary documents ever published on Pike's life and times. This definitive edition includes journals, letters, government documents, and newspaper editorials relating to the lieutenant's two expeditions in the West. In the introduction, Jackson admitted what Hollon refused to admit: "[Pike] was a spy—and proud to be one."[33] Such forthrightness was tantalizing enough, but the teaser ends there. By "spy," Jackson meant that Pike's loyalties to General Wilkinson appeared to be "more boyish than sinister." There was no duplicity in Pike; he was not part of a conspiracy. Rather, Pike was a soldier who was sent to spy on the Spanish during "a sensitive time when war was possible" between the United States and Spain. For Jackson, Pike was guilty of a lot of things, including poor judgment and bad luck, but not treason.[34]

Jackson's writings were well written and well informed, but they did not put an end to the debate on whether Pike was an innocent explorer or a spy with greater ambitions. Just two years after Jackson's work was published, a prolific author of the American West, John Upton Terrell, offered the most provocative analysis of Pike's activities. In *Zebulon Pike: The Life and Times of an Adventurer,* he argued that it was implausible that Pike was just an explorer reconnoitering the Louisiana hinterlands. Pike left on his southwestern journey in mid-July, which meant that he could not have possibly made it to the Red River before the winter chill set in, because the weather patterns were "widely known in the east" and Pike would have known that it would have been too cold by the time he arrived at his destination that fall. For Terrell, the only conclusion to make was that Pike had no intention of seeking the genesis of any river. He had a bigger prize in mind; he wanted to "spy for either the United States Army or General Wilkinson and Aaron Burr, or perhaps for both."[35]

Terrell offered two additional points to support his case. First, he claimed the Red River was already known in the East, and for Pike to state that as one of his objectives made no sense. Second, Pike had only a small number of men on his journey, which is "proof" that he wanted to "commit depredations against Spanish outposts and settlements," in an attempt to start a war with New Spain. If Pike had succeeded, Terrell intoned, he would have fulfilled the wishes of General Wilkinson and Aaron Burr, who wanted to take the region by bloodshed. But Pike did not succeed, and Terrell could only conclude that from "almost every standpoint, the expedition was a failure. He drove no British trader from the North. He won no Indian allies for the United States." Additionally, in scientific affairs, "he accomplished almost nothing." In Terrell's judgment, Pike was a failure on all accounts.[36]

Terrell's book was the last full-length study published on Pike. It was not reviewed in any major academic journals, and it is hardly known among scholars today. But it is an important work, for it challenges Hollon's and Jackson's assertion that Pike was a "lost explorer." More broadly, it raises the possibility that Pike's reconnaissance was part of a larger mission to sever the southwestern borderlands from U.S. control. Finally, and most importantly, it raises the possibility that Pike was a willing participant in a treasonous act—that he knew what he was doing and for whom he was working. Thus, with these bold claims, Terrell moved beyond the earlier arguments that Cox and Crichton had made connecting Pike to the conspiracy.

In the final analysis, though (and as tantalizing as Terrell's allegations are), historians do not know enough about Pike's relationship with Wilkinson and Burr to assert with any reliability that he was doing their bidding. The evidence is simply too sketchy to proclaim his guilt. Indeed, there is much truth to historian Patricia Limerick's claim that "historical conspiracies are no easier to document than contemporary ones."[37] What we are left with, then, is Pike's own words, and he was quite emphatic about where he stood. He vehemently denied being a part of the "sinister designs of general Wilkinson," and he vigorously denounced

the idea that he had anything to do with "colonel Burr's conspiracies."
He learned about the conspiracy "for the first time," he said, when he
was in Spanish custody. Until more evidence surfaces, Pike deserves the
final word.[38]

. . .

In this volume, we have tried to move beyond the labels of "spy" and
"lost pathfinder" and offer a fresh perspective of Pike's life. We seek to
place Pike's life and times within a broader context and explain his significance as an explorer in the American West. Pike's story is a compel-
ling one. He was an empire builder, field scientist, mapmaker, explorer,
spy, and soldier. More important, he was a significant cog in the opening
of the American West. His two expeditions set in motion a pattern of
conquest and settlement that would forever alter the political, environmental, and geographic landscape of the region.

The chapters in this volume capture those changes. They explore Pike's
contributions to science and mapmaking, address his relationship with
Native peoples and Spanish officials, compare him to other Jeffersonian
explorers, discuss the impact of his expeditions on the environment, assess his relationship with General Wilkinson and his connection to the
Burr conspiracy, and, above all, evaluate his role as an empire builder
in the trans-Mississippi West. *Zebulon Pike, Thomas Jefferson, and the
Opening of the American West* begins with two chapters placing Pike
within a larger national context. Jay Buckley's chapter, "Pike as a Forgotten and Misunderstood Explorer," provides a rich and nuanced portrait
of Pike's life, discussing his family, experiences on the rugged frontier,
and rise in the military. Buckley also traces Pike's two expeditions in the
American West, demonstrating the hardships and travails that Pike and
his men experienced, in addition to exploring his relationship with Native peoples and his affection for James Wilkinson, Pike's commanding
officer.

The next chapter, "Pike and Empire," by the distinguished historian
James Ronda, argues that Pike was part of a long and distinguished tra-
dition of empire building that began during the American Revolution.
Ronda explains that Pike contributed significantly to a larger effort to

spread democracy across the American landscape, fulfilling Jefferson's vision of an "empire of liberty." For Jefferson, this empire would not be ruled by force or fear, nor would it seek imperialistic gains through compulsory means (as had empires of old). It would be characterized by a different mission: Americans, sharing a love for liberty and a respect for republican institutions, would be bound into the empire through a shared language, culture, and commitment to liberty.

Historical geographer John Logan Allen's chapter, "Pike and American Science," posits that Pike played a greater role in exploring the West than critics have acknowledged. Allen tells us that although Pike's maps contain many errors about the natural history of the region, they provided a general outline of the Southwest that other mapmakers, including William Clark, followed. Specifically, Pike published the first map of what became the Santa Fe Trail, and the information he provided later served as an important roadmap for the thousands of migrants who made their way west into the Kansas, New Mexico, and Texas territories. Finally, Allen dispels the idea that Pike knew he was on the Rio Grande in Spanish territory when he was captured by the Spanish in the spring of 1807. Pike was influenced by the German Baron Alexander von Humboldt's flawed map, which was nothing more than his conjecture of where the Rio Grande valley was.

Jay Buckley's chapter titled "Jeffersonian Explorers in the Trans-Mississippi West: Zebulon Pike in Perspective" situates Pike within a larger pantheon of Jeffersonian explorers. Buckley compares the expeditions that Thomas Jefferson and James Wilkinson commissioned to explore the western tributaries of the Mississippi River that were part of the Louisiana Purchase—the Missouri, Arkansas, and Red rivers. In addition to Pike, he examines the Lewis and Clark, Dunbar and Hunter, and Freeman and Custis expeditions and analyzes their objectives, logistics, Indian relations, scientific and cartographical contributions, publication efforts, and historical significance. Buckley reminds us that each of these men had ambitions of establishing Jefferson's empire of liberty in the West, of creating spaces where U.S. citizens could farm and till the land unencumbered by British, Spanish, or American Indian nations.

Jared Orsi provides a provocative new paradigm for understanding the early American republic and Jefferson's "empire of liberty." His

*Thomas Jefferson,* by Charles Willson Peale, from life, 1791–1792. Courtesy of Independence National Historical Park.

chapter, "An Empire and Ecology of Liberty," focuses on the ecosystems of the West, arguing that Pike's journey exploring the Louisiana hinterland allows one to reconstruct flows of energy and commodities in that region during a critical time in the nation's political and economic development. Orsi treats capitalism as a system that converts the energy of plants, animals, and minerals into marketable products, and he contends that the new American nation achieved political and economic preeminence in North America, in part, by capturing the stored energy of the West in profitable commodities. Budding merchants and ambitious entrepreneurs then directed these profitable commodities into a burgeoning North American and trans-Atlantic world economy, making the United States government the broker of this new and exciting material world. This was possible, Orsi writes, because of explorers such as Zebulon Pike, who blazed a trail mapping, exploring, and writing about their scientific observations of the region.

Leo Oliva examines the relationship between Pike and Facundo Melgares, the Spanish lieutenant who had a hand in capturing Pike near the Rio Grande. In "Enemies and Friends: Pike and Melgares in the Competition for the Great Plains," Oliva traces the expeditions that both men made in exploring the region and explains that they were part of a larger imperial effort to control the Great Plains—a region rich in importance to the national interest of the United States and New Spain. Under orders from their respective governments to curry favor with the Native peoples of the region through trade and diplomacy, both men, Oliva observes, became enmeshed in a competition to chart the western limits of the Louisiana Territory. This competition had a lasting effect on the region. It opened up the American West to generations of future Americans but, more importantly, led to the annexation of Texas in 1845 and the Mexican-American War in 1846–48.

Finally, William Foley evaluates James Wilkinson's role in the Burr conspiracy, offering keen insights about his character and code of ethics. In "James Wilkinson: Pike's Mentor and Jefferson's Capricious Point Man in the West," Foley asserts that the sale of the Louisiana Territory, with its "culturally diverse frontier," provided a conduit by which Wilkinson could spy for both the Spanish and U.S. governments. With Spain distrustful of the French for selling the Louisiana Territory to the Americans and Americans distrustful of the Spanish for their reluctance to acknowledge U.S. sovereignty in the Southwest, Wilkinson drew on this anger and mistrust to advance his political career and enhance his financial prospects. Wilkinson joined the Spanish payroll as "Agent 13," spying for the Spanish while serving as the highest-ranking military officer in the United States Army. Further, he aligned himself with the crafty and overzealous former vice president Aaron Burr in an effort to detach the southwestern borderlands from American control. In this endeavor, Foley writes, the evidence is not clear whether Pike was connected to the Wilkinson-Burr conspiracy; more likely, he claims, Wilkinson used Pike for commercial purposes. He commissioned Pike's two expeditions in the West not for the purposes of filibustering the Spanish but to explore the potential of tapping into the rich and lucrative trade market that the Spanish had developed with the Native Americans in the region.

We hope that this book will not only provide readers with a new reconceptualization of the explorer Zebulon Pike, a fresh and exciting retrospective assessment of his life and legacy, but also spark further research into Pike's considerable accomplishments as a major player in building Jefferson's "empire of liberty."

## NOTES

1. There were no full-length books published on Pike during the bicentennial, but Mark L. Gardiner wrote a new foreword to *The Southwestern Journals of Zebulon Pike, 1806–1807*, ed. Stephen Harding Hart and Archer Butler Hulbert, reprinted by the University of New Mexico Press in 2006 (the journals were first published in 1932). The pomp and circumstance surrounding the Lewis and Clark Bicentennial is discussed in *Across the Continent: Jefferson, Lewis and Clark, and the Making of America*, ed. Douglas Seefeldt, Jeffrey L. Hantman, and Peter S. Onuf (Charlottesville: University of Virginia Press, 2005), ix–x, 1–15. The author thanks Jay H. Buckley for his perceptive comments on this chapter.

2. The best accounts of Jefferson's "empire of liberty" include Boyd, "Jefferson's 'Empire of Liberty'"; Tucker and Hendrickson, *Empire of Liberty*; and, especially, Onuf, *Jefferson's Empire*.

3. Hyslop, *Bound for Santa Fe*, esp. ch. 1 ("The Ambiguous Venture of Zebulon Pike").

4. Pike describes the Southwest, then known as the Internal Provinces of New Spain, in great detail in Jackson, ed., *Journals of Pike*, 2:47–51. Pike was not impressed by the region he explored. "These vast plains," he commented, "may become in time equally celebrated as the sandy deserts of Africa; for I saw in my route, in various places, tracts of many leagues, where the wind had thrown up the sand, in all the fanciful forms of the ocean's rolling wave and on which not a speck of vegetable matter existed." Ibid., 2:27. See also Goetzmann, *Exploration and Empire*, 52.

5. Gardiner, introduction to Hart and Hulbert, *Southwestern Journals of Pike*, 4.

6. For a beautifully written account of Burr's life, see Isenberg, *Fallen Founder*. For two reliable studies of Burr and the election of 1800, see Sharp, *Deadlocked Election of 1800*; and John Ferling, *Adams vs. Jefferson: The Tumultuous Election of 1800* (New York: Oxford University Press, 2004). Besides Isenberg's *Fallen Founder*, the best discussion of the duel is Joanne B. Freeman, *Affairs of Honor: National Politics in the New Republic* (New Haven, Conn.: Yale University Press, 2001).

7. Kathleen DuVal writes that Pike's orders to escort the Osage Indians back to their homelands were part of an effort by the U.S. government to rectify a past mistake for not protecting the Osages against their enemies. See DuVal, *Native Ground*, 186–87.

8. David J. Weber discusses the realities of war between the United States and Spain in *The Spanish Frontier in North America*, but he concedes that "Wilkinson's exact purpose in sending Pike into Mexico, like many other shadowy dealings of this double agent, continues to elude full explanation" (292). See also Cook, *Flood Tide of Empire*; and Lewis, *American Union*. One historian writes that Pike and his men "assumed that Mexico would become independent and even that some of its Internal Provinces would join the Union," but there is scant evidence to support that assertion. See Stagg, *Borderlines and Borderlands*, 153.

9. This story is fleshed out in Linklater, *Artist in Treason*, 4–5, 209.

10. Richard White, *It's Your Misfortune and None of My Own: A New History of the American West* (Norman: University of Oklahoma Press, 1991), 121. See also Smelser, *Democratic Republic*, 130–31; and Goetzmann, *Exploration and Empire*, 49–50.

11. In 1806, Wilkinson wrote several letters to Jefferson informing him of Burr's role "to seize on New Orleans, revolutionize the territory, and carry an expedition against Mexico by Vera Cruz," in a plan to separate the southwestern borderlands from the United States. Convinced that Wilkinson's intelligence was legitimate, the president had Burr arrested. For Wilkinson's letters to Jefferson, see Wilkinson, *Memoirs*, vol. 2, appendixes 95 and 100.

12. For a good account of the Burr conspiracy, see Abernethy, *Burr Conspiracy*. It has been supplanted, more recently, by Hoffer, *Treason Trials*. Also informative is Melton, *Aaron Burr: Conspiracy to Treason*; and Isenberg, *Fallen Founder*.

13. Secretary of War Henry Dearborn, in a letter to Pike dated February 24, 1808, assured the soldier that he had been exonerated from any wrongdoing. In Jackson, *Journals of Pike*, 2:300–301.

14. Hollon, *Lost Pathfinder*, 165–66; and Hollon, "Zebulon Montgomery Pike," 455.

15. *Natchez Weekly Chronicle*, July 27, 1809.

16. In Nile, *Life of Perry*, 374.

17. Whiting, "Life of Pike," 277–83, quotations on 277. Whiting's account was also published in Jared Sparks, *The Library of American Biography*, 2nd ser., 25 vols. (Boston: Little, Brown, 1834–48), 5:217–314.

18. R. Thomas, *The Glory of America, Comprising Memoirs of the Lives and Glorious Exploits of Some of the Distinguished Officers Engaged in the Late War with Great Britain* (New York: E. Strong, 1834); and Charles Jacobs Peterson, *The Military Heroes of*

*the War of 1812, with a Narrative of the War* (Philadelphia: W. A. Leary, 1848). For other accounts, see Renwick, Whiting, and Mackie, *Lives of Rumford, Pike, and Gorton;* and Jenkins, *Daring Deeds of American Generals.* For counties and towns named after Pike, see Michael L. Olsen's splendid article, "Zebulon Pike and American Popular Culture." For poems written on Pike's behalf, see these newspapers: the *Columbian* (New York), October 2, 1813; *Daily National Intelligencer* (Washington, D.C.), September 5, 1822; and *Louisville (KY) Public Advertiser,* October 2, 1822.

19. Greely, *Men of Achievement,* 193.

20. Coues, *Expeditions of Pike,* 1:vi.

21. Herbert Bolton published a portion of these papers in the *American Historical Review* 13 (July 1908): 798–827. Snippets of these papers were also published as "Notes and Documents: Zebulon Montgomery Pike's Lost Papers," in the *Mississippi Valley Historical Review* 34 (September 1947): 265–73. The editor, Eugene Hollon, wrote, "As long as these documents were not recovered, many believed that they contained the real clue to the Wilkinson-Burr conspiracy. The history of the lost papers is more interesting than their content" (265).

22. Cox, *Early Exploration of Louisiana,* 111, 113, 115.

23. Crichton, "Zeb Pike," 464–65.

24. Leroy R. Hafen, review of *Zebulon Pike's Arkansas Journal,* in *Mississippi Valley Historical Review* 20 (June 1933): 118. See also M. M. Quaife's review in *American Historical Review* 38 (July 1933): 774–75; Quaife did not think the editors should have dignified Crichton's "muckraking" article.

25. Hart and Hulbert, *Southwestern Journals of Pike,* 34–35.

26. Ibid., 38.

27. See LeRoy R. Hafen's review of *Lost Pathfinder,* by Hollon, in *William and Mary Quarterly,* 3rd ser., 7 (April 1950): 333–35; and Isaac J. Cox's review in *Mississippi Valley Historical Review* 36 (March 1950): 706–707.

28. Hollon, *Lost Pathfinder,* 135–36.

29. Ibid., 170.

30. Ibid., 163.

31. Jackson, "The Question Is: How Lost Was Zebulon Pike?" *American Heritage Magazine* 16 (February 1965): 11–15, 75–80. Jackson republished a variation of this essay as chapter 12 of his book *Thomas Jefferson and the Rocky Mountains: Exploring West from Monticello.*

32. Jackson, "The Question Is," 79.

33. Jackson, *Journals of Pike,* 1:viii.

34. Ibid., 1:vii–viii.

35. Terrell, *Zebulon Pike,* 16–17.

36. Ibid., 17, 48.

37. Patricia Nelson Limerick, *The Legacy of Conquest: The Unbroken Past of the American West* (New York: W. W. Norton, 1987), 229. Limerick writes that Pike "might have been acting as Wilkinson's agent."

38. In the preface he wrote for the publication of his journals in 1810, Pike denied being part of Wilkinson's designs. He thought it was "groundless calumny" to suggest he was involved in the conspiracy (Jackson, *Journals of Pike,* 1:xxv). While in custody, Pike claimed that he read a Spanish newspaper, the *Gazettes of Mexico,* that apprised him "for the first time" of the "rumors of colonel Burr's conspiracies" (1:411; see also 2:334).

# 1

# Pike as a Forgotten and Misunderstood Explorer

*Jay H. Buckley*

Zebulon Montgomery Pike's legacy remains mired in limbo. He is best remembered for a Colorado mountain peak that he neither climbed nor named; few today know much if anything about his adventurous life or his important historical contributions. For two centuries, critics have maligned the hapless explorer (often unfairly) as a lost pathfinder, an American spy, or even a poor man's Lewis and Clark. Others have brusquely characterized Pike as a young, inexperienced, and uneducated soldier whose expeditions were ill timed and poorly planned, even though the funding and timing of those expeditions were not decisions he had control over. James Ronda has characterized Pike as "a young army officer cursed by galloping ambition, an inadequate education, and a misplaced loyalty to his commanding officer, General James Wilkinson." Donald Jackson sympathized: "Nothing that Pike ever tried to do was easy, and most of his luck was bad."[1]

Although Lewis and Clark commanded a single epic journey that is well known, Pike's two similar ventures went largely unnoticed even though he published his map and journals well before the captains did. That America's collective memory of Pike's exploratory achievements and soldiering prowess continues to languish in historical obscurity is thus somewhat surprising. The bicentennial of Pike's expeditions was a mild affair compared to the celebratory tone that marked the bicentennial commemoration of the journey of his more famous contemporaries.[2]

Pike deserves a fresh reappraisal. Although long overshadowed by Lewis and Clark and vilified for his alleged involvement in a shadowy conspiracy to wrest Louisiana Territory from U.S. control or to acquire the Spanish Borderlands, Pike can be seen, upon closer examination, to have been a patriotic and indefatigable explorer intent on advancing Thomas Jefferson's "empire of liberty" in the trans-Mississippi West. Contrary to popular belief, some of Pike's luck was pretty good. He was a dutiful son, a devoted husband, and a caring father. A capable army officer, Pike did not lose a man on either expedition, advanced to the military rank of general, published his observations, and died defending his country in the War of 1812. With little government support, he successfully conducted what he considered as three expeditions, survived harsh winter conditions in the frozen north and the Rocky Mountains, negotiated with half a dozen Indian nations, sparred with Spanish and British diplomats, and was a true American standard bearer. Pike's expeditions helped form the foundation of the political, commercial, diplomatic, and military circumstances that culminated in the United States' solidifying its northern border with Britain and securing the southern borderlands with New Spain. Despite the challenging circumstances he faced from Mother Nature, British and Spanish personnel, Indian nations, and his misunderstood association with James Wilkinson, Pike emerges from the forgotten memory of his country as a patriotic explorer filled with grit and determination and personally willing to sacrifice everything—including his life—to advance the cause of liberty.[3]

Pike's father, also named Zebulon Pike, hailed from New Jersey and fought in General George Washington's army during the Revolutionary War. On April 17, 1775—two days before the shots heard round the world were fired at Lexington and Concord—the elder Pike married Isabella Brown of New York in New York City. As the war between the American colonists and the British soldiers and Indian allies commenced, Captain Pike achieved prominence for his courage in battle, and some Indians called him the "Great Brave." The Pikes' first daughter, Mary, died in infancy. Their second child, Zebulon Montgomery Pike, was born on January 5, 1779, in the port city of Lamberton (Trenton, New Jersey).[4]

Not much is known of young Pike's early life. He spent his child-hood near the Delaware River on the Pennsylvania frontier, where he received a rudimentary education. A lifelong learner, Pike loved books. He bought or borrowed them whenever he could and devoured them as occasion allowed. He also learned French and a smattering of Spanish. Standing 5 feet 8 inches tall, Pike compensated for his slim physique by developing physical stamina through regular rigorous exercise. He had striking blue eyes and habitually tilted his head to one side. The Pike family moved frequently, traveling from a succession of posts in western Pennsylvania until they reached the newly constructed Fort Washing-ton (near present-day Cincinnati) in 1790. Intent on following in his father's footsteps, the teenage cadet joined the elder Pike's regiment, commanded by General Anthony Wayne, during Little Turtle's War.[5]

Pike spent most of the mid to late 1790s at Fort Massac (in what is now Illinois), where he helped make repairs on the fort and once saved his father from drowning in the Ohio River. He studied math and French whenever he could find the time and continued to expand his knowledge through reading. On March 3, 1799, at the age of twenty, Pike accepted a second lieutenant's commission in the Second Infantry regiment and earned a promotion to first lieutenant in the First Infantry regiment be-fore the year's end, on November 1, 1799. He won notice for his loyalty to superiors, his zeal for discipline, his marksmanship, and his reputa-tion as a teetotaler. Fond of sports, he exhibited a strong, independent will and dignified confidence tinged with a little self-righteousness. Po-litical persuasion mattered during this era, and Pike, a devout Federal-ist, apparently lent his support to the public whipping of a Republican newspaper editor at Reading, Pennsylvania, in 1799. As a young officer, he shaped up his men, served as regimental paymaster, and supervised supply distribution and transportation between frontier fortifications.[6]

In addition to his military duties, Pike turned his attention to court-ship. While traveling to the Ohio River forts, Pike often stopped at the Sugar Grove plantation, fifteen miles below Cincinnati. The object of his interest—a dark-haired beauty named Clarissa "Clara" Harlow Brown—cut a striking figure, but Clara's father, Captain John Brown of Boone County, Kentucky, was Pike's maternal uncle. Uncle John tried to discourage Pike from courting his cousin, because Brown desired more for his daughter Clara than the transient life of an army wife. Against Brown's wishes, in 1801 the cocksure twenty-two-year-old soldier and his spirited eighteen-year-old betrothed eloped to Cincinnati, where they married. Brown never forgave his nephew, now son-in-law, for his insolence and forbade him to visit the Brown estate ever again.

The army regularly transferred Pike, who went to Fort Knox (Vincennes, Indiana) in April 1802 and Kaskaskia (Illinois) in 1803. Clara missed her home, her family, and Cincinnati society. Her husband urged her to "cheer up and try to be lively and laugh," but the lonesome life her father had warned her about became a reality. The birth of a healthy daughter, Clarissa, on February 24, 1803, brought her only temporary solace.[7]

## MISSISSIPPI EXPEDITION

Sixteenth-century Spanish explorers Alvar Nuñez Cabeza de Vaca and Hernando de Soto called the Mississippi the "Rio del Espiritu Santo." French explorers Louis Jolliet and Jacques Marquette descended it only as far as the Arkansas River in 1673, but in 1682 Robert Cavalier Sieur de La Salle reached the delta and claimed all lands drained by it for France and named the region "Louisiana." France claimed the "right of discovery" to this central river except for a brief period between 1762 and 1800, when Spain exercised dominion. Reports and maps from American explorers such as Jonathan Carver whetted American desires to know more about the Mississippi, particularly after the 1783 treaty of Paris made it the western boundary of the United States and again in 1803 when the United States purchased the Louisiana Territory from Napoleon.

America's largest river, the Mississippi, extended 2,350 miles from northern Minnesota to its delta, but no one knew for certain where its elusive headwaters originated. After the Louisiana Purchase, Americans began to redirect their focus from Europe to North America's continental interior. Jefferson's desire for an agrarian republic required sufficient land to satisfy the demands of a growing population, and that expansion required national control over the continent's interior waterways and trade routes.

General James Wilkinson—one of the great scoundrels in American history—has received the fitting moniker of "the general who never won a battle and never lost a court-martial." Placed on the Spanish payroll as "Agent 13" as early as 1787, Wilkinson received a "retainer" or pension from them for more than two decades, even as he ascended the ranks in the U.S. Army to become the nation's highest-ranking military officer. As a secret agent, the American general offered officials in Madrid valuable intelligence in exchange for monetary or land compensation. Wilkinson's appointment as commanding general of the army in 1802 increased his interest in locating the source of the Mississippi. While stationed at New Orleans in 1803, the general accepted the transfer of Louisiana from France on behalf of the United States. With assistance from Vice President Aaron Burr, Wilkinson was reassigned to St. Louis, where he assumed his new duties as governor of Louisiana Territory in 1805.[8]

Wilkinson, who had commanded Pike's father during the Indian wars of the Old Northwest, took an interest in his former subordinate's ambitious son, who was by then serving as district paymaster for the First Infantry Regiment at Fort Massac. During the summer of 1805, the general enlisted the twenty-six-year-old Lieutenant Pike's services to undertake a reconnaissance mission to ascend the Mississippi to its source. Wilkinson instructed his young protégé to survey the commercial prospects of fur and mineral resources, gather useful geographical and scientific information, and assert U.S. sovereignty along the upper Mississippi in conformity with the terms of John Jay's 1794 treaty with Great Britain. The assignment called for him to monitor British fur-trading activities, evict foreign interlopers, and lure Indians from the British to the American side. He directed Pike to select sites for future military and commercial establishments that would sustain America's imperial aspirations and to seek the approbation and permission of the Indians, whose leaders Pike was to invite to St. Louis to parlay with Wilkinson.[9]

Pike quickly assembled his team of twenty enlisted men (Sergeant Henry Kennerman, two corporals, and seventeen privates) and was allowed two thousand dollars' worth of supplies from St. Louis and Fort

Bellefontaine—the westernmost army outpost, located at the mouth of Coldwater Creek overlooking the Mississippi about fifteen miles north of St. Louis. Pike bade a fond farewell to Clara and their two-year-old daughter Clarissa. With four months of provisions aboard the seventy-foot keelboat, Pike departed on August 9, 1805.[10]

As Pike hastily embarked on his arduous ascent up the Mississippi, he had cause for concern. The lateness of his departure ensured that he would have to confront snow and cold, but he failed to properly prepare for a winter expedition. In all likelihood, the haste stemmed from Wilkinson's desire for Pike to observe the British fur traders in the region during the winter trapping season. Pike did not have the benefit or assistance of an aide, a slave, a scientist, or an interpreter, nor did he benefit from the preparation, training, or funding afforded other Jeffersonian exploratory parties. Pike's scientific instruments consisted of a thermometer, a theodolite (for determining latitude), and a watch.

The keelboat made slow but steady progress up the river by sailing, poling, and pulling, sometimes making twenty miles a day. The river presented many dangers; shoals, submerged logs, sandbars, rock ledges, and rapids impeded their ascent. Supplying the men with enough calories to sustain their arduous labors depended on the hunting skills of expedition members, and Pike proved to be the best shot and did most of the hunting. On August 24, Pike and his two dogs went on shore to hunt, but the dogs grew tired and lay down to rest. When the animals did not come back to camp, two men volunteered to search for them. When neither duo returned, Pike's party spent several anxious days before a kind Frenchman known as Blondeau found the two men and reunited them with the party. The dogs never returned. In camp, Sergeant Kennerman attempted to help the men forget their fatiguing labor through listening to his fiddle playing.[11]

A group of Sac (Sauk) Indians, including Black Hawk, came out to assist the expedition's ascent by helping haul the craft up the rapids near Rock River. A few weeks later, Pike surveyed the lead deposits at the Dubuque mines and pressed on through the Mississippi rapids through a howling gale. Just before arriving at Prairie du Chien, Pike noticed some five-hundred-foot-high bluffs with a commanding view of the river that he noted would be a good place for a fort.[12]

Pike continued upstream and arrived at Prairie du Chien, the major fur trade entrepôt, at the junction of the Wisconsin and Mississippi rivers, and his men engaged in an athletic contest with the Indians assembled there. Pike made two excellent decisions while at the French village. First, he exchanged his keelboat for two smaller watercraft better suited for plying the shrinking river. Second, he hired mixed-blood guide Pierre Rousseau and interpreter Joseph Renville to facilitate his interactions with the Dakota Sioux. Within the week, as he entered modern Minnesota, Pike put Rousseau's skills to work. Pike arrived at a Sioux village and met with Chief Wabasha. Some days later he had a council with Chief Hupahuduta ("Wing of the Wild Swan Dyed Red," namesake of Red Wing, Minnesota). A few weeks later, while camped on Pikes Island at the confluence of the Minnesota and Mississippi rivers, Pike held a major council with Indian leaders. Using the sail to form an awning, Pike elicited a land deal with a collection of Sioux leaders on September 23 to procure 100,000 acres for a military site (future Fort Snelling, near present-day Minneapolis). After the treaty council, Pike distributed two hundred dollars' worth of presents.[13]

The Falls of Saint Anthony—the major falls of the upper Mississippi—forced Pike's party to endure a laborious portage around the falls before proceeding on. Winter overtook the party several hundred miles above St. Anthony Falls, at the Little Falls of the Mississippi. Pike had pushed his men to the breaking point. The October cold, combined with wading in the frigid, freezing water to propel the boats, exhausted and numbed the men; one of the toughest of the party, Sergeant Kennerman, exerted himself sufficiently to break a blood vessel, and he vomited a half gallon of blood. Pike wrote "that [even] if I had no regard for my own health and constitution, I should have some for these poor fellows, who were killing themselves to obey my orders."[14] The men's deteriorating condition and the adverse weather forced Pike to establish a winter camp. From October 28 to December 10, they labored to construct a stockade near present Little Falls, Minnesota, approximately 1,500 miles upstream from St. Louis.

Leaving the boats, half the party, and most of the supplies under the care of Sergeant Kennerman, Pike led a dozen men northward, employing snowshoes and pulling sleds to venture up the mud, snow, and ice along and upon the frozen river. One sled fell through the ice, soaking Pike's baggage and books. With the real threat of frostbite on exposed fingers, noses, and toes, Pike walked ahead to light fires for his men to warm themselves when they caught up. In February 1806, Pike received a hospitable welcome by trader Hugh McGillis at the Montreal-based North West Company post at Leech Lake, the third largest lake in Minnesota. McGillis probably regretted it later when Pike castigated him for illicitly trading for furs in the United States without a proper license and reprimanded the British traders for trespassing on U.S. soil. To make matters worse, when Pike's host refused to lower the Union Jack, Pike ordered one of his men to shoot the flag down! His patient host reciprocated with kindness by supplying Pike with a map of the area and providing several sled dogs and two voyageurs to guide Pike and one companion to Red Cedar or Cass Lake in February 1806. Upon his arrival there, Pike was euphoric: "I will not attempt to describe my feelings on the accomplishment of my voyage, this being the main source of the Mississippi." Thinking he had accomplished his task of finding the headwaters, Pike turned south, gathered his men at Leech Lake Post, and set off to rejoin Kennerman on February 18.[15]

Upon his return to the Little Falls stockade on March 5, Pike found things in disarray. Having concluded that Pike would not likely return, Sergeant Kennerman had rifled through the lieutenant's personal belongings, used up most of the supplies, and emptied the whiskey barrel. Instead of shooting him, Pike demoted Kennerman to a private, packed up what was left of the supplies, and headed downstream with the spring thaw on March 18, arriving in St. Louis on April 30, 1806.[16]

Pike enjoyed a brief reunion with his young family and labored for six weeks reworking his Mississippi River journal for submission to Wilkinson. Pike's round-trip journey of several thousand miles had taken less than nine months. He had ascended the Mississippi to a point very near its source, warned the British to stop their illegal trading, parleyed with representatives of the Sac, Fox, Menominee, and Sioux tribes, and negotiated the purchase of a site for a future fort.

Some historians unfairly dismiss Pike's Mississippi exploration as falling short because he did not thwart British traders from continuing their trade, did not win over Indian allies, and did not escort any Indian leaders to meet with Wilkinson. They complain that Pike's notes are difficult to follow, his maps are poorly drawn, and he did not add much new geographic or scientific information.[17] A clearer picture is emerging that Pike did a remarkable job, considering the circumstances, and that his notes and maps are adequately done, contain important scientific and geographic information, and represent significant historical contributions. Moreover, his journey to the headwaters of the Mississippi tempered Pike's mettle and prepared him for future exploration. General Wilkinson, satisfied with Pike's northern jaunt, was busily outlining plans for Pike to embark on a journey into the southern reaches of the Louisiana Purchase along the Spanish Borderlands.

## SOUTHWESTERN EXPEDITION

Wilkinson's combined roles as commanding general of the U.S. Army and governor of Upper Louisiana proved insufficient to assuage his intense ambition. Two centuries later, historians continue to puzzle over the purpose of his machinations with Spain and his duplicitous dealings with Aaron Burr. While providing sensitive American military intelligence to Spanish officials in return for compensation, Wilkinson effectively worked both sides of the ledger. He corresponded with Burr (Jefferson's former vice president, who was then campaigning in New York to become governor). Following his defeat in that contest, Burr laid the blame at Alexander Hamilton's doorstep and challenged his nemesis to a duel. After mortally wounding Hamilton, Burr fled New York to escape murder charges.[18]

Burr's subsequent dealings with Wilkinson remain shrouded in mystery, but as the former vice president proceeded down the Mississippi, he amassed a private army. Most historians believe that Burr (with Wilkinson's encouragement) planned to either separate the trans-Appalachian region from the United States or invade northern New Spain and instigate a military coup d'état to wrest control of Spain's northern provinces (especially East and West Florida and Texas) without official U.S. military involvement. Meanwhile, Wilkinson traveled to New Orleans to repel any attack from Spanish Texas over the Sabine River boundary

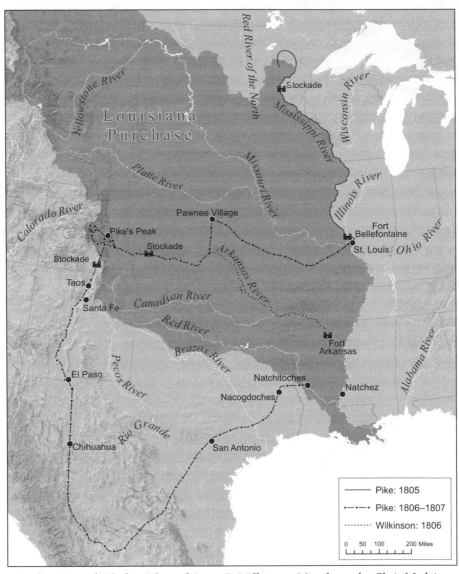

Explorations of Zebulon Pike and James B. Wilkinson. Map drawn by Chris Madeira and Scot Godfredson.

dispute. On November 6, 1806, he partially settled the indefinite nature of the boundary between the United States and Spain in an agreement with Lieutenant Colonel Simón de Herrera establishing neutral territory on both sides of the river.[19]

Pike most likely did not know about the Burr-Wilkinson intrigues, but he enthusiastically agreed to undertake Wilkinson's assignment to gather intelligence about New Spain that would be helpful in the event that war broke out between the United States and Spain or, alternatively, that would facilitate General Wilkinson's designs for trade with Santa Fe.[20] Wilkinson's instructions to Pike for a second expedition called upon the need to ascertain the southwestern boundary of the Louisiana Purchase by exploring the sources of the Arkansas and Red rivers and gathering intelligence in the Spanish Borderlands region. La Frontera—the northern Internal Provinces of New Spain—functioned as an extended buffer zone between other European and Indian groups and the rich silver mines of Mexico. The Spanish restricted foreign trade or travel to the region and did not share information about the country with anyone. They also viewed any intrusion as a direct threat, particularly when those groups involved military personnel, note taking, and mapmaking. Wilkinson had somehow purloined a rendition of a "General Map of the Kingdom of New Spain" by the German cartographer Alexander von Humboldt in addition to another map depicting a 1797 trek by three French traders from St. Louis to Santa Fe. Wilkinson warned Pike to "move with great circumspection, to keep clear of any hunting or reconnoitering parties from that province and to prevent alarm or offense" but to scout near Santa Fe. In the event that Pike was captured, he should simply explain that he was lost along the contested boundary of Louisiana.[21]

Pike's reconnaissance of the borderlands also involved creating friendly alliances with Plains tribes such as the Arapahos, Cheyennes, Comanches, Kansas, Osages, Pawnees, and Utes. Wilkinson ordered Pike to escort back to their homes fifty-one Osage captives recently ransomed from the Potawatomis and a delegation of Pawnee, Osage, and Oto leaders returning from a trip to visit President Thomas Jefferson. Wilkinson admonished Pike to negotiate peace between the Kansa and Osage nations and to seek a U.S. alliance with the Comanches. Although

Jefferson did not learn of Pike's expedition until after it had departed, he gave the venture his official blessing on the grounds that it provided for the safe return home of the Indians and also, no doubt, because his two previously authorized attempts to send military and scientific expeditions up the Arkansas and Red rivers had been thwarted by the Spanish.[22]

The plan involved Pike going off the map to explore a world wherein the geographical knowledge was largely conjectural, primarily because of Spain's reluctance to share such information. Wilkinson ordered Pike to ascend the Arkansas River, proceed south to the Red River, and descend it to the Mississippi, making careful observations of the geography, natural history, Indian residents, and anything of scientific interest.[23] Leaving his two-year-old daughter Clarissa and pregnant wife at Fort Bellefontaine, Pike departed with twenty-two companions on July 15, 1806. Nineteen of the men consisted of the "Dam'd set of Rascels" who had accompanied him on the Mississippi expedition.[24] The noncommissioned officers were Sergeant Henry Kennerman, Corporal Samuel Bradley, and Corporal William Meek. Three notable additions to the southwestern expedition included his second in command, Lieutenant James Biddle Wilkinson (the general's son, who intended to travel with Pike partway and return with a small detachment down the Arkansas River), civilian physician Dr. John H. Robinson, and interpreter Antoine Baronet Vasquez of St. Louis.

Pike's entourage of soldiers, civilians, and Indians traveled west across present-day Missouri along the Missouri and Osage rivers in two boats (one for the soldiers, one for the Indians) before arriving at the Osage villages near the Lake of the Ozarks. The Osages warmly welcomed Pike, who recorded some ethnographic information and helped instigate a temporary peace between the Osage and Kansa nations. Pike exchanged the two boats for fifteen horses and, with thirty Osage and Kansa companions, headed northwest, angling toward the Pawnee villages along the Republican River (near present-day Red Cloud, Nebraska).[25] Along the way, Private Kennerman (whom Pike had demoted from sergeant to private for his dereliction of duty during the Mississippi expedition) deserted, perhaps anticipating another grueling trip or fearful of the reputably ferocious Pawnees.

While camped on the Republican River, Pike wrote a letter to Wilkinson that reveals the general may have given Pike some verbal instructions to ascertain whether an American force could invade northern Mexico via Santa Fe if the northern Mexican colonies revolted, if war between Spain and the United States erupted, or if disagreements between the United States and Spain over contested mineral claims emerged. Pike opined, "Any number of men . . . would find no difficulty in marching by the route we came with baggage waggons, field artillery, and all the usual appendages of a small army." He continued that "if all the route to Santa Fe should be of the same description, in case of war I would pledge my life (and what is infinitely dearer, my honor) for the successful march of a reasonable body of troops, into the province of New Mexico."[26]

When Pike arrived at the Pawnee villages, he learned that a Spanish force of several hundred mounted troops led by don Facundo Melgares had recently been there. The Spaniards' show of force impressed the Pawnees, who willingly consented to Melgares's request for their assistance in preventing any Americans from penetrating the interior. When Pike arrived, the truculent Indians attempted to force him to retreat. Pike, with his meager band, countered, saying that if anything happened to him or his friends, "the great American father" would send out many warriors "to gather our bones and revenge our deaths." After an uneasy two weeks of thrust and parry by both sides, Pike insisted that they replace the Spanish flag flying above their village with a American one (he allowed them to keep the Spanish flag in case the Spanish returned and they needed to use it again), return the horses they had taken from him, and allow the party to continue their journey west. The Pawnee chief Sharitarish, however, indicated to Pike that the Pawnees still adhered to their friendship with the Spanish and were not willing to accept claims of U.S. sovereignty, and he told the Americans they could not proceed westward. Nevertheless, Pike retorted courageously and with exuberant confidence that should the Pawnees try to stop them, the Americans were men who would "*sell our lives* at a dear rate." He threatened that "our *great father* would send our young warriors" to the Pawnees "to gather our bones and revenge our *deaths* on his people." Pike's boldness to the point of recklessness swayed the Pawnees sufficiently to allow the Americans to trade for additional horses and leave their village a few days later to continue their westward journey. With the Stars and Stripes waving over the village, Pike sent out across the central Plains following a clear trail—one made by Melgares's cavalry—and headed directly toward Santa Fe.[27]

The Osage and Pawnee villages had provided Pike with horses, food, geographic information, and guides, but how other Indian nations would receive him was unclear. Crossing the Solomon and Smokey Hills forks, Pike finally arrived at the Arkansas River; Lieutenant James B. Wilkinson, five men, and the last remaining Osage guide left the party (as previously planned) and descended the Arkansas to the Mississippi in two canoes, transporting some of Pike's notes and observations to Wilkinson's father, the general.[28] Despite lacking the proper clothing, equipment, and supplies for a winter expedition, Pike and his fifteen troopers faced westward into the winter wind in the waning days of October, ascending the Arkansas and following the trail left by the Spanish cavalry. On November 22, sixty Pawnee warriors stopped Pike and—after deciding that the tobacco and presents he had offered them were insufficient as a toll for passing through their country—began taking his remaining supplies and equipment. Pushed to his limit, the hypersensitive Pike jeopardized his entire enterprise by threatening to shoot the next Pawnee who touched their baggage. Fortunately, the Pawnees gathered up what they had acquired and rode away, leaving Pike in a sour mood and a cloud of dust. On November 23, Pike's party halted to construct a winter shelter and fortification along the Arkansas near present-day Pueblo, Colorado.[29]

Leaving a dozen men to finish the stockade, Pike, John Robinson, and two others set out to explore the "Mexican Mountains," or Front Range of the Rockies, and attempted to reach the summit of the blue mountain rising in the distance that he had first spied in his telescope a week earlier. Called Ta-Wa-Ah-Gath (Sun Mountain—the first mountain to greet the sun) by the Southern Utes and El Capitán by the Spaniards who grazed their sheep along its slopes, the mountain rises vertically some 7,000 feet from the valley floor to a height of 14,115 feet. Arriving near present-day Colorado Springs, the foursome hiked for several days to get nearer to the "Highest Peak." Short of food and with only thin linen shirts and pants to protect them from the waist-deep snow and

On November 15, 1806, Zebulon Pike caught his first glimpse of the mountain peak that later carried his name. His journal entry stated: "Marched early. Passed two deep creeks and many high points of the rocks; also, large herds of buffalo. At two o'clock in the afternoon I thought I could distinguish a mountain . . . to our right, which appeared like a small blue cloud. . . . When our small party arrived on the hill they with one accord gave three cheers to the Mexican mountains." Pike, Dr. John Robinson, and Privates Theodore Miller and John Brown set out to ascend it. Several days later, from the top of an adjacent mountain, they viewed the towering peak still beckoning. Because of their inadequate provisions and clothing, they made the sensible choice to turn back. Painter E. Cameron created this image for the *St. Louis Globe-Democrat* in 1902. Courtesy of the Colorado Springs Pioneer Museum.

frigid temperatures, they abandoned their quest to ascend "Pikes Peak" and returned to their base camp. After ascending Mount Rosa, Pike recalled that "it would have taken a whole day's march to have arrived at its base" and that the snowy, wintry conditions would have proven a challenge for any man attempting to "reach its pinnacle."[30]

Back at the Pueblo breastwork, Pike made an executive decision and ordered his force to ascend the Arkansas River. They arrived at Royal

Located in the Front Range of the Rocky Mountains west of Colorado Springs, Pikes Peak rises 14,115 feet above sea level. This view taken from the Garden of the Gods conveys the majesty of this sublime granite mountain. Although Pike was unsuccessful in his 1806 ascent, in 1820 botanist and geologist Edwin James reached the summit. Photo courtesy of Wikimedia Commons.

Gorge, constructed another breastwork (near present-day Cañon City), then traveled north on 4 Mile Creek toward Cripple Creek and South Park during the first week of December. Pike traveled overland to the north and discovered a river he correctly identified as the South Platte on the 13th. Pike confidently asserted that he could visit the source of any of the major western rivers in a day's journey from the highest peak. Baffled by the never-ending ranges of the Colorado Rockies, which failed to conform to his geographic expectations, Pike realized that he was temporarily lost. "The geography of the country had turned out to be so different from our expectations we were at a loss which course to pursue," he confided in his journal. Crossing a mountain pass and thinking he was now on the Red, Pike had inadvertently rejoined the Arkansas River about seventy miles upstream from where they had left it two weeks previously.[31]

Pike traveled north with Robinson to modern-day Leadville, Colorado. As the snow piled up, Pike grew frustrated over his inability to definitively locate the headwaters of the Arkansas River, which begins as a trickle from several springs near the top of the Continental Divide near Fremont Pass. For Christmas dinner, the party dined on bison steak near present-day Salida, Colorado. As they descended the stream through the monumental thousand-foot vertical walls of Royal Gorge, Pike was mortified to realize that they had traveled in one big circle and were not on the Red but on the Arkansas instead. Bewildered by the mountains, with no Indian guide, few provisions, difficult terrain, inclement weather, and exhausted men, Pike confided that his twenty-eighth birthday had not been stellar, "and most fervently did I hope never to pass another so miserably."[32]

Pike conceded that he "now felt at considerable loss how to proceed." Unfortunately, his situation turned from bad to worse. Determined to cross the snow-capped mountains, the party stored its baggage and supplies and left interpreter Vasquez and Patrick Smith to care for the horses in a small wooden stockade on the Arkansas, while Pike and the others shouldered seventy-pound loads and set out on foot on January 14, 1807, in search of the Red River's headwaters. During the arduous and agonizing ordeal, nine of the fourteen men suffered frostbitten feet, which forced Pike to leave three of them in a temporary camp. The men sent parts of their frostbitten fingers and toes to him to make sure he did not forget them in their travails. The waist-deep snow and bitter cold made the going slow and laborious for the remaining ten on what must have seemed like a death march.[33]

His men had reached their breaking point. John Brown complained that it was "more than human nature could bear, to march three days without sustenance, through snows three feet deep, to carry burdens only fit for horses." Knowing the fasting could not go on without devastating effects, Pike traveled ahead and shot a buffalo to assuage their hunger. As they feasted, Pike seized the teaching moment to harangue Brown for his seditious comment, reminding him and the other men that Pike had endured even more than they. He promptly forgave Brown but assured him and everyone else that if any of them uttered a mutinous comment again, they would receive "instant death." Pike capped off the evening by thanking them for their obedience and sacrifice and promised that he would do all in his power to see that the government rewarded them for their service.[34]

Turning south, they crossed the Sangre de Cristo Mountains into the Spanish territory of New Mexico, traversed the Great Sand Dunes, and arrived at the San Luis Valley of the upper Rio Grande. They found a stand of timber along the Rio Conejos south of present-day Alamosa, Colorado, and constructed a small thirty-six-foot-square stockade out of cottonwood logs in early February. Thinking that he had found the elusive Red River, Pike sent back two relief parties to try to reunite his entire party.[35] Meanwhile, Dr. John Robinson asked Pike for permission to journey to Santa Fe to collect a debt from Baptiste LaLande owed to Kaskaskia merchant William Morrison. He would be protected under international law as an American citizen seeking to recover a debt in a foreign country. Moreover, his visit would allow him to examine the defenses of Santa Fe and take the pulse of its citizenry regarding their feelings toward the Spanish crown, and ascertain the possibilities of future trading relations for American merchants. Robinson's arrival in the middle of the winter alerted New Mexico's Spanish governor, Joaquín del Real Alencaster, of the Americans' presence. The governor reported the incident to his superiors and dispatched Spanish troops to search out and apprehend the American "hunting" party trespassing in Spanish territory.[36]

Pike and a companion were out hunting when two Spanish cavalrymen intercepted and questioned them on February 16, 1807. Ten days later, a hundred-man Spanish force of dragoons and militiamen rode up to Pike's fort and arrested the Americans. Pike feigned surprise and insisted that he thought he was on the Red River. Upon being informed that he was in Spanish territory, Pike "immediately ordered [his] flag to be taken down and rolled up." They departed on the 28th for Santa Fe while Spanish patrols finished rounding up the rest of the American stragglers. Pike's captors were also his rescuers, a fact acknowledged when he expressed embarrassment for his expedition's shabby dress, appearance, and helpless condition.[37]

After Pike arrived in the provincial capital of some five thousand inhabitants on March 3, Governor Alencaster interrogated Pike. Although shabbily dressed without coat, shoes, or a hat, Pike stood his ground before Alencaster and demanded to be treated as a representative of the United States. The governor offered to resupply Pike, give him mules and horses, and take him to the headwaters of the Red River and release him, but Pike refused because of his concern for his men. Alencaster treated Pike and his men amicably; in fact, they were treated not as prisoners but as guests, and Pike was housed in a cartographer's home. Alencaster reoutfitted Pike's party with clothes and supplies and confiscated and examined Pike's records.[38] Unable to find any proof that Pike was an American spy, the governor sent Pike under military escort to General Nemesio Salcedo for further questioning.[39]

Pike carefully observed the people, geography, natural resources, and military resources he witnessed during his 550-mile march along the old Camino Real, or Royal Road, linking Santa Fe with Chihuahua. Stopping at missions, pueblos, and presidios along the route, Pike queried priests and residents to gather additional information and kept careful mental and written notes of military defenses, garrison strength, and individuals of importance. When they left Albuquerque, Pike's former nemesis, Facundo Melgares, took charge of escorting the Americans southward, and the two became fast friends. The Spanish treated Pike with great hospitality and kindness, and local communities hosted numerous feasts and fandangos for the entourage.

Nemesio Salcedo, commandant general of the Internal Provinces, interrogated Pike upon the arrival of the American party in the provincial capital of Chihuahua. General Salcedo expressed concern about the repeated American military incursions into the Spanish Borderlands, which he rightly viewed as a deliberate attempt to undermine Spanish control over the region. With information supplied by Agent 13 (Wilkinson), the Spanish had successfully blocked or apprehended similar American expeditions sent west into Louisiana Territory. Salcedo used Wilkinson's intelligence to prevent William Dunbar from undertaking his Red River venture in 1804 and to halt and turn back Thomas Jefferson's Red River expedition led by surveyor Thomas Freeman and physician George Custis in 1806. Although the Spanish did not apprehend Meriwether Lewis and William Clark on the Missouri, they made at least four attempts to do so. Spanish Lieutenant Colonel

Simón de Herrera y Leyva and James Wilkinson had narrowly averted war along the Sabine River by agreeing to create a buffer zone called the Neutral Ground between Texas and Louisiana, but the boundaries, jurisdiction, and governance of West Florida remained contentious and controversial.[40]

On the morning of April 2, 1807, Salcedo met Pike, a U.S. military officer who attributed his trespass on Spanish soil to his having lost his bearings. To make matters worse, Pike had just been given a personal tour of the Spanish Borderlands. The king would not be pleased. Salcedo tried to control the damage done by confiscating some of Pike's papers. Nevertheless, not wishing to provoke war with the United States, Salcedo sent Pike, Robinson, and six privates under military escort through the Texas borderlands via the Old San Antonio Road and released him at Natchitoches, Louisiana, on July 1, 1807. Pike recorded, "Language cannot express the gaiety of my heart, when I once beheld the standards of my country waved aloft!"[41]

Despite a safe return to the United States, bad news awaited him after his year-long sojourn. Pike learned that his infant son had died a few months after he had left on his southwestern expedition.[42] Moreover, Pike found himself not merely linked to the Burr conspiracy but already declared guilty in the court of public opinion because of his ties to Wilkinson. Instead of receiving a hero's welcome, he returned under a cloud of suspicion. When Spain decided not to declare war despite repeated American provocations (including Pike's intrusion), Wilkinson concluded that Burr's scheme was lost and seized the opportunity to ingratiate himself with Jefferson by foiling it.[43]

Jefferson ordered Burr arrested for treason and returned to Richmond, Virginia, to stand trial. Although Jefferson carefully orchestrated the government's case from behind the scenes, Chief Justice John Marshall defined the case narrowly and limited the evidence the government could present. While there was sufficient proof to show that Burr had planned to invade New Spain, his failure to carry out those plans precluded a conviction for treason. Following his acquittal, Burr fled to Europe for a brief period before he returned to New York to practice law.[44] Wilkinson, a master prevaricator, escaped indictment for treason on a nine to seven grand jury vote in 1807 and subsequently received exoneration in his court-martial in 1811 largely because of his willingness to testify against the unpopular Burr. The general continued his military service until he was relieved of command for shoddy leadership during the Montreal campaign in the War of 1812.[45]

After Clara and Clarissa joined Pike at New Orleans, they sailed to New York in September. There the disappointed Pike learned that his alleged complicity with Burr and Wilkinson precluded the kind of recognition and remuneration that a grateful nation had bestowed upon Lewis and Clark a year earlier. Although Pike's lackluster reception did not quell his vanity, the suspicion and innuendo slowly abated after Jefferson separated Pike from Wilkinson and Burr in his State of the Union address and Secretary of War Henry Dearborn officially exonerated Pike of any wrongdoing.[46] But the insinuations and speculation did not die easily. One person cannot stop a thousand rumors. Dearborn and a House of Representatives committee recommended special compensation of land and pay for Pike and his men, but Congress refused to appropriate the funds. His competence as a soldier was nonetheless reconfirmed when he received a promotion—one of only three Federalist officers on the list—when President Jefferson supported an expansion of forces in the army in 1807.[47]

Promoted to major for the new Sixth Infantry regiment on May 2, 1808, and stationed near Baltimore at Fort McHenry, Pike remained upset that Congress had denied his request for land and monetary compensation for his men. He sought to reclaim his reputation and perhaps even generate some profit from his ventures by publishing his official reports. In this, however, he faced numerous disadvantages. He lacked a flair for writing as well as the scientific eye or training of a Meriwether Lewis, the cartographic skills of William Clark, or the scientific acumen of William Dunbar. Pike nevertheless commenced writing, using his notes, journals, and maps to re-create his Mississippi journey. Recapturing his western and Spanish Borderlands expeditions (Pike considered them separate ventures) required additional effort, because the Spanish had confiscated many of his documents. Relying on his memory and the few notes he had smuggled out of New Spain, including some secretly hidden inside the gun barrels of his men, Pike reconstructed his confiscated journals. Pike's correspondence with General Wilkinson, his Indian speeches, and his recounting of the three expeditions appeared in 1810 as a massive 503-page tome entitled *An Account of Expeditions to the Sources of the Mississippi and through the Western Parts of Louisiana*.[48]

Despite the popular acclaim it received, numerous grammatical and spelling errors, insufficient editing, poor organization, and a lack of scientific information marred the publication. Nevertheless, Pike's *Account* provided an informed narrative of British fur-trading operations on the upper Mississippi, ethnographic information about numerous Plains tribes, and extensive observations about military, commercial, and political conditions in the Spanish Borderlands—key information for America to possess in order to expand its empire westward. Moreover, Pike whetted enterprising entrepreneurs' interest by expounding on the commercial potential of the fur trade of the upper Mississippi and the overland trade with Mexico. His valuable information also benefited the United States and its citizenry during Mexican Independence, the settlement of Texas, and the Mexican Revolution.

Pike's geographical information about the southern plains and Rockies provided a clearer image of the southern portion of the Louisiana Purchase. Pike's 1810 map, "A Chart of the Internal Part of Louisiana, Including All the Hitherto Unexplored Countries," incorporated information supplied by William Dunbar's Ouachita expedition and Thomas Freemen's truncated Red River expedition. Pike's maps contained numerous errors, partly because he erroneously embraced the cartographic concept perpetuated by Jonathan Carver and Alexander von Humboldt that all the great western rivers (Yellowstone, Platte, Colorado, Arkansas, and Red rivers, and the Rio Grande) arose from a single height of land within a day's journey of each other. From Pike's perspective, this "highest point," or pyramidal height of land, was the mountain later named in his honor. Pike's information and observations contributed to William Clark's perpetuating this error by compressing the Wyoming and Colorado Rockies into one region to have all the western streams flowing from a central core region. Nevertheless, Pike's maps provided some of the first American knowledge derived from actual exploration along Louisiana's northeastern and southwestern boundaries and one of the earliest renditions of the Santa Fe Trail.[49]

Pike also compared the southern plains to the sandy deserts of Africa, describing "tracts of many leagues, where the wind had thrown up the sand, in all the fanciful form of the ocean's rolling wave, and on which not a speck of vegetable matter existed."[50] His commentary suggesting that the "scarcity of wood and water, almost uniformly prevalent, will prove an insuperable obstacle in the way of settling the country" and that the Plains were fit only for the buffalo and the Indians who pursued them likely deterred American expansion, enabled the future creation of an Indian Territory, and led to the mistaken notion of the southern plains as the Great American Desert.[51]

The limitations of Pike's publications in no way diminished his attributes as a soldier. The War Department promoted Pike to lieutenant colonel of the Fourth Infantry on December 31, 1809. Pike's next military assignment was the riled hornet's nest of West Florida. Roughly consisting of the area bounded by the Mississippi River, the 31st parallel, and the Perdido River, West Florida's residential makeup grew more complex when Choctaws, French Acadians, British Loyalists, and Spanish residents were joined by American settlers who openly resisted Spanish control. The Anglophones led a rebellion in 1810 and established a short-lived Republic of West Florida. The first and only governor, Fulwar Skipwith, had helped negotiate the Louisiana Purchase. President James Madison's October 27 proclamation annexed portions of West Florida to the United States, who claimed the region as part of the Louisiana Purchase. Madison sent William C. C. Claiborne to take possession of the territory. Military and civil leaders alike expected that violence might spread amidst the turmoil of the transition. By the first part of December, Orleans territorial governor Clairborne and Mississippi territorial governor David Holmes were coordinating with Colonel Zebulon Pike (alternately stationed between Natchez, Cantonment Terre aux Boeufs, and Baton Rouge) and Colonel Leonard Covington to establish a military presence on both sides of the river. Enduring the heat, humidity, mud, and mosquitoes, they eventually established order over the Baton

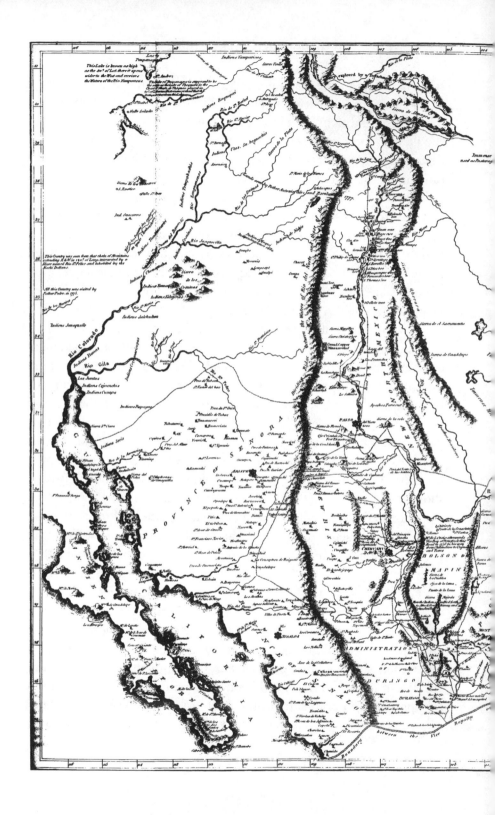

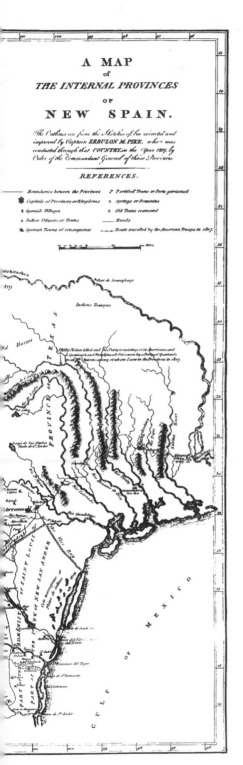

Pike's map, "A Chart of the Internal Part of Louisiana from an Account of Expeditions to the Sources of the Mississippi and through the Western Parts of Louisiana" (Philadelphia: C. and A. Conrad, 1810). Courtesy of the Library of Congress.

Rouge and Orleans region. Pike constructed forts, commanded the West Florida troops, arrested bandits, removed intruders from neutral territory, and was even recommended as a gubernatorial candidate for West Florida.[52]

## WAR OF 1812

As the tension between the United States and Spain over East and West Florida cooled, American relations with Britain heated up. Britain's war with Napoleonic France heightened tensions on the high seas. The 1807 British assault on an American frigate, the *Chesapeake,* created a diplomatic crisis. British naval impressments of sailors on American vessels constituted an infringement of U.S. sovereignty, and the war hawks in Congress demanded action.[53]

Concurrently, Indians along the American frontier organized to protect and defend tribal lands being overrun by settlers' westward advance by forming a defensive alliance under Tecumseh and his brother Tenskwatawa. Lieutenant Colonel Pike fought with the Fourth Infantry Regiment in the Battle of Tippecanoe on November 7, 1811, during a preemptive strike orchestrated by Indiana governor William Henry Harrison. They and a thousand militia and regulars attacked Tecumseh's Prophetstown at the confluence of the Tippecanoe and Wabash rivers while the venerable Indian warrior was away. The Battle of Tippecanoe led to a weakening and breakup of the British-allied Indian Confederacy arrayed against the U.S. forces and was one of the causes of the War of 1812.[54]

Louisiana joined the Union on April 30, 1812, as the eighteenth state. On June 1, President James Madison requested a formal declaration of war on Great Britain, and Congress complied seventeen days later. Wars often make generals, and Pike viewed this as his opportunity. Having received a promotion from quartermaster general of the army to colonel in the Fifteenth Infantry on July 6, 1812, he was poised to attain the coveted status of general. He recruited and trained over seven hundred recruits at Staten Island and endured a cold winter with inadequate supplies at Plattsburgh, New York. Military leaders deemed Pike's men the best prepared for the impending battle near the Great Lakes and dispatched his regiment on a grueling overland march through three feet of snow that took them to Sackets Harbor, New York, on the east end of Lake Ontario. At least one man died of exposure, and others lost limbs to frostbite. On March 12, 1813, Madison crowned Pike with one of the military's highest ranks—brigadier general—and additional duties as adjutant-general (chief administrative officer) and inspector-general (a post meant to ensure that the army operated within governmental policies and charged with preventing corruption).[55]

Many Americans believed that an invasion of Canada would crush the Indian resistance and extend U.S. control over the Great Lakes. Conquering Canada would also allow military leaders to use it as leverage to force the British to alter their maritime practices. General Pike spearheaded a springtime invasion across Lake Ontario in an assault against Fort York, the principal defense for Toronto, the capital of Upper Canada (later Ontario). The task was a formidable challenge. Fort York had been the main naval defense for Upper Canada for two decades. It guarded against the most vulnerable western land approach and was defensible against a land assault because it was nearly surrounded by water. Moreover, the better-trained British troops and their Indian allies had already achieved military victories at Mackinac, Detroit, and Chicago.

Secretary of War Henry Dearborn realized that the key to victory required cutting Upper Canada off from Lower Canada. This strategy meant capturing Kingston and Montreal to secure the St. Lawrence and the British naval base at York (Toronto) to control the Great Lakes. Hoping to pluck York first, the army and navy began amassing forces at Fort Tompkins, at Sackets Harbor, New York. Commodore Isaac Chauncey commanded the naval squadron, comprising fourteen vessels sporting eighty-three guns and manned by 700 sailors. General Pike commanded the land force, consisting of 1,500–1,700 soldiers. Before the battle, Pike wrote a letter to his father: "I embark tomorrow in the fleet at Sacketts Harbor at the head of fifteen hundred choice troops, on a secret expedition. If success attends my steps, honor and glory await my name—if defeat, still shall it be said we died like brave men; and conferred honor even in death on the American name."[56]

*The Death of U.S. General Pike at the Battle of York, 27 April 1813.* These two American engravings of later date bear little resemblance to the actual 1813 fortifications, which Brigadier General Pike captured at the battle of York in Upper Canada (now Toronto). The town of York was actually out of sight farther to the east. Pike was killed by flying debris from the explosion of a powder magazine as the British scuttled the fort as they vacated. Courtesy of Canadian Military History Gateway and Library and Archives Canada.

They set sail on Sunday, April 25, 1813, and arrived on Monday evening. Dawn on the 27th revealed their day's task. British officer Sir Roger Sheaffe had 700–800 troops to defend the fort, as well as additional Indian auxiliaries from the Glengarry, Mississauga, and Ojibwe (Chippewa) tribes. Sheaffe sent his Indian supporters to greet the U.S. forces as they approached the landing site. Instead of staying on the warship *Madison,* Pike earned the respect of his men by leading three companies toward the beach. Facing deadly fire from on shore, the bloody battle of York commenced. Heavy casualties soon forced the British grenadiers and Indian troops to retreat, allowing the Americans to land en masse. With the fifes and drums playing "Yankee Doodle," Pike marched his men toward the battery. Pike's Fifteenth Infantry regiment surrounded Fort York and unleashed a blistering artillery attack. Unbeknownst to the Americans, the British had quietly evacuated the fort while the U.S.

forces waited outside the walls for their surrender. After the British had slipped away, Sheaffe ordered the grand magazine blown up. The resulting explosion shook the earth violently and propelled debris in all directions, wounding or killing 250 Americans in a single blow. Although Pike had captured the fort—the first important American victory of the war—he suffered his coup de grâce from a rock projectile or falling debris. The thirty-four-year-old explorer, patriot, soldier, and war hero died with his boots on.[57]

Through no fault of his own, Zebulon Montgomery Pike is one of the most unappreciated American explorers. Although he may have indeed been unlucky, few could match his personal drive and stubborn determination to complete a mission. His association with Wilkinson and the ignominy of becoming lost and being captured undeservedly doomed his reputation. The only explorer to successfully travel to the headwaters of the Rio Grande and the Mississippi, Arkansas, and Red rivers, Pike is entitled to greater recognition for his services. U.S. negotiations for international borders with Britain in 1818 and Spain in 1819 utilized his missions to the country's advantage. Somewhat of a martinet, Pike demanded discipline, but his men respected him for enduring all the fatigues and dangers they did, and they willingly followed him into blinding blizzards, snow-capped mountains, and the heat of battle. His exemplary military service reveals a brave and zealous officer who performed extraordinary feats of service on his country's behalf. He spent his life defending his country and died doing so. Pike held his own in diplomatic encounters with British, Spanish, and Indian leaders. He was one of the first Americans to see, describe, chart, and publish information on the upper Mississippi and the Spanish Borderlands. Pike's southwestern route became an important commercial avenue of the Santa Fe Trail. His journals and maps, however imperfect, provided some of the first American intelligence and observations of the Rocky Mountains, southern Great Plains, and northern Mexico. His notion of the "Great American Desert" being too arid for agricultural settlement and only suited to buffalo and their pursuers likely slowed American expansion and contributed to the creation of a permanent Indian Territory.

Although never receiving the fame or acclaim of other explorers, Pike's dogged determination and his military service ultimately helped build Jefferson's "empire of liberty" rather than Burr and Wilkinson's "empire of the Southwest." Pike's courage and endurance were second to none, but his great sin lay in his unquestioning loyalty to—and faith in—his commanding officer and his overzealous patriotism for flag and country. It is true that Pike lacked the professional training of a Meriwether Lewis, the gregariousness of a William Clark, and the scientific mind of William Dunbar. Moreover, Pike was repeatedly ill-prepared (mostly because of insufficient funds) for undertaking consecutive winter explorations and often failed to achieve the objectives of his expeditions. Yet his contributions of knowledge pertaining to the northeastern and southwestern regions of the Louisiana Purchase and his firsthand tour through the Spanish Borderlands, combined with the publication of his journals and maps, mark him as an important player in the imperial struggle to control the continent and expand American commercial and territorial interests into the trans-Mississippi West. His explorations of the Mississippi and its major southern tributaries have earned him a rightful place in the pantheon of American explorers.

## APPENDIX A: MEMBERS OF PIKE'S MISSISSIPPI EXPEDITION, 1805–1806

Sgt. Henry Kennerman
Cpl. Samuel Bradley
Cpl. William E. Meek
Pvt. John Boley
Pvt. Peter Brandon
Pvt. John Brown
Pvt. Jacob Carter
Pvt. Thomas Daugherty
Pvt. William Gordon
Pvt. Solomon Huddleston

Pvt. Jeremiah Jackson
Pvt. Hugh Menaugh
Pvt. Theodore Miller
Pvt. John Mountjoy
Pvt. David Owens
Pvt. Alexander Roy
Pvt. Patrick Smith
Pvt. John Sparks
Pvt. Freegift Stout
Pvt. David Whelpley

## APPENDIX B: MEMBERS OF PIKE'S SOUTHWESTERN EXPEDITION, 1806–1807

Capt. Zebulon Pike (orig. Lt. Pike, promoted during expedition)
Lt. James B. Wilkinson (second in command; son of General James Wilkinson)
Antoine Baronet Vasquez (civilian interpreter)
Dr. John H. Robinson (volunteer surgeon)
Sgt. Joseph Ballinger (returned with Wilkinson party)
Cpl. Jeremiah R. Jackson
Cpl./Sgt. William C. Meek (volunteer for rescue detail; killed Theodore Miller in Santa Fe)
Pvt. John Boley (also on Lewis and Clark expedition; returned with Wilkinson party; deserted)
Pvt. Samuel Bradley (returned with Wilkinson party; deserted)
Pvt. John Brown

Pvt. Jacob Carter

Pvt. Thomas Daugherty (Pike's waiter; frostbite victim)

Pvt. William Gordon

Pvt. Solomon Huddleston (returned with Wilkinson party; deserted on return)

Pvt. Henry Kennerman (deserted in Missouri)

Pvt. Hugh Menaugh (frostbite victim; returned to stockade with relief party)

Pvt. Theodore Miller (volunteer for rescue detail; killed in Mexico by William Meek)

Pvt. John Mountjoy

Pvt. Alexander Roy

Pvt. Patrick Smith

Pvt. John Sparks (hunter; frostbite victim)

Pvt. Freegift Stout

Pvt. John Wilson (returned with Wilkinson party)

## ACKNOWLEDGMENTS

The author thanks the Charles Redd Center for Western Studies at Brigham Young University for a research grant and the staff at the Denver Public Library, Colorado Historical Society, and Colorado Springs Pioneers Museum for their assistance and William E. Foley, Harvey Hisgen, and Matthew L. Harris for their insights and comments on this chapter.

## NOTES

1. James P. Ronda, "Exploring the American West in the Age of Jefferson," in *North American Exploration,* vol. 3, *A Continent Comprehended,* ed. John L. Allen (Lincoln: University of Nebraska Press, 1997), 40–41; Donald Jackson, *Thomas Jefferson and the Stony Mountains* (Urbana: University of Illinois Press, 1981), 263.

2. The Colorado Springs Pioneers Museum, located in the shadow of Pikes Peak, spearheaded a regional effort to commemorate the two-hundredth anniversary of Pike's 1806 western expedition. The museum's major exhibits, numerous programs, and dynamic lectures in 2006 and 2007 were first-rate, yet relatively few outside of Colorado

knew about them. The Pike National Bicentennial Commission, Zebulon Pike National Historic Trail Association, and the Pike Family Association of America played vital roles in the commemoration. See http://zebulonpike.org. I extend my thanks to Matt Mayberry, Leah Davis Witherow, and Kelly Murphy of the Colorado Springs Pioneers Museum for their research assistance.

3. Compared to that on Lewis and Clark, the literature on Pike is scant. See Hollon, *Lost Pathfinder*; Terrell, *Zebulon Pike*; and, especially, Jackson, *Journals of Pike*. See also Hyslop, *Bound for Santa Fe*, ch. 1; Jackson, *Thomas Jefferson*, ch. 12; and Olsen, "Zebulon Pike." Historians have written about Jefferson's "empire of liberty," but they have not studied Pike's role in it. See Tucker and Hendrickson, *Empire of Liberty*; Onuf, *Jefferson's Empire*; and chapters in Douglas Seefeldt, Jeffrey L. Hautman, and Peter S. Onuf, eds., *Across the Continent: Jefferson, Lewis and Clark, and the Making of America* (Charlottesville: University of Virginia Press, 2005).

4. Zebulon Pike (September 18, 1751–July 27, 1834) and Isabella Brown (July 5, 1753–December 25, 1809) had eight children, but half of them died in infancy (likely from tuberculosis). Three sons and one daughter survived: Zebulon Montgomery, James Brown (May 1, 1784–April 8, 1855), Maria Herriot (August 22, 1789–September 11, 1844), and George Washington (April 7, 1793–January 30, 1812). Emblazoned on the Pike coat of arms are three words: *L amour—La Vertu—La Paix* (Love—Virtue—Peace). The Pike Family Archives reside in the Salisbury Massachusetts Library. A. Pike, *Family of "John Pike*," 96–97.

5. Alan D. Gaff, *Bayonets in the Wilderness: Anthony Wayne's Legion in the Old Northwest* (Norman: University of Oklahoma Press, 2004), 103.

6. Heitman, *Historical Register and Dictionary*, 1:792.

7. A. Pike, *Family of "John Pike*," 142–44. Clarissa "Clara" Harlow Brown (1783–1847) and Zebulon Pike had five children, but only their daughter Clarissa reached maturity. Pike was stationed at Fort Kaskaskia, located on the Mississippi River some fifty miles south of St. Louis, during the first week of December in 1803 when Lewis and Clark came to the fort to recruit a dozen soldiers for their expedition. Because they were not seeking officers, Pike was not a candidate to accompany them. Lewis later wrote a letter to him asking if Pike would like to lead a western expedition, "to which [he] answered in the affirmative." This is one of the only documents linking Pike to Jefferson's plans to explore Louisiana Territory. Deposition of Zebulon Pike, November 17, 1808, in Donald Jackson, ed., *Letters of the Lewis and Clark Expedition*, 2nd ed. (Urbana: University of Illinois Press, 1978), 2:722.

8. Foley, "James A. Wilkinson." For biographies of the general, see Jacobs, *Tarnished Warrior*; Hay and Werner, *Admirable Trumpeter*; and Linklater, *Artist in Treason*. See also chapter 7 in this volume.

9. Wilkinson to Pike, July 30, 1805, in Jackson, *Journals of Pike*, 3–4.

10. At least three manuscript versions of Pike's "Journal of the Mississippi River Expedition" were prepared; two have survived. See Jackson, *Journals of Zebulon Pike*, 5. Clarissa Brown Pike (February 24, 1803–February 1, 1837) married John Cleves Symmes Harrison, the son of President William Henry Harrison. John Brown, Clarissa "Clara"

Harlow Brown Pike, and Clarissa Pike Harrison are all buried in the Sugar Grove Cemetery near Ludlow, Kentucky. A. Pike, *Family of "John Pike,"* 142–44. Pike's keelboat was probably the largest craft that had ascended the upper Mississippi. Appropriately, in August 1817, the *Zebulon M. Pike* became the first steamboat to ascend the Mississippi River to St. Louis. See the Web sites http://zebulonpike.org/zebulon-pike-links.htm and http://www.nps.gov/archive/jeff/LewisClark2/Circa1804/WestwardExpansion/Early Explorers/ZebulonPike.htm.

11. Pike, journal entry, August 24, 1805, in Jackson, *Journals of Pike,* 1:16.

12. The fort on the Iowa bluffs was never built, but the area is now Pikes Peak State Park.

13. Jackson, *Journals of Pike,* 1:37–38, 245–46. Army engineers praised Pike's choice as the best fort location on the upper river and constructed Fort Snelling in 1819. The location became an important commercial center for the fur trade, the meat-packing and wheat industries, and the railroad and contributed to the growth of the Twin Cities, Minneapolis–St. Paul. Incidentally, Pike's treaty was never ratified, and the Indians did not receive any compensation until 1838.

14. Pike, journal entry, October 15, 1805, in Jackson, *Journals of Pike,* 1:47–48.

15. Pike, journal entry, February 1, 1806, in ibid., 1:87. Later explorers corrected this error by pinpointing Lake Itasca as the true source of the Mississippi in 1832. Pike missed the headwaters by two lakes (Bemiji and Itasca/Elk) and about twenty-five miles. Later explorations added to Pike's knowledge of the Mississippi's headwaters: Lewis Cass (1820); Giacomo Constantino Beltrami (1824); Henry Rowe Schoolcraft (1820 and 1830), who determined that Lake Itasca (the name derives from three of the five syllables of the Latin, *ve*ritas *ca*put, or true source) was the headwaters and announced his discovery to the world in 1832; Jean Nicollet (1830s); Charles Lanman (1847); and Willard Glazier (1881). See Glazier, *Headwaters of the Mississippi.*

16. Wilkinson complained to Secretary of War Henry Dearborn that Pike had "stretched his orders." James Wilkinson to Dearborn, in Jackson, *Journals of Pike,* 2:250.

17. See introduction to this volume.

18. A group of disgruntled Federalists detested Jefferson and the Louisiana Purchase. They argued that the influence of New England would wane as the power of the West and South increased. Known as the Essex Junto, these Massachusetts politicians sought to curry favor with New Jersey and New York to join them in a Northern Confederacy. Hamilton, an ardent nationalist, refused their overtures. Burr, however, listened, although whether he made an agreement to join the secessionist cause if they assisted him in being elected governor remains unclear. Hamilton publicly accused Burr of plotting treason, and when Burr lost the election, he blamed Hamilton's spurious remarks as the cause. See James E. Lewis, Jr., *The Louisiana Purchase: Jefferson's Noble Bargain* (Charlottesville, Va.: Thomas Jefferson Foundation, 2003), 62–66.

19. Most Americans anticipated war to break out with Spain. All that was required was an incident to ignite the fuse—such as a military expedition caught trespassing in New Spain. For recent treatments of the conspiracy, see Melton, *Aaron Burr;* Isenberg, *Fallen Founder;* and Linklater, *Artist in Treason.* See also Carter, "Burr-Wilkinson Intrigue."

20. Pike to Wilkinson, July 22, 1806, in Jackson, *Journals of Pike,* 2:124.

21. Wilkinson and Pike correspondence on June 24 and July 12 and 22, 1806, in ibid., 1:285–89, 2:124. While the maps proved helpful, they also contained errors that contributed to Pike's disorientation in the Rockies.

22. Wilkinson to Pike, June 25, 1806, in ibid., 1:285–86. For a comparative account of these explorations, see chapter 4, this volume.

23. Wilkinson authorized a meager six hundred dollars for Pike's expense and trading account, which meant he was scarcely able to procure the bare minimum of supplies.

24. Pike to Bissell, June 15, 1806, in Jackson, *Journals of Pike,* 2:114. The fact that so many of the men who had accompanied Pike up the Mississippi did so again could indicate their appreciation for Pike as a fair and competent leader whom they respected.

25. The Osages later complained that the horses purchased by Pike and Wilkinson were never paid for by the government. William Clark to Secretary of War Dearborn, May 18, 1807, in Carter, *Territorial Papers,* vol. 14, *Louisiana-Missouri, 1806–1814,* 122–23.

26. Pike to Wilkinson, October 2, 1806, in Jackson, *Journals of Pike,* 2:150–53. Wilkinson indicated to others that Pike was ignorant of the general's plan to have Dr. Robinson inform the Spanish about Burr's planned insurrection. If a Mexican revolt occurred in the interim, Pike's military reconnaissance would be useful for a filibuster. Bolton, "Papers of Pike," 801–802.

27. Pike, journal entry, October 1, 1806, Jackson, *Journals of Pike,* 1:329–30. See also Munday, "Pike-Pawnee Village Site." Unbeknownst to Pike, during his late summer trek across the Great Plains he was promoted to captain in the U.S. Infantry on August 12, 1806. Heitman, *Historical Register and Dictionary,* 1:792.

28. Lt. Wilkinson was accompanied by Sgt. Joseph Ballinger and privates John Boley, Samuel Bradley, Solomon Huddleston, and John Wilson. Boley, Bradley, and Huddleston deserted before the Wilkinson group arrived at St. Louis seventy-three days later.

29. Pike, journal entries for late November, in Jackson, *Journals of Pike,* 1:347–49. Pike probably should have constructed a permanent winter camp near the future site of Bent's Fort. If Pike's mission was espionage or capture, that helps explain why he jeopardized the health and lives of his men by proceeding into the Rockies in the dead of winter.

30. Pike, journal entry, November 27, 1806, in Jackson, *Journals of Pike,* 1:350–51. Located on the edge of the Great Plains, Pikes Peak offers a phenomenal view of the countryside and inspired Katharine Lee Bates to write her patriotic poem "America the Beautiful" in 1893, published on July 4, 1895. Lynn Sherr, *America the Beautiful: The Stirring True Story behind Our Nation's Favorite Song* (New York: Public Affairs, 2001). Although the mountain's signs read 14,110 feet, the 1988 National Geodetic Survey measured 5 additional feet of elevation. John Robinson's 1819 map was probably the first to call it "Pike's Mountain."

31. Pike, journal entries, December 13 and 14, 1806, in Jackson, *Journals of Pike,* 1:357–58. Although they were aware of Pike's presence, the Mouache, Capote, and Tabeguache bands of Southern Utes chose not to make contact with Pike during the winter, but Pike saw evidence of their presence, including large piles of their horses' dung along the Arkansas.

32. Pike, journal entry, January 5, 1807, in ibid., 1:365–67.

33. Pike, journal entries, January 14 and 17, 1807, in ibid., 1:368–69.

34. Pike, journal entry, January 24, 1807, in ibid., 1:371–73.

35. Privates Thomas Daugherty, Hugh Menaugh, and John Sparks suffered frost-bite. Menaugh recovered sufficiently to travel, but Daugherty and Sparks remained too incapacitated to move; they sent their gangrenous toes to Pike, pleading not to be abandoned or forgotten.

36. Dr. Robinson joined the expedition as a civilian physician a few days before it embarked and may have been planted as an emissary of Wilkinson to alert the Spanish to Pike's journey. Robinson later served as a brigadier general in the Mexican revolutionary army, making his presence with the party all the more intriguing. Jackson, *Journals of Pike*, 1:377–78, 2:132n. For an in-depth analysis of Robinson's role as a potential filibusterer, see Narrett, "Liberation and Conquest."

37. Pike considered this the end of his southwestern expedition and the beginning of his expedition through the Internal Provinces of New Spain. Pike, journal entries, February 16 and 26, 1807, in Jackson, *Journals of Pike*, 1:379–81, 1:383–85, 2:122–26.

38. Herbert Eugene Bolton discovered Pike's papers in the Mexican archives a century later and published them in the *American Historical Review* in 1908. The Mexican government eventually returned them to the United States. "Pike's Notebook of Maps, Traverse Tables, and Meteorological Observations," in Records of the Adjutant General's Office, 1780s–1917, Archives Division of the Adjutant General's Office, Record Group 94, National Archives.

39. While in Santa Fe, Pike met fur trader James Purcell, who told him of placer gold deposits in the South Platte River that brought gold rush Argonauts to the Front Range in 1858, touting "Pike's Peak or Bust." Jackson, *Journals of Pike*, 2:59–61. At Warm Spring, Pike finally met Baptiste LaLande, who refused to pay William Morrison's debt and justified his actions by claiming that the Spanish held him captive. Pike seized LaLande and accused him of being sent by the Spanish governor to betray Pike. Under duress, the frightened French creole confessed that he had been employed to ascertain Pike's intentions. Pike chastised him and then set him free. Pike, journal entry, March 2, 1807, in Jackson, *Journals of Pike*, 1:387–90.

40. Isaac Cox, *The West Florida Controversy, 1798–1813: A Study in American Diplomacy* (Baltimore, Md.: Johns Hopkins University Press, 1923), 158–68; Kastor, *Nation's Crucible*, 68–75.

41. Pike, journal entry, July 1, 1807, in Jackson, *Journals of Pike*, 1:447. The Spanish retained the rest of Pike's men for two years. One of them, Sgt. William Meek, was kept until 1821 for killing Pvt. Theodore Miller in a drunken altercation. The Freeman-Custis and Pike expeditions nearly sparked a border war and elicited a strong Spanish response, demanding an American apology, which Secretary of State James Madison refused to give, nor would the United States reimburse the Spanish for the substantial amount of food, wine, clothes, supplies, animals, and money they had provided Pike. The king relieved Alencaster of his command for releasing Pike and sending him deeper into Spanish territory and reprimanded General Salcedo.

42. Pike's son was born either just before or soon after Pike left because the boy died on November 23, 1806, and was buried without a name. Later, his remains were interred at Jefferson Barracks National Cemetery. See also A. Pike, *Family of "John Pike,"* 142–44.

43. James Wilkinson to Thomas Jefferson, October 9, 1806. Jefferson sent orders for Wilkinson to arrest Burr on November 8 and issued a general proclamation denouncing Burr to the public on November 27. Paul L. Ford, ed., *The Works of Thomas Jefferson*, 12 vols. (New York: G. P. Putnam's Sons, 1904–1905), vols. 10 and 11.

44. Hoffer, *Treason Trials*. See also "The Aaron Burr Trial," http://www.law.umkc .edu/faculty/projects/ftrials/burr/burr.htm.

45. Pike, who had completed one of Wilkinson's most successfully orchestrated espionage missions (albeit with different motives) was eventually exonerated of any wrongdoing. The embarrassing international incident with Spain caused the two nations to end diplomatic relations and forced Jefferson to scuttle his plans for other military expeditions to explore Louisiana. Those explorations resumed in 1819 with Stephen Long's expedition, conducted during the same year the United States and Spain formally settled the boundary of the Louisiana Purchase with the Adams-Onís Transcontinental Treaty. The Santa Fe Trail opened up two years later when Mexico gained independence from Spain. Wilkinson eventually died in Mexico City awaiting an empresario land grant to settle colonists in Texas. Wilkinson's interpretation of his long military career, which included a cabal against George Washington, his plan to separate the trans-Appalachian frontier, and his involvement in the Burr conspiracy to invade northern Spain, receives a different light in James Wilkinson's three-volume *Memoirs of My Own Times* (Philadelphia: Abraham Small, 1816). In it, Wilkinson called Pike a man of "great hardihood and enterprise" (1:413). Wilkinson's correspondence with the Spanish can be found in Reyes Siles Saturnino, *Archivo general de Indias: Sección papeles de Cuba: Correspondencia y documentación oficial de los gobernadores de Luisiana (años 1777–1803)*, vol. 2 in *Documentos relativos a la independencia de norteamérica existentes en archivos españoles* (Madrid: ES, 1980); Purificación Medina Encina and Reyes Siles Saturnino, *Archivo general de Indias: Sección papeles de Cuba: Correspondencia y documentación oficial de varias autoridades de Luisiana y de las dos Floridas (años 1778–1817)*, vol. 7 in *Documentos relativos a la independencia de norteamérica existentes en archivos españoles* (Madrid: ES, 1981); and idem, *Archivo general de Indias: Sección papeles de Cuba: Correspondencia y documentación oficial de autoridades de Luisiana y de Florida occidental (años 1764– 1819)*, vol. 9 in *Documentos relativos a la independencia de norteamérica existentes en archivos españoles* (Madrid: ES, 1986). See also Portal de archivos españoles, http://pares .mcu.es/. The author thanks colleague George Ryscamp for his assistance.

46. Dearborn to Pike, February 24, 1808, in Jackson, *Journals of Pike*, 2:300–301.

47. U.S. House of Representatives, "Report of . . . Compensation." Jefferson's inability to link Pike to the conspiracy makes it quite clear that he was not involved. Although Lewis and Clark upstaged Pike considerably in gathering scientific information, Pike bested them in his "scientific" presents sent to Jefferson. The two captains sent Jefferson a prairie dog and several magpies from their journey. Pike presented Jefferson with two grizzly bear cubs (male and female) that he had acquired on his march through New

Spain. Jefferson thanked Pike for the bears and sent them to Philadelphia museum curator Charles Willson Peale on January 28, 1808. Both bears eventually ended up as stuffed exhibits in Peale's museum. Thomas Jefferson to Zebulon Montgomery Pike, November 6, 1807, Thomas Jefferson Papers Series 1, General Correspondence, 1651–1827; see Ford, *Works of Thomas Jefferson,* vol. 11. Sometime after the bears arrived at Peale's museum in 1808, Pike took the opportunity to sit for the famous portraitist, who painted the twenty-nine-year-old officer in full dress uniform; this, the only existing contemporary image of Pike, hangs in Philadelphia's Independence Hall.

48. An 1811 edition appeared in London and was subsequently translated into French, German, and Dutch. Zebulon Montgomery Pike, *An Account of Expeditions to the Sources of the Mississippi, and through the Western Parts of Louisiana, to the Sources of the Arkansaw, Kans, La Platte, and Pierre Jaun Rivers; Performed by Order of the United States during the Years 1805, 1806, and 1807; and a Tour of the Interior Parts of New Spain, When Conducted through These Provinces, by Order of the Captain-General, in the Year 1807* (Philadelphia: Cornelius and Andrew Conrad and Co., 1810). An atlas containing five maps of Pike's travels and charts on western commerce and tables on Indian populations was available for separate purchase. Pike and Gouverneur Kemble Warren, *Atlas Accompanying An Account of Expeditions . . .* (Philadelphia: C. and A. Conrad and Co., 1810). Pike did not profit from either of these publications, because his publisher filed for bankruptcy before he received any compensation.

49. Nicholas King, a British immigrant noted for completing the survey for Washington City, performed an important function as Jefferson's editorial choice for the redaction of the journals and re-creation of the maps of explorers John Sibley, William Clark, William Dunbar, George Hunter, Thomas Freeman, Peter Custis, and Zebulon Pike to make them ready for publication. William Clark trusted the information about the region from Pike, who had not verified it himself but instead had trusted the information from a German cartographer who had never been north of Mexico! Using Pike's field notes and sketch maps, Anthony Nau compiled a large, four-sheet manuscript map of the upper Mississippi drainage system. Pike's reports influenced the maps of William Clark, the geographical textbook of Elijah Parish, and the expedition of Stephen Long. Wheat, *Mapping the Trans-Mississippi West* (1958), 2:60; Allen, *Passage through the Garden,* 376.

50. Pike, "Pike's Dissertation on Louisiana," in Jackson, *Journals of Zebulon Pike,* 2:27.

51. Wheat, *Mapping the Trans-Mississippi West,* vol. 2, *From Lewis and Clark to Fremont, 1804–1845* (1957–63; repr., Mansfield Center, Conn.: Martino Publishing, 2004), 16–30; and Goetzmann, *Exploration and Empire,* 62.

52. Carter, *Territorial Papers,* vol. 9, *Territory of Orleans,* 909, 927–28, 998–1001; and Cox, *West Florida Controversy,* 158–68.

53. Hickey, *War of 1812.*

54. R. David Edmunds, *Tecumseh and the Quest for Indian Leadership* (Lincoln: University of Nebraska Press, 1983); and Robert M. Owens, *Mr. Jefferson's Hammer: William Henry Harrison and the Origins of American Indian Policy* (Norman:

University of Oklahoma Press, 2007). William Henry Harrison was Pike's daughter's future father-in-law.

55. Heitman, *Historical Register and Dictionary,* 1:38–39, 792.

56. Zebulon M. Pike to his father Zebulon Pike, April 22, 1812, Charles B. Pike Collection, Chicago Historical Society Archives.

57. On his body was a field book with a page addressed to his son. Although only two sentences, it encapsulates Pike's core beliefs on living a good life. The first line read, "Preserve your honor free from blemish." The second said, "Be Always ready to die for your country." Cited in A. Pike, *Family of "John Pike,"* 146. In 1814, the British cited the burning of York as the pretext for burning Washington. A good account of the battle of York is in Benn, *Historic Fort York,* 50–58. Pike's body was preserved in a whiskey barrel before being pickled and buried in an iron casket near the site of Fort Pike on Black River Bay. Pike's body was exhumed in 1818 and moved to a new military cemetery at Madison Barracks before being moved yet again in 1909 to a new location east of Sackets Harbor, New York, and received a stone marker. Colorado Springs residents have made half a dozen unsuccessful attempts to have Pike's body interred in Colorado. Richard Melzer, *Buried Treasures: Famous and Unusual Gravesites in New Mexico History* (Santa Fe, N.Mex.: Sunstone Press, 2007), 262–63; and Warner, "Death of Zebulon Pike," 105–109.

# 2

# Pike and Empire

*James P. Ronda*

Early in March 1807, in a small village outside Santa Fe, two men talked quietly about the future of New Spain and the ambitions of the young American republic. Lieutenant Zebulon Montgomery Pike had come to Santa Fe just days before under guard from his post on the Conejos River. The man Pike often called "my friend" was Bartholemew Fernandez, a Santa Fe resident and someone Pike once thought was an officer in the Spanish army. But in the snowy stillness of that March night, Fernandez sounded more like a civilian and a merchant than a soldier as he told Pike about the "great desire they felt for a change of affairs, and an open trade with the United States." Sensing an opportunity, Pike seized the moment, took a piece of chalk, and began to draw a map on the floor. What he sketched out were the routes and connections between Louisiana and "North Mexico." Then, as if to say that the wish for a "change in affairs" might happen sometime soon, Pike gave "Mr. Bartholemew" a certificate addressed to American citizens and identifying Fernandez as a friend and "man of influence."[1] Fernandez was convinced that an American army would invade New Spain no later than spring. Pike assured him that no invasion was in the works, but the certificate seemed to say "not this spring but sometime soon."

Where did this memorable conversation come from? Why was a junior officer in the U.S. Army deep in Spanish territory talking about the future shape of the continent? Answers to those questions take us back to the origins of Manifest Destiny, the imperial rivalries that dominated North America for two centuries, and the tangled life of sometime empire builder Zebulon Montgomery Pike. Pike traveled a long road to

Santa Fe; the ideas he championed had been on the road even longer. If I may borrow a term from geology, Pike moved in a world of "suspect terrain" where boundaries, loyalties, and identities were constantly shifting and always uncertain.

Whether he knew it or not, young Lieutenant Pike was part of a long tradition of empire building. For Americans, that tradition had its beginnings in seventeenth-century England. English nationalism was an explosive mixture of religious passion and economic necessity, all fueled by an intense hatred of Catholic Spain. It was religion that most fully shaped the ideas that swirled around English expansionism. In sermon after sermon, both Puritan and Anglican clergy preached that the English nation had a special mission, a divine obligation to spread the Protestant faith throughout the world. "God is English," said one preacher, emphasizing that sense of the English as the new Israel, the chosen people of God.[2] That powerful feeling of mission and "chosenness" clung to English colonists, whether they were bound for Massachusetts Bay or Virginia. One Puritan divine caught the temper of the time when he declared that God had sent the English on an "errand into the wilderness" to spread the true faith, making the world both godly and English.[3]

As religious passions cooled in the eighteenth century, that English sense of sacred mission was steadily transformed. At a time of constant imperial conflict with France, the mission took on a more secular tone. Now it was Great Britain's national destiny to defeat France, wrest land from Indian hands, and become a real empire. Once it was the clergy who preached God's empire; now it was pamphleteers and politicians who promoted an imperial Britain.

No one better exemplified that secular British-American imperialism than Benjamin Franklin. A recent Franklin biographer has written that "to Franklin the rise of the British Empire was the greatest phenomenon of the eighteenth century."[4] While some political theorists took a darker view of empire and its consequences, Franklin and most others defined the word in positive terms. Empire promised power and prosperity. To build an empire was to take out an insurance policy for the future. In Franklin's view, America was at the very heart of the British Empire. Writing his "Observations Concerning the Increase of

Mankind, Peopling of Countries, Etc." in 1751, Franklin predicted that America "will in another Century will be more than the people of England, and the greatest Number of Englishmen will be on this Side [of] the Water." But this was not an argument for American independence. Instead, Franklin exclaimed, "[W]hat an Accession of Power to the British Empire by Sea as well as Land!"[5]

The American Revolution changed the location of power and destiny from Britain to the new nation. Once Britain had imagined itself exceptional among the nations of the world; now the American republic took on that role. God's will and the territorial expansion of the nation were fused in the fires of war and nation-building. South Carolinian William Henry Drayton captured that sense of American imperial mission and its religious overtones when he wrote in 1776 that "the Almighty has made choice of the present generation to erect the American Empire."[6] Drayton looked to God for imperial validation; Boston revolutionary Samuel Adams substituted Nature for the deity. "We shall never be upon a solid Footing till Britain cedes to us what Nature designs we should have."[7] Just what Nature had in store for a land-hungry republic was a bit clearer in Jedediah Morse's influential 1789 *American Geography*. "We cannot but anticipate the period, as not far distant, when the AMERICAN EMPIRE will comprehend millions of souls, west of the Mississippi." As for Nature's American limits, Morse argued that "the Mississippi was never designed as the western boundary of the American empire."[8] Revolutionaries and geographers soon found their words echoing in the popular press. On the eve of the Louisiana Purchase, the *New York Evening Post* boldly announced that "it belongs of *right* to the United States to regulate the future destiny of *North America*. The country is *ours*; ours is the right to its rivers and to all the sources of future opulence, power and happiness."[9] God's empire promised salvation in heaven; the American empire promised heaven on earth. During the debate on the ratification of the Constitution, old revolutionary Patrick Henry paused to consider the nation's future. "Some way or other," he mused, "we must be a great and mighty empire."[10]

These prophets of empire could define American expansion by their words, but they lacked the power to transform ideas into political and diplomatic action. That power rested in Thomas Jefferson, third president of the United States. Like Franklin, Jefferson used the word "empire" in glowing terms. Perhaps his most famous expression of imperial ambition came in the phrase "empire for liberty." Writing to James Madison in 1809, Jefferson predicted that "we should have such an empire for liberty as she has never surveyed since creation: and I am persuaded no constitution was ever before so well calculated as ours for extensive empire and self government."[11] Behind those high-flown words was a harsh reality. As president, Jefferson had used all the powers of his office to gain Indian land by whatever means. If the empire of liberty had no place for Native people, it also meant shoving aside Spanish, French, or British claims in the West. Jefferson made his imperial ambitions plain in an 1803 letter to Senator John C. Breckinridge. "When we are full on this side," he told Breckinridge, "we may lay off a range of States on the Western bank [of the Mississippi River] from the head to the mouth, and so, range after range, advancing compactly as we multiply."[12] Here was the vision of an irresistible march across the continent, a march justified by the spread of liberty and made inevitable by the very design of Nature. As Jefferson declared in his Second Inaugural Address (1805), "[I]n my view, is it not better that the opposite bank of the Mississippi should be settled by our own brethren and children, than by strangers of another family?"[13] And those strangers might be French, Spanish, British, or American Indians.

Long before New York journalist John L. O'Sullivan coined the term "Manifest Destiny" in 1845, there was a fully formed expansionist ideology to energize and justify what George Washington had called "the rising American empire."[14] That ideology, drawn from religious conviction, superheated nationalism, and a fierce land hunger, was part of Zebulon Montgomery Pike's intellectual inheritance. Pike came to maturity in a world whose very language defined empire and territorial expansion as goals worthy of the best efforts anyone could muster. Pike embraced those ideas and blended them with his own restless ambition and exaggerated sense of self-importance. In the larger scheme of things, empire gave Pike a field on which to play out all his dreams of national honor and personal glory.

Pike was shaped by the climate of opinion that swirled around him. But it took one individual to draw him into the suspect terrain of imperial rivalry. Meriwether Lewis and William Clark had President Thomas Jefferson; Pike had General James Wilkinson. There was perhaps no more complex and dangerous figure on the early nineteenth-century western frontier than James Wilkinson.[15] Commander of U.S. forces in the West, sometime governor of Louisiana Territory, Spanish secret agent, and co-conspirator with Aaron Burr, Wilkinson was what a recent historian has called "the perfect chameleon."[16] But on one matter Wilkinson remained true to his colors—the color of money and personal advancement. By the time Pike met Wilkinson, the general already had a long history in the shadowy world of deception and intrigue.

The summer of 1805 found Pike at Fort Massac in the Illinois country serving as district paymaster for the First Infantry Regiment. It was hardly a promising assignment for an officer hungry for advancement and eager for glory. Sometime during that summer, Wilkinson visited the post and selected Pike to lead a reconnaissance party up the Mississippi River. What drew Wilkinson to Pike remains unclear. The general did know Pike's father, Colonel Zebulon Pike, and the younger Pike's wife, Clarissa, was the daughter of a Kentucky friend. Wilkinson always had an entourage of young officers around him, and perhaps he was looking to add another to that company. Without question or hesitation, Pike became Wilkinson's man. It was a decision that would haunt him for the rest of his life. It still haunts him.

The exploration assigned to Pike seemed straightforward enough. Mapping the rivers of the Louisiana Purchase was high on Jefferson's list of western priorities. But Pike's journey up the Mississippi was not at the direction of the commander-in-chief but on orders from Wilkinson. And Wilkinson's reasons for sending Pike up north remain elusive. However, as Donald Jackson reminds us, Wilkinson was not "completely a charlatan," and Pike's first expedition may have been just what it seemed—a genuine military probe up an important river.[17]

Whatever the reasons, Pike got his instructions for exploration from Wilkinson on July 30, 1805. He and his crew were to head up the Mississippi, plot the course of the river, and pay attention to what Jefferson always called "the face of the country." Pike was also handed important Indian missions, including the purchase of land for two military posts and arrangements for Indian delegations to visit the Great Father. In addition, Pike was instructed to note the current state of the fur trade on the upper Mississippi.[18] But nothing in those orders directed him to launch a diplomatic offensive against British traders doing business in what is now Minnesota and the western Great Lakes region. Although Pike is often said to have gone north in search of the headwaters of the Mississippi, Wilkinson did not think this was an important expedition objective, for he simply told Pike that finding the headwaters would be useful if it could be done in one season. Taken together, these instructions were not much different (if less detailed) than those Jefferson prepared for Lewis and Clark and the Freeman-Custis expeditions.[19] How Pike interpreted them would be another matter.

In so many ways, the Minnesota country at the beginning of the nineteenth century was a borderland frontier. There the borders—both national and personal—were fluid and ill-defined. More important, Minnesota was a "middle ground," a place where peoples from diverse cultures met to trade and sometimes make war. The Minnesota country would be Pike's first borderland, the first place to give life to the ideas of empire he had inherited.[20]

Pike had no experience in the complex world of Indian diplomacy. He had never been a participant at a major council, he knew little about the protocols and rituals that shaped such meetings, and he spoke no Native language. Nonetheless he was ordered to represent the United States at a gathering on contested ground and with Indians who were not much impressed by the power of the new nation. Heading upriver, Pike did not doubt that he could mold Native realities to American patterns.

Perhaps the most important meeting Pike had with Native people came near the end of September 1805 when he held council with representatives of the Santee and Mdewakanton Sioux. Pike and the Indian delegates met on an island at the confluence of the Minnesota and Mississippi rivers within what are now the city limits of St. Paul. Pike blandly announced the Louisiana Purchase and then in a candid moment said he represented not the Great Father but General Wilkinson. Two issues then occupied Pike, both of them imperial in character. Like Lewis and Clark, Pike had been instructed to scout out suitable locations for military establishments. Claiming that such posts would benefit Native people, Pike asked the assembled representatives to sign a land purchase draft treaty. Thinking he had accomplished that, he then moved to an issue not covered by his instructions. Intertribal peace had long been a centerpiece for British Indian policy. Now it was on the American agenda as well. Taking matters into his own hands, Pike attempted to negotiate a peace between the eastern Sioux and their Chippewa neighbors. After listing all the advantages peace might bring, Pike concluded with a threat. "If the chiefs do not listen to the voice of their father and continue to commit murders on you and our traders," Pike warned that "they will call down the vengeance of the Americans."[21]

At the end of the day, two Sioux chiefs signed a brief treaty document granting land for building the posts Pike sought. Pike later told Wilkinson that he had bought the land "for a Song."[22] But he had neglected to fill in that portion of Article Two that specified the amount to be paid for the land. When Wilkinson wrote Secretary of War Henry Dearborn about the treaty, he tartly observed that Pike was "a much abler Soldier than Negotiator."[23] But Pike thought he had done well, only later beginning to suspect that the peace he believed existed was no more than a temporary truce.

Nothing more fully reveals Pike's expansive view of American empire than his ill-conceived foray into international diplomacy in the snows of northern Minnesota. During the first months of 1806, Pike and a small party sledded their way north in search of the headwaters of the Mississippi. What they found instead was a country fully in the hands of traders from Canada's North West Company. Established in 1787, the expansionist-minded Nor'westers had pushed west toward the Pacific and south into the Great Lakes region. The Minnesota country was dotted with North West Company posts doing a brisk business with many Indians. This British presence was perfectly legal under the conditions of the 1794 Jay Treaty, which allowed traders from both nations to "freely carry on trade and commerce with each other" and the several nations of Indians. But there were widely recognized problems. Tensions between British and American traders were compounded by charges that Nor'westers were smuggling trade goods and furs past the U.S. customs house at Michilimackinac. And many in the federal government were persuaded that the Canadian company was a front for British imperial designs. Rumors of flags and medals being given to Indians by British traders only increased the troubles in Minnesota. Wilkinson had taken action against British interests on the Missouri River, but nothing had been done on the upper Mississippi. Pike was about to change that.

Few things more deeply offended Pike than the sight of the flags of other nations on lands claimed by the United States. For him, flags were the premier symbol of national sovereignty. They also had deep personal meanings linked to honor and identity. In early January 1806, Pike and his men visited British trader James Grant at his Cedar Lake post. Pike reported what happened next. "When we came in sight of his House, [I] discovered the Flag of Great Britain flying. I felt indignant, and cannot say what my feelings would have excited me to." Pike complained to Grant, prompting the trader to smoothly reply that the flag was not his but belonged to nearby Indians. "This was not much more agreeable to me," recalled Pike, and he decided to watch Grant and other traders carefully.[24]

What he saw at other North West Company posts convinced Pike that British traders were indeed politicking among the Indians and posed a real threat to U.S. sovereignty. In a certain way, Pike was right. Until the Treaty of Ghent in 1814, the British held on to their Great Lakes military posts in open defiance of agreements made at the end of the American Revolution. And they had not abandoned efforts at making alliances with Indians throughout the Old Northwest. At Leech Lake, Pike and trader Hugh McGillis had a spirited exchange about the presence of British flags. For Pike, those flags were more than a question of law and sovereignty; they were a personal insult to American honor. Sensing that the matter was a sensitive one, McGillis asked Pike if the British flag could be raised "by way of complement to ours, which had nearly arrived." Just as the Jay Treaty had allowed traders from both nations to work in the country, McGillis pragmatically thought two flags might be acceptable. Pike was silent on this, explaining later that "I had not yet explained to him my Ideas."[25]

Those ideas became dramatically clear in a letter Pike addressed to McGillis on February 7, 1806. Pike brusquely informed McGillis that he and other company traders were in U.S. territory and had to obey import laws and customs regulations established by the federal government. While admitting that the Jay Treaty permitted the British to

do business in the Minnesota country, Pike insisted that foreign traders had to pay appropriate customs duties, obtain trade licenses, and
conform to all U.S. laws. The explorer's winter tour had convinced him
that the North West Company's trade networks extended "to the center
of our newly acquired territory of Louisiana."[26] Pike knew that American traders often complained about unfair competition from their British rivals. In his mind, the North West Company not only challenged
American power but also cut into a vital part of the national economy.
As Pike later explained to Wilkinson, "[T]he Dignity and Honor of our
Government requires that those Scoundrels be taught to geather [sic]
their Skins in quiet . . . , added to which those are the very instigators
of the War between the Chiefs and Scioux [sic] in order that they may
monopolize the trade of the Upper Mississippi."[27]

Wilkinson once wrote that Pike "stretched his orders," but what the
explorer did next went far beyond them.[28] He brazenly deceived McGillis about the nature of his mission, telling the trader, "I have found, sir,
your commerce and establishments, extending beyond our most exaggerated ideas, and in addition to the injury done our revenue, by the
evasion of duties, other acts which are more particularly injurious to
the *honor* and *dignity* of our government."[29] Acting entirely on his own
authority, Pike then issued a comprehensive set of demands. The North
West Company was to stop distributing flags and medals to Indians,
trade goods had to be registered and duties paid at Michilimackinac,
and no company post could fly the British flag. None of this was ever
part of Pike's official instructions. Instead, the letter represented Pike's
deeply felt personal and emotional sense of American empire. Pike had
his first taste of imperial politics and diplomacy in northern Minnesota.
It would not be his last.

When Wilkinson complained that Pike had "stretched his orders,"
the general was writing specifically about the explorer's ill-fated attempt
to find the headwaters of the Mississippi. But for Wilkinson there was
something appealing about an officer willing to go beyond the letter of
the law. Perhaps it seemed to show initiative and the willingness to take
risks. And in the spring of 1806 when Pike returned to St. Louis, Wilkinson was all about taking risks in a high-stakes game. The nature of his
game has never been fully clear. Wilkinson continued to spy for Spain as

Agent 13, collecting a handsome pension from his handlers. At the same time, he entertained a personal and financial interest in opening a direct trade toward Santa Fe despite New Spain being closed to American merchants. But most complex and murky was his relationship with ex–vice president Aaron Burr. The Wilkinson-Burr conspiracy has long been the subject of scholarly debate. This much is plain: Burr and Wilkinson had invested their personal and political fortunes in the West. Over time they would fashion different plans, adopt different strategies, and then tell different stories to different audiences. Whatever their plans— whether invading Mexico to spark a war between the United States and Spain or the establishment of an independent republic in what was once New Spain—the conspirators needed to know more about Spain's empire to the southwest.[30]

The schemes hatched by Wilkinson and Burr played on the mutual fears and suspicions shared by Spain and the United States. Wilkinson was especially adept at pitting one nation against the other. Although Spain had allied itself with the United States during the revolution, Spanish officials were increasingly convinced that the new republic had designs on Spanish territory. As early as 1783, one Spanish official warned that "a new and independent power has now arisen on our continent. Its people are active, industrious, and aggressive. It would be culpable negligence on our part not to thwart their schemes for conquest."[31] Writing in 1796 from New Orleans, Governor Carondelet predicted that the Americans would soon invade Spanish territory. On the eve of the Louisiana Purchase, frontier army officer Jose Vidal described the Americans as "ambitious, restless, lawless, conniving, changeable, and turbulent."[32] And news about the Lewis and Clark expedition supplied by Wilkinson as well as the successful interception of the Freeman-Custis expedition on the Red River only served to give substance to Spanish fears.

If Spanish officials worried about an American invasion by either civilian adventurers or the U.S. Army, Jefferson and his cabinet were equally unsettled when they looked south. The borders of the Louisiana Purchase between the United States and Spanish territory were open to question and definition. Spain and the United States had vastly different views on the territorial reach of the purchase itself. And there were many unruly characters such as Philip Nolan to trouble the contested border between Louisiana and Spanish Texas. No one was more skilled at increasing those tensions than James Wilkinson. In a series of letters written during 1805, Wilkinson filled Secretary Dearborn with stories of Spanish treachery and the possibility of imminent attack. Early in the year, Dearborn ordered a secret reconnaissance into Texas, thus providing at least some official authority for what would become Pike's second borderland exploration. In one especially explosive letter written in the fall of 1805, Wilkinson suggested strategies and operations "should it be judged expedient to take possession of New Mexico."[33] Dearborn promptly responded, agreeing that such military operations were entirely possible.

It was in that atmosphere of intrigue, suspicion, and shadowy conspiracy that Wilkinson prepared for Pike's southwestern expedition. Wilkinson's instructions for Pike, dated June 24, 1806, gave the explorer three missions. His first objective was to return fifty-one Osage captives to their homes. Wilkinson always maintained that this was Pike's "primary object," but neither the general nor the lieutenant ever believed that tale. The second mission was more clearly imperial—a peace treaty between the Osage and Kansa Indians. But Pike's third goal was the one that proved most difficult and ultimately most controversial; Wilkinson ordered the explorer to find and negotiate with the Comanches, a search that would surely take Pike into Spanish territory. Pike was told to "move with great circumspection," a polite way to say that he was on a spying mission.[34] But the nature of that spying and who would benefit from it remain unexplained. Wilkinson probably knew that Pike would be captured, although there is no evidence that he betrayed Pike as he had Lewis and Clark by informing Spanish officials of their presence in the West. How would the Spanish react to the presence of a U.S. Army officer and his party found on Spanish territory? Would that frontier incident spark a war between the two nations? What is clear is that Pike uncritically accepted his role as a spy. For him, this was one more way to serve the greater cause of American empire. He had faced the British in Minnesota; now he was prepared to confront the Spanish on the southwestern frontier.

Imperial expansion in North America always involved diplomatic relations with Native nations. Empire builders sought Indians as allies and trading partners and—in the case of the Anglo-Americans—as sources for land. Pike was not an especially skilled or experienced diplomat, but he did have a sure grasp of American imperial aspirations and how Native people fit into the republic's scheme of things. Peace, trade, and a wholehearted acceptance of the Great Father in Washington were the essentials that Pike and his superiors demanded from the nation's "red children."

At the end of September 1806, the second Pike expedition was camped on a rise overlooking the Kitkehahki or Republican Pawnee village in what is now Webster County, Nebraska. On September 27, Pike's interpreter Antoine F. Baronet Vasquez (known in Pike's *Account* as Barony) came to camp with Pawnee chief Sharitarish, or White Wolf (known in Pike's *Account* as Characterish), and three other chiefs. Always alert to signs of rival empires, Pike could not miss seeing the large Spanish medal White Wolf was wearing around his neck. And if he did not see it at that moment, Pike soon learned that the chief had a commission from Spanish officials dated mid-June 1806. If the British were moving into the very center of Louisiana, then these objects were sure signs that Spain was also trespassing on the Purchase and luring Indians away from their new Great Father. Eager to impress the Pawnees, Pike offered food and gifts. The gifts were more than presents; they were symbols of imperial authority. Like other diplomats and explorers, Pike thought that when Indians accepted such gifts they were also acknowledging American authority and sovereignty. Native leaders undoubtedly saw the gifts in another light. Pike gave White Wolf a gun, a gorget, and "other articles." The otherwise unidentified "second chief" got a small American medal, while the remaining Pawnees received gorgets. Writing several days later to Wilkinson, Pike hoped that the gifts "would have a good effect, both as to attaching them to our government, and in our immediate intercourse."[35]

While Pike was eager to get on with his Pawnee diplomacy, there was the matter of arranging peace between the Osage and Kansa Indians. He pursued that matter on September 28. No record survives of that negotiation, but Pike was convinced that the Indians had "smoked the pipe

This painting, *Uncertain Welcome,* by Darrell Combs, hangs in the Pawnee Indian Village Museum near Republic, Kansas. General James Wilkinson instructed Pike to broker a peace between the Pawnees and their neighbors. Pike's small party of two dozen soldiers visited the Pawnee village on the Republican River between the present-day towns of Red Cloud and Guide Rock on September 25, 1806. During the next two weeks, they held a grand council. The Pawnees initially tried to dissuade Pike from continuing on, yet his perseverance, courage, and luck enabled his entourage to continue their journey to the Rocky Mountains. Pike acquired horses, supplies, and information and then followed a trail left by a Spanish force that was returning to Santa Fe after their recent visit to the Pawnees. Courtesy of Darrell Combs.

of peace."[36] Like so many others, he easily confused peace with truce. On the Great Plains, there was no permanent peace but only a long series of truces easily broken. Native leaders understood that; Pike did not.

The next day, September 29, was fully taken up with the great Pawnee council. Pike estimated that some four hundred warriors were present in the large village. As the Americans entered, something immediately caught Pike's eye. It was a Spanish flag, hanging in the door of the council lodge. Pike had a long history with flags, and he was about to add another chapter. No sooner had the gathering begun than Pike demanded the Spanish flag be hauled down and handed over to him, and an American flag put in its place. Pike admitted later that this was "carrying the pride of nations a little too far."[37] The Pawnees had been impressed by the recent presence of a large Spanish force commanded by Lieutenant Facundo Melgares. Tipped off by Wilkinson, the Melgares expedition was in the field hoping to intercept Lewis and Clark just as Francisco Viana had recently halted the Freeman-Custis party. Although Melgares did not visit the Republican Pawnees, a junior officer made known the Spanish presence and the desire to stop all American interlopers. After replying to Pike's other requests, there was stony silence about handing over the Spanish flag. Pike decided to press the issue just as he had with the Nor'westers. He told the Indians that "it was impossible for the nation to have two fathers; that they must either be the children of the Spaniards or acknowledge their American father."[38]

Two flags now carried the weight of rival empires. Like it or not, the Pawnees were caught between the Spanish and the Americans. After a long and painful silence, a Pawnee elder got up and quietly took down the Spanish ensign. Pike then triumphantly raised the American standard over the village. The American officer may have thought he had won the day, but the Pawnees were both angry and fearful. As Pike later recalled, "every face in the council was clouded with sorrow, as if some great national Calamity was about to befall them."[39] At that moment, Pike must have known he had overreached. Realizing that he had embarrassed the Indians and put them at risk of Spanish reprisals, Pike offered a quick compromise. He returned the Spanish flag but insisted that it not be flown so long as the American expedition was present.

Pike was right about one thing. In the contest for empire in the West, flags were more than mere fabric: they represented imperial ambition and national honor. Pike once described flags as "the standard of an European power."[40] For him, flags and medals were markers, emblems of empire. His Pawnee adventure suggests just how far Pike was willing to place those markers, as well as the limits of American influence. The Pawnees got their compromise; in later years, Native people would not be so successful.

The rest of Pike's journey into the Southwest is an often-told story. It is a tale of geographic confusion, courage in the face of adversity, and eventual arrest at the hands of the Spanish.[41] Pike once wrote to Wilkinson that a journey to Santa Fe under Spanish guard "would gratify our most sanguine expectations."[42] Whatever those expectations, Pike and his men got that wish.

Historians and other scholars have paid much attention to the origins of Pike's second expedition and his various geographic bewilderments. But in the larger story of empire in the West, those are sideshows. Perhaps Pike would have us look closer at the ideas and strategies embedded in his "Observations on New Spain." Written in 1808 and printed as an appendix to his *Account,* the "Observations" is a summary of what he learned about Spain's empire in the American Southwest. More important, it presented Pike's geopolitical thinking about relations between Spain and the United States as well as the means to effect what his friend Bartholemew Fernandez called "a change of affairs." That meant political revolution and the extension of American power into what had been Spanish territory. Beyond anything else Pike ever wrote, "Observations on New Spain" reveals his vision of empire.[43] To understand that document is to grasp something about the essential Pike.

Most of "Observations on New Spain" is a routine recounting of what Pike knew or thought he knew about large parts of Spanish North America. There are the predictable comments about terrain, climate, local customs, and military forces. And there are occasional flashes of unintended humor, as when Pike compared Spanish women to "Turkish ladies."[44] But near the end of the essay, Pike suddenly shifted focus and began a detailed geopolitical discussion of southwestern North America.

That analysis began with Pike's views on the consequences of Spanish rule. Betraying all the preconceptions and prejudices of a culture that was deeply anti-Spanish and profoundly anti-Catholic, Pike portrayed New Spain's government as filled with petty tyrants and greedy aristocrats who oppressed a generous, sober, and hospitable people. New Spain, so Pike believed, labored under the burdens of "restrictions, monopolies, prohibitions, seclusions, and superstition." Pressing this theme, Pike argued that Spain kept its American possessions "so carefully secluded" from "all light" that her citizens "have vegetated like the acorn in the forest."[45]

But Pike believed that change was in the air. Echoing what Bartholemew Fernandez told him, Pike insisted that opening the doors to free trade would make the country "rich and powerful." Yet more than the power of the marketplace would be needed to produce political change. A Spanish official once wrote that so long as the United States and New Spain were neighbors, they would be enemies. Pike turned that argument on its head. "The approximation of the United States, with the gigantic strides of French ambition, have begun to rouse their dormant qualities, and to call into action the powers of their minds, on the subject of their political situation." Believing that the people of New Spain would not turn to the British for help, Pike was convinced that only the United States could extend the empire of liberty to "North Mexico." Here Pike pulled no punches. "*They therefore have turned their eyes towards the United States,* as brethren of the same soil, in their vicinity, and who has within her powers ample resources of arms, ammunition, and even men to assist in securing their independence."[46] For Pike, the choice was clear. Either the United States would support a revolution, or Spanish rule might continue. And if Napoleon's brother Joseph became king of Spain, a revived French empire would suddenly become the republic's dangerous southern neighbor.

Pike never pretended that American empire building in Spanish America would be done for the ideal of liberty alone. The economic rewards were sure to be substantial and enduring. American merchants from St. Louis would have ready partners in men such as Bartholemew Fernandez, and American ships would fill Mexican ports. "Even on the coast of the Pacific," Pike was sure, "no European nation could vie with us." Summing up all the prosperity that empire seemed to promise, Pike confidently predicted, "[W]e would become their factors, agents, guardians, and, in short, tutelary genius."[47] But Pike was not prepared to see Spanish-speaking Catholics as U.S. citizens. A liberated New Spain would become a separate client state, a permanent but junior partner in "the rising American empire."

But none of this could happen without military intervention. And Pike openly promoted his plan for invading Spanish territory and prompting a revolution. Twenty thousand U.S. troops "under good officers," fighting in concert with a force of "Mexican independents," would be needed to "create and effect the revolution." The entire cost of the adventure would be borne by the new government in Mexico City. Convinced that such an invasion would have widespread popular support, Pike insisted that the army act as "friends and protectors, not as plunderers."[48] This was conquest without guilt, empire without shame.

Generations of preachers, politicians, and pamphleteers had offered their distinctive visions of empire that sounded almost millennial in passion and promise. The conquerors were really liberators, the conquered were grateful victims, and all would enjoy the benefits of heaven on earth, a glorious empire of liberty. Pike concluded his "Observations" with a prophetic vision that was at once remarkable yet representative of things to come: "Should an Army of Americans ever march into the country, and be guided by these maxims, they will have only to march from province to province in triumph, and be hailed by the united voices of grateful millions as their deliverers and saviors, whilst our national character would resound to the most distant nations of the earth."[49]

Zebulon Montgomery Pike has suffered a strange and undeserved fate. Dismissed as either a young officer with little talent and consumed by ambition or the unwitting accomplice of an unscrupulous commander, Pike now seems a mere shadow. He appears an uncomplicated man of action with neither ideas nor intellect. In American memory, Pike is recalled for a piece of the western landscape he neither climbed nor named.[50] We trace his journeys but not the grand theories and bitter conflicts that shaped them. On the simplest level, Pike stands at the beginning of a long American fascination with the Southwest, one that finally exploded in the Mexican-American War and continues into our own time. The publication of his *Account* in 1810 revived interest in the Santa Fe trade and inspired an entire generation of soldier-explorers, including the redoubtable William H. Emory.[51]

But it is in the elusive world of ideas that we can understand something deeper about Pike. Thomas Jefferson's empire of liberty faced four powerful opponents: France, Spain, Great Britain, and Native nations. Unlike Lewis and Clark, Pike dealt directly with three of the four. What he said, what he wrote, and what he did were inspired by a venerable tradition of empire building, a tradition that Pike fully accepted and enthusiastically advanced. In Pike as geopolitical thinker, we can see all the twists and turns, fantasies and fabrications that made the West part of the United States. Pike really meant it when he talked about "the national objects" that guided his journeys.[52] More than most other explorers of the age, Pike stands as the perfect emblem in the imperial war for the West.

# NOTES

1. Pike, journal entry, March 4, 1807, in Jackson, *Journals of Pike*, 1:397.

2. John Alymer, 1558, quoted in Gary Nash, *Red, White, and Black: The Peoples of Early America* (Englewood Cliffs, N.J.: Prentice-Hall, 1974), 1. For an extended treatment of this theme, see the documents and editorial remarks in Conrad Cherry, ed., *God's New Israel: Religious Interpretations of American Destiny*, rev. ed. (Chapel Hill: University of North Carolina Press, 1998).

3. The phrase is taken from the title of Samuel Danforth's *A Brief Recognition of New-Englands Errand into the Wilderness* (Cambridge, Mass.: Printed by S. G. and M. J., 1671).

4. Gordon S. Wood, *The Americanization of Benjamin Franklin* (New York: Penguin, 2004), 72.

5. Franklin, "Observations Concerning . . . ," in J. A. Leo Lemay, ed., *Benjamin Franklin: Writings* (New York: Library of America, 1987), 373.

6. William Henry Drayton, *A Charge on the Rise of the American Empire* (1776), quoted in Richard W. Van Alstyne, *The Rising American Empire* (New York: Oxford University Press, 1960), 1.

7. Samuel Adams to James Warren, November 3, 1778, in Harry Alonzo Cushing, ed., *The Writings of Samuel Adams*, 4 vols. (New York: G. P. Putnam's Sons, 1908; repr., New York: Octagon Books, 1968), 4:88–90; see also DeConde, *This Affair of Louisiana*, 35.

8. Jedediah Morse, *The American Geography; or, A View of the Present Situation of the United States of America* (Elizabethtown, N.J.: privately published, 1789), 469.

9. *New York Evening Post*, 1803, quoted in DeConde, *This Affair of Louisiana*, 138.

10. Patrick Henry, speech before the Virginia Ratifying Convention, June 5, 1788, in John Kaminski and Gaspare J. Saladino, eds., *The Documentary History of the Ratification of the Constitution*, vol. 9, *Ratification by the States: Virginia, no. 2* (Madison: Wisconsin Historical Society Press, 1990), 959; see also DeConde, *This Affair of Louisiana*, 247.

11. Jefferson to Madison, April 27, 1809, in James Morton Smith, ed., *The Republic of Letters: The Correspondence between Thomas Jefferson and James Madison, 1776–1826*, 3 vols. (New York: W. W. Norton, 1995), 3:1586. For an extended treatment, see also Onuf, *Jefferson's Empire;* and Tucker and Hendrickson, *Empire of Liberty*.

12. Jefferson to Breckinridge, August 12, 1803, in Merrill D. Peterson, ed., *Thomas Jefferson: Writings* (New York: Library of America, 1984), 1138.

13. Ibid., 519.

14. Van Alstyne, *Rising American Empire*, 1.

15. There has not been a good scholarly study of Wilkinson. For a popular account of his life, see Hay and Werner, *Admirable Trumpeter*.

16. Kukla, *Wilderness So Immense*, 121.

17. Jackson, *Journals of Pike*, 2:102n.

18. For Pike's instructions, see Wilkinson to Pike, July 30, 1805, in Jackson, *Journals of Pike*, 1:3–4.

19. For Jefferson's instructions to Lewis and Clark, see his letter of June 20, 1803, in Donald Jackson, ed., *Letters of the Lewis and Clark Expedition, with Related Documents*, 2nd ed. (Urbana: University of Illinois Press, 1978), 60–66. For Jefferson's instructions to Freeman and Custis, see his letter of April 14, 1804, in Dan Flores, ed., *Southern Counterpart to Lewis and Clark: The Freeman and Custis Expedition of 1806* (Norman: University of Oklahoma Press, 2002), 320–25.

20. White, *Middle Ground*.

21. Pike, Council with the Sioux, September 23, 1805, in Jackson, *Journals of Pike*, 1:243.

22. Pike to Wilkinson, September 23, 1805, in ibid., 1:238.

23. Wilkinson to Dearborn, November 26, 1805, in ibid., 1:250.

24. Pike, journal entry, January 3, 1806, in ibid., 1:76.

25. Pike, journal entry, February 6, 1806, in ibid., 1:90.

26. Pike to McGillis, February 6, 1806, in ibid., 1:256.

27. Pike to Wilkinson, September 23, 1805, in ibid., 1:239.

28. Wilkinson to Dearborn, November 26, 1805, in ibid., 1:250.

29. Pike to McGillis, February 6, 1806, in ibid., 1:257. Italics in original.

30. The Wilkinson-Burr "conspiracy" is most fully explained in the editorial notes in Kline, *Political Correspondence of Burr*. Isenberg, *Fallen Founder*, esp. 272, 288, 299–301, and 306–309, is also helpful. See also Abernethy, *Burr Conspiracy*.

31. Juan Gassiot to Felipe de Neve, October 9, 1783, quoted in Weber, *Spanish Frontier*, 271.

32. Jose Vidal to Jose Joaquin Ugarte, October 4, 1803, quoted in ibid., 291.

33. Wilkinson to Dearborn, September 8, 1805, in Jackson, *Journals of Pike*, 2:101.

34. Wilkinson to Pike, June 24, 1806, in ibid., 1:286.

35. Pike to Wilkinson, October 2, 1806, in ibid., 2:151. See also Pike's journal entry for September 27, 1806, in ibid., 1:327.

36. Pike, journal entry, September 28, 1806, in ibid., 1:328.

37. Pike, journal entry, September 29, 1806, in ibid., 1:328. The Pawnee council is also treated in Lt. James Wilkinson's Report, April 6, 1807, in ibid., 2:6–7.

38. Pike, journal entry, September 29, 1806, in ibid., 1:328.

39. Pike, journal entry, September 29, 1806, in ibid., 1:329.

40. Pike to McGillis, February 6, 1806, in ibid., 1:257.

41. For a brief recounting of the story, see Donald Jackson, *Thomas Jefferson and the Rocky Mountains: Exploring the West from Monticello* (repr., Norman: University of Oklahoma Press, 2002), 242–67.

42. Pike to Wilkinson, June 22, 1806, in Jackson, *Journals of Pike,* 2:124.

43. Pike, "Observations on New Spain," in ibid., 2:42–97.

44. Ibid., 2:83.

45. Ibid., 2:94–95.

46. Ibid., 2:95–96. Italics in original.

47. Ibid., 2:96.

48. Ibid., 2:96.

49. Ibid., 2:97.

50. For a brief explanation of Pike and American memory, see Olsen, "Zebulon Pike."

51. Pike's southwestern journals have been reprinted in Hart and Hulbert, *Southwestern Journals of Pike.*

52. Pike, journal entry, October 17, 1806, in Jackson, *Journals of Pike,* 1:336.

# 3

# Pike and American Science

*John Logan Allen*

On the evening of April 18, 1804, two of the world's greatest scientific minds met in Washington City. Based on a long-standing invitation arising from their frequent correspondence over the preceding fifteen years, Baron Alexander von Humboldt, the scion of one of the oldest aristocratic families in central Europe, joined Thomas Jefferson, founder of American liberty and champion of the common man, for an elegant dinner at "the President's house," accompanied by the best French wines.[1] The combination might appear to have been unlikely: the young Prussian aristocrat tied firmly to the wealth and privilege of the Old World and the elderly author of the Declaration of Independence, prime mover in the creation of a New World republic. But on things scientific, these two men thought remarkably alike. We know next to nothing of their conversation on the evening of April 18, as they enjoyed what Jefferson referred to as an "agreeable" meal.[2]

Indeed, we know little of their other exchanges over the next three weeks while von Humboldt was Jefferson's house guest. What we can surmise is that the conversations between these two intellectual giants must have been fascinating and wide-ranging—and almost certainly included information on von Humboldt's recent "tour" in South and Central America.[3] The great German geographer-explorer presented Jefferson with a statistical table giving population and other data on New Spain and quite probably relayed what information he could on how the Spanish viewed their border with the new American territory of Louisiana.[4] Von Humboldt had with him a manuscript map of the "Internal Provinces of New Spain" that, upon its publication in Europe, would become the first widely available map of Spanish possessions in North America.[5] Earlier Spanish maps of the Southwest existed, most notably those from the Dominguez-Escalante expedition into the Great Basin in the 1770s, and von Humboldt used these to construct the northern portions of his map.[6]

It is important to note that von Humboldt did not *give* Jefferson a copy of this map, as it was not yet prepared for publication. But he *loaned* the map to Jefferson's secretary of the treasury, Albert Gallatin, with instructions that it was not to be copied. Gallatin, who had been active in acquiring cartographic data for Lewis and Clark, returned the map to the German baron before von Humboldt left the United States. Despite von Humboldt's directions, a copy of the map was made; it ended up in the possession of General James Wilkinson, the commander of Zebulon Montgomery Pike and the sponsor of Pike's explorations into the borderlands of the United States and New Spain.[7] Jefferson, of course, would later disavow any unethical copying of the von Humboldt map.[8]

Whatever else might have transpired between von Humboldt and Jefferson during the European savant's stay in Washington must be left entirely to the imagination. But a meeting between perhaps the two most important scientists of their day cannot have been inconsequential. These men helped shape the process of changing scientific thought we call "the Enlightenment." Born out of French rationalism of the eighteenth century, the Enlightenment was nothing less than a new approach to inquiry about the natural and cultural world.

Prior to the 1700s, the explanations of nearly all natural phenomena had been framed primarily in religious terms and nearly all questions about the natural world answered in terms of divine origin.[9] But by the late eighteenth century, those who inquired into the workings of the world sought the answers to questions in natural law rather than religion. Scientific inquiry moved from the clerical realm to the secular.[10] With the emergence of this new approach to science, the nature of exploration also changed—and given that von Humboldt had just returned from what was a quintessential Enlightenment expedition, we can expect that this new mode of exploration formed the core of his and Jefferson's conversations.

Pre-Enlightenment exploration was largely commercial and imperial, driven by a need to seek new sources of raw materials and new markets for European products and by a desire on the part of European countries to control non-European parts of the world as colonial empires. There was some leavening of the commercial and imperial objectives of exploration by the missionary impulse that accompanied some European national explorations.

In general, however, the religious motivation for exploration was significantly less important than either the commercial or the imperial objective. But with the change in the view of the world and its workings represented by the Enlightenment, at least a portion of exploratory objectives in the nineteenth century would be defined in terms of inquiry into the characteristics of unknown lands.[11] And this is what von Humboldt and Jefferson would have visited about. Von Humboldt's scientific exploration in South and Central America was a far-flung enterprise that took him from deep in the tropical forests of what is now Venezuela and Brazil to the upland basins and plateaus of Mexico.[12]

During von Humboldt's travels, he gathered samples of plants and animals previously unknown to science, made observations about the soils and climate of these areas new to European scholars, and attempted to relate the natural conditions to human cultures by observing native customs and traditions in differing environmental settings. Within a week of von Humboldt's departure from Washington on his way back to his Prussian estate, an expedition conceived and sponsored by Jefferson— the Lewis and Clark expedition—would depart on a trek across North America, armed with a set of instructions from Jefferson that were just as much based in Enlightenment science as had been the South American and Mesoamerican travels of the great German scholar.

Von Humboldt's travels and those of Lewis and Clark and other Jeffersonian explorers were a logical outgrowth of the traditional Enlightenment approach to inquiry about the natural world: first collect, catalogue, identify; then attempt to analyze the "encyclopedia" of information gathered.[13] It was in this intellectual framework that the science that underlay the explorations of Zebulon Montgomery Pike was framed. But it was framed in a uniquely American context in which some of the more traditional views of exploration involving commerce and empire also were part of the exploratory goals.[14]

The contemporaneous explorations of Lewis and Clark and Zebulon Pike were uniquely American explorations. Their goals were based on both Enlightenment science and the logical extension of American commerce and empire. There was, in American thought of the early nineteenth century, nothing contradictory in an explorer being some strange combination of merchant, scientist, and diplomat. After all, American science—as well-grounded in the European Enlightenment as it was—was still American. The chief scientific organization of the time was the American Philosophical Society, "held in Philadelphia for the purpose of advancing useful knowledge"[15]—a name that suggests that in the American Enlightenment, high value was placed on utilitarian knowledge gathered for the promotion of American commercial or territorial objectives.

The goals of the society were linked with those of the republic: indeed, Thomas Jefferson served concurrently as president of the United States and president of the American Philosophical Society. Even though Pike (unlike Lewis and Clark) was not a direct product of Jefferson's administration, he was certainly no less committed to the concept of "useful" or utilitarian knowledge (science) as the bulwark of American scientific inquiry.

On the eve of his explorations up the Mississippi and into the American Southwest, Pike was under the command of General James Wilkinson,[16] commander of U.S. military forces in the West and governor of Louisiana Territory. Wilkinson, one of American history's most shadowy figures, had an intriguing past. He was a product of the University of Pennsylvania, where his studies seemed destined to lead him to a medical career. He was, therefore, exposed to the same scientific thinking that drove Jefferson and von Humboldt and had a significant understanding of what was then termed "natural history" (an amalgam of today's geography, geology, biology, and anthropology). He served with minimal distinction in the American Revolution and after war's end, headed for Kentucky. There, as a private citizen, he became involved in a Spanish conspiracy to separate the territories south of the Ohio River from the new republic and add them to what was then the Spanish-held Territory of Louisiana—the western portion of the Mississippi's drainage basin.

When the conflict between the United States and the Indian nations of Ohio broke out, Wilkinson rejoined the U.S. Army. He soon became the commander of the U.S. Army in the West—all the while maintaining his status as an agent of the Spanish colonial government in Mexico City. When Jefferson dispatched Lewis and Clark, Wilkinson urged his Spanish employers to intercept the American explorers.[17] But at the same time, the general seemed bent upon engaging in exploration of his own. Was he concerned that Lewis and Clark would grab all the glory, leaving none for an expedition—equally scientific, commercial, and imperial in scope as that of Lewis and Clark—sponsored by Wilkinson or, perhaps, by his employers in New Spain?

While we can know almost nothing about Wilkinson's true objectives in dispatching Pike, what we do know is that he had a long-term interest in the Louisiana–New Spain borderlands. Wilkinson wrote to Jefferson in June 1804 expressing his disappointment in missing von Humboldt and not having the opportunity to query the baron about the New Spain–United States borderlands.[18] But there is additional evidence of Wilkinson's links to von Humboldt's view of New Spain and, therein, connections between the German scholar and the explorations of Zebulon Pike.

Enter another of the more shadowy figures of American history— one who surpasses even General James Wilkinson in notoriety: Aaron Burr, who nearly became president of the United States, served as vice president during Jefferson's first administration, killed Alexander Hamilton in a duel, was arrested for murder but not convicted, and was later brought to trial on conspiracy charges dealing with a plot (in which Wilkinson was also implicated) to found a republic in the Southwest.[19]

If anyone in the United States in 1804 would have been interested in getting a look at Alexander von Humboldt's maps, it would have been Aaron Burr and his probable coconspirator, General James Wilkinson. Current thinking suggests that Burr had somehow obtained the original of the von Humboldt two-sheet map loaned to Gallatin by the German scholar. This map was then copied by an army sergeant in Wilkinson's command,[20] identified as Antoine Nau, a cartographer of some skill who later produced the maps that accompanied the published edition of Zebulon Pike's journals of his southwestern expedition. Had Zebulon Pike seen the copied von Humboldt map before he departed? It would be amazing if he had not. He may have even had a copy of it in the field.

Whatever Wilkinson's motives in sending Zebulon Pike out as an explorer, clearly he was dealing with a young army officer who had a fascination with the West—particularly the new Territory of Louisiana. Pike grew up in an army family and received little formal education, although his continual efforts to improve himself were apparent by his reading lists while a young lieutenant on the Ohio frontier. His letters and journals make clear that, although sensitive about his lack of education, Pike was no less well educated than most Americans or even most officers in the U.S. Army. And his reading obviously included material on the trans-Mississippi West, as evidenced by his submission of a letter in the summer of 1803 to the *Medical Repository*, a respected periodical among the American intellectual community that often contained letters of interest on Louisiana Territory.[21]

Pike's letter, printed in 1804, supported the actions of the administration in purchasing Louisiana Territory from the French by describing the wonders of this new American territory.[22] Pike described the geography and natural resources of the West and noted that the Missouri River was the key to discovering a passage to the Pacific. In doing so, he reinforced an existing belief that somewhere in the interior of the continent was a height-of-land from which all major western rivers flowed. Pike also volunteered some new information: namely, that the mines of New Mexico were on the same line of latitude as St. Louis and that the journey from St. Louis to New Mexico was "one-third . . . through the woods, and the rest through an immense prairie, where not a tree, shrub or knoll is seen to bound the prospect and the horizon only terminates the traveller's view for many a successive day."[23]

All in all, this is not a bad description of the southern Great Plains, albeit an abbreviated one. Pike made no attempt to address a scientific question that was being debated at the time: was the newly acquired territory a vast trackless wasteland as the Spanish and some British scientific publications seemed to suggest? Or was it, as American and French literature posited, a rich gardenlike area, barren of trees—in Jefferson's phrase—"because the soil was too rich for the growth of forest trees"? But in Pike's description of an area where "not a tree, shrub, or knoll is seen," we see a harbinger of his later descriptions of the southern Great Plains, which foreshadowed the myth of the Great American Desert.[24]

In this letter to a leading American periodical—one read by the most prominent thinkers in the country—Pike demonstrated an interest in science and a grasp of the basics of western "natural history." This letter may have been what drew Pike to Wilkinson's attention—or, perhaps, in the small army garrison in St. Louis it would have been natural that even officers as widely separated in rank as a lieutenant and a general could share their common interests in the natural history of the trans-Mississippi West. We do know that by July 1805, Wilkinson had selected Pike to lead an army exploration up the Mississippi River to attempt to ascertain the source of that river.[25] It is apparent from the same letter in which Wilkinson informed Secretary of War Henry Dearborn that he was sending Pike "for the Head of the Mississippi" that the general was also thinking of an expedition to the West, particularly to the Comanches, who, in Wilkinson's opinion, constituted "the most powerfull Nation of Savages on this Continent, and have it in their power to facilitate or impede our march to New Mexico, should such movement ever become Necessary."[26] Concluding a treaty with the Comanches could also facilitate a march from New Mexico to St. Louis, should Wilkinson's Spanish employers find *that* movement necessary.

During the winter of 1805–1806, Pike led an expedition to the upper Mississippi that failed in its central objective of locating the Mississippi's source but did provide field maps and notes that gave American science its first really clear look at the upper Mississippi valley. More important, perhaps, it gave Pike some experience in the art and science of exploration.[27]

Shortly after his May 1806 return to the St. Louis garrison from the Mississippi River expedition, Pike had from Wilkinson orders to embark on his southwestern expedition with a set of exploratory objectives that had largely to do with Indian diplomacy—particularly establishing

favorable relationships with the Comanches. This apparent focus on Indian diplomacy was misleading in the context of the other objective that
Wilkinson laid down for Pike: to continue west to determine the sources
of the Red and Arkansas rivers. Here Wilkinson's instructions revealed
both the tidy mind of someone trained in and dedicated to Enlightenment science and the devious thinking of a man who may have been
attempting to serve two masters—the governments of the United States
and New Spain—at the same time.

In language that began as if it were simply an afterthought, Wilkinson
suggested to Pike that because his contacts with the Comanches would
probably lead him to the headwaters of the Red and Arkansas rivers,
he might just as well reconnoiter that territory and make a report. Of
course, as Wilkinson instructed, he should move with the greatest circumspection because "the affairs of Spain, & the United States appear to
be on the point of amicable adjustment, and more over it is the desire
of the President, to cultivate the Friendship & Harmonious Intercourse,
of all the Nations of the Earth, & particularly our near neighbours the
Spaniards."[28]

This is General James Wilkinson at either his best or his worst—de-
pending on your point of view. In one fell swoop, he instructed Pike to
move toward (and possibly beyond?) the very fringes of the legal definition of Louisiana Territory (the headwaters of the Mississippi's western
tributaries) and at the same time warned the young explorer of the "desire of the President" for peace and harmony with all nations. Of all the
people on the western frontier, no one knew better than General James
Wilkinson how the Spanish officials would view an American exploring
party moving anywhere near the sources of the Red or Arkansas rivers—
they would certainly not view it as "amicable." By invoking the wishes
of Jefferson to preserve peace, tucked away in a message that instructs a
U.S. Army officer to tread gingerly into territory occupied by a foreign
power, Wilkinson lent a degree of official approbation to Pike's expedition that it simply did not possess. What is even more intriguing is that
the remainder of Wilkinson's instructions had nothing to do with either
the Indians or the Spanish. Using language similar to that of Jefferson's
instructions to Meriwether Lewis, the general provided Pike with the
kind of blueprint for exploration that gave the southwestern expedition

the scientific flavor that, when the diplomatic and commercial intrigue was added in, made of Pike a quintessential explorer of the American Enlightenment. "In the course of your tour," Wilkinson instructed Pike,

> you are to remark particularly upon the Geographical structure, the Natural History; and population; of the country through which you may pass, taking particular care to collect & preserve, speci-mens of every thing curious in the mineral or botanical Worlds, which can be preserved & are portable: Let your courses be regu-lated by your compass, & your Distances by your Watch, to be noted in a field Book, & I would advise you when circumstances permit, to protract & lay down in a separate Book, the march of the Day at every evenings halt. The Instruments which I have furnished you; will enable you to ascertain the variation of the magnetic needle and the Lattitude with exactitude, and at every remarkable point I wish you to employ your Telescope in observeing the Eclipses of Jupiters Satillites, having previously regulated your Watch by your Sextant, takeing care to note with great nicety the periods of im-mersion & emersion of the eclipsed Satillite. These observations may enable us after your return, by application to the appropriate Tables, to ascertain the Longitude. It is an object of much Interest with the Executive, to ascertain the Direction, extent, & navigation of the Arkansaw, & Red Rivers.[29]

The instructions for Pike to explore the upper reaches of the Arkan-sas and Red rivers were, as Wilkinson worded them, meant to appear to come from the president himself—"an object of much Interest with the Executive."[30] These were slippery directions to give a young man who probably had no idea what he was in for. But they also indicate that Wilkinson's intentions—irrespective of his motivations regarding the borders of the United States and New Spain and the potential for conflict that travel into that borderland might bring—were not without scientific merit. For Wilkinson instructed Pike to do for the Southwest much of what Jefferson had instructed Meriwether Lewis to do for the Northwest: to come finally to grips with what was probably the most es-sential scientific question about the western interior of North America.

Was there a common source region for all major western streams, as suggested by cartography of the late eighteenth and early nineteenth centuries?[31]

This was surely one of the questions Wilkinson would have directed to von Humboldt had the opportunity presented itself. But Wilkinson already possessed at least part of the answer von Humboldt would have provided: on Nau's copy of the von Humboldt map, there appeared western streams such as the Red, Arkansas, and Rio Grande, with their sources very close to those of the Missouri and Columbia.[32] More important, this source region was close to Santa Fe, the heart of New Spain's Internal Provinces. Lewis and Clark were searching for this common source area far to the north during their 1804–1806 expedition. General Wilkinson, unaware in the summer of 1806 of the success or failure of Jefferson's explorers, wanted to locate the source region himself—either in connection with the plotting that he and Burr had done to create their own fiefdom in the Southwest or in the interests of his Spanish employers. The instrument of Wilkinson's desire was to be Zebulon Montgomery Pike.

Let us then try to place Zebulon Pike into the correct scientific context on the eve of his southwestern expedition and view the common state of knowledge of the interior of the American Southwest in 1806. We must first note that American knowledge of the area between St. Louis and Santa Fe, or between the Platte and the Rio Grande, was extremely sketchy. No American explorer had yet managed to penetrate more than a few hundred miles up the Red River valley.[33] The Spanish knew the area relatively well, but persisting in the geographical delusion of the proximity of the sources of the Rio Grande and Missouri and, therefore, viewing the Missouri River as a highway for the invasion of New Spain from the north and east, they kept their maps and journals and notes and military reports locked away in unreachable archives in Mexico City and Seville in Spain.

The best geographical understanding of the area was probably to be found on von Humboldt's map—and it was filled with conjecture and bad cartography based on limited Spanish explorations beyond the Rio Grande valley. Given the secretive and nonscientific nature of Spanish exploration—not yet influenced by Enlightenment science—von

Humboldt's map was little better than the maps produced by the French in early Louisiana Territory a century earlier. Unlike his maps of areas that he had actually explored, von Humboldt's map of New Spain's northern borderlands contained geographical features and descriptions that appear to have been entered more to fill blank space than to illustrate known topography or rivers or Native settlements or vegetative regions.[34]

To be fair to von Humboldt, where blank spaces exist on maps, the imagination of cartographers of the time was more than ready to fill them. No clearer example exists than that of the core geographical feature of the American West on most maps of the period—including von Humboldt's. Compressed into a single small area on most maps was what American adventurer and promoter Jonathan Carver called the "pyramidal height-of-land,"[35] the common source area for western rivers that had been created out of rather flimsy evidence by American and British opportunists and bought eagerly by ambitious imperialists like Thomas Jefferson—and James Wilkinson.

This was the reason for the section in Wilkinson's instructions to Pike that the general deviously threw in as an afterthought and made appear to be consistent with Jefferson's wishes: "an object of much Interest with the Executive."[36] Well, of course. Whoever discovered the direction, extent, and navigation of the Arkansas and Red rivers would also discover the location of the sources of the Rio Grande, Missouri, Columbia, and other western streams and open up half a continent to water travel by conquering armies or eager merchants. Armed with such intelligence, Pike had reason to appear confused and lost in the field.

Other components of existing science on the Southwest also had a bearing on Pike's expedition and its results. Not the least of these were the conflicting notions of the "utility" of the land—was it fertile soil suitable for the expansion of Jefferson's yeomanry or a desert expanse similar to the deserts known to the Spanish farther west between the Rio Grande and the Colorado? The Spanish had their opinions, based on the experiences of settlements in Texas and elsewhere: it was grassland suitable for raising livestock. But the Spanish information was not part of the general fund of knowledge and was kept, like the Spanish maps, in secreted depositories.

French geographical information from the French occupation of Louisiana Territory from the early 1700s to the end of the French and Indian
War in 1763 suggested that the great grasslands were somewhat more
productive but were still largely "meadows" where the "hump-backed
kine," or buffalo, roved in such numbers that the area surely would support large herds of domesticated cattle and sheep and horses. The British, with their experience confined largely to the cooler, more humid
northern country, tended to see the area as desertlike because it did not
produce trees. American opinion was molded most directly, perhaps, by
Thomas Jefferson, who recognized the treeless nature of the southern
plains but also viewed the area as a potential agricultural garden.[37]

We do not know Pike's opinion of these conflicting geographies, but
we can guess: his letter to the *Medical Repository* bore more overtones
of the Spanish desert than of the Jeffersonian garden. And so young Zebulon Montgomery Pike, in the summer of 1806 on the eve of his departure into the Southwest, possessing little real scientific knowledge of
the area he was about to traverse, supplied with faulty maps, provided
with misleading (and perhaps illegal) instructions, and proving loyal to
a commander who did not deserve his loyalty, serves as a poster child
on how not to prepare an explorer embarking on what should have been
a great expansion of Enlightenment science but ended up, on the whole,
rather badly.

There is no need to retrace Pike's steps here, for doing so would be
both superfluous and redundant: the story is well known to scholars.
One critical event in the journey is worthy of note because of its impact
on subsequent images of the West. When, in December 1806, Pike made
his aborted attempt to climb "the highest peak" that would later bear his
name,[38] he reached a point where he looked down on what he thought
was the source region of the Platte, the Arkansas, the Rio Grande—and
the Yellowstone. Spread out before his imagination was the pyramidal
height-of-land, the source of western rivers and the locus of future commercial travel in the West.

Throughout much of the remainder of Pike's journey, his field notes
inform us that he often "felt at considerable loss how to proceed." Indeed, that is the case: almost nothing that Pike could have done from

the time he viewed the supposed common source region would have eliminated the confusion in his physical and political geography. There was no easy way out of this dilemma as Pike sorted through the disjunctions between imaginary and real geography—through his confused attempts to identify which rivers he was actually seeing. When Spanish soldiers arrived at Pike's winter cantonment, they mercifully ended his geographical confusion by informing him that he was on the Rio Grande and, therefore, decidedly not in the U.S. territory of Louisiana. Informed of this fact, Pike exclaimed, "[W]hat ... is not this the Red river?"[39]

There has been conjecture that Pike knew exactly where he was, was under no illusions about not being in Spanish territory, and was simply dissembling. This is doubtful. The best geographical information available to Pike—the von Humboldt map—led inescapably to the conclusion that he was on the upper Red River and in U.S. territory. But a small and very weary American force was not going to argue with a larger, better-fed, and better-equipped force of Spanish soldiers. For the next four months, Pike and his men were the "guests" of the government of New Spain, not returning to the United States until June 1807. Bad luck, poor planning, questionable objectives, and a disastrous grasp of geography had all combined to make of Zebulon Pike a failure.

Although he beat Lewis and Clark to press by four years,[40] Pike never was seen as a heroic figure, as they were. His reports did not capture the imagination of the American public as did those of John C. Frémont, and although most Americans would recognize the name "Pike's Peak," few knew anything about its namesake. His bad luck continued when he was killed at the age of thirty-seven in the War of 1812; history, in general, has not been kind to his reputation. Donald Jackson, editor of the definitive edition of Pike's journals, noted, "Nothing that Zebulon Pike ever tried to do was easy, and most of his luck was bad."[41]

While Pike's accomplishments as an Enlightenment explorer fall far short of those achieved by Lewis and Clark, his role in the development and assessment of the American West was still a significant one—but, as seems to be typical of Pike, that role was significant largely because of errors of understanding and imagination. In the published reports of

Pike's journeys, there were two primary pieces of information and interpretation that continued to perpetuate myth and, by doing so, became significant in a historical context.

The first of these was Pike's assessment of the land quality of the area between the Mississippi and the Rocky Mountains. Although Pike provided detailed information on the "natural history" of the southern Great Plains, unfortunately much of this information was either flat wrong or, at best, exaggerated. In his letter to the *Medical Repository* in 1804, Pike had suggested the treelessness of the southern plains but had not used the word "desert." In his daily journals during the crossing of the plains in 1806, he consistently referred to the plains as "prairie"—a term equated in the American mind of the Jeffersonian Age to the English word "meadow." In fact, during his entire trek, Pike used the word "desert" only sparingly.[42]

Four years after his return, however, the published version of Pike's journals carried more-negative descriptions of the southern plains, descriptions that some historians contend signal the beginning of the "Great American Desert" myth: "These vast plains of the western hemisphere," Pike's published journals concluded, "may become in time equally celebrated as the sandy deserts of Africa; for I saw in my route, in various places, tracts of many leagues, where the wind had thrown up the sand, in all the fanciful forms of the Ocean's rolling wave, and on which not a speck of vegetable matter existed."[43]

The Native inhabitants of this vast wasteland Pike compared to the "tribes of Tartary," and little was said about the herds of buffalo, deer, and antelope that flavor other early descriptions of the southern and central Great Plains. Pike's plains were very far indeed from the Jeffersonian Garden of the World—and Pike took a step further: "Our citizens being so prone to rambling and extending themselves, on the frontiers," he wrote, "will, through necessity, be constrained to limit their extent on the west, to the borders of the Missouri and Mississippi."[44] If James Wilkinson had wanted to exclude an American population from the Southwest to preserve it for a Spanish population over which he might rule, he could not have made a better argument than did Zebulon Pike. We are left to wonder whether Pike's self-realized failings as an explorer colored his impressions of a landscape in bleak desert pastels, whether the "prairies" of the westbound journey were converted, by sheer disillusionment, to the "wastes of the Zahara" at journey's end.

Pike's second grand error was in his perpetuation of the concept of the core drainage area, the pyramidal height-of-land that gave rise to all major western streams. In his journals and in his maps, Pike persisted in the opinion that the sources of northern plains rivers such as the Missouri and Yellowstone headed in the same region as the southern plains rivers of the Arkansas and Rio Grande. On the second sheet of his major map, Pike showed the northernmost sources of the Platte and, across a range of mountains to the west, the "sources of the Arkansaw." Going by the scale of the map, about forty miles north of the sources of the Platte and Arkansas was the "Yellow Stone River Branch of the Missouri."[45]

This is the area depicted in the northwestern corner of the "Chart of the internal parts of Louisiana," which Pike referred to in his journal as "the grand reservoir of snows and fountains."[46] The significance of this is not simply that Pike was wrong in compressing the nearly six hundred miles between the Yellowstone and Arkansas/Rio Grande headwaters. What makes the error significant is that Pike believed he had actually seen this drainage area, an impression picked up by William Clark, who was, at the time Pike's map was published, preparing his own map summarizing the results of the Lewis and Clark expedition. On Clark's manuscript map of 1810 and his published map of 1814, immediately to the south of the southernmost portion of the Yellowstone drainage may be seen a replica of the northwest corner of Pike's "Chart"—with the sources of "Rio de la Platte," the "Arkansaw," and the "Rio del Norte" (Rio Grande), the "Block House U.S. Factory in 1806" (Pike's winter cantonment), and just to the north of the "Block House," the label "Highest Peak."[47]

For the area that William Clark and Meriwether Lewis had seen and surveyed, Clark's map is highly accurate. For other areas, Clark relied on information from others, including a fellow army officer and resident of St. Louis who must have been well known to him—Zebulon Montgomery Pike. By accepting Pike's erroneous and wishful cartography, Clark was guilty of perpetuating the myth of the common source area. Would he have done so had he not had Pike's map—from a source that he probably judged to be highly reliable?

There is no real way to measure the importance of Pike's two grand errors: the evaluation of the southern plains as desert and the "grand reservoir of snows and fountains" from which issued all major western rivers. What we can say is that the errors have done Pike's reputation as a scientific explorer little good and much damage. He has, consequently, long been dismissed as either a tool of Wilkinson's imperial (and illegal) ambitions or an afterthought of Jeffersonian exploration who managed to get himself lost and confused, captured by the Spanish and hauled away in ignominy to Chihuahua, and then, finally and perhaps mercifully, killed by a stray British cannonball.

But for all that, Pike was actually much more important as a shaper of the view of the American West in the late Jeffersonian and early Jacksonian periods than he has been given credit for. Accused even during his own lifetime of being a spy (an allegation that Jefferson vehemently denied),[48] Pike nevertheless did provide noteworthy intelligence: for example, the first map of what became the Santa Fe Trail. People may have forgotten Pike's maps quickly. But they did not forget William Clark's map that was the master map of the American West until the 1840s—still containing the geographical misinformation from Pike. And potential migrants into West Texas and Kansas and New Mexico as late as the 1850s may have found Pike's descriptions of what another explorer of questionable talent, Stephen Long, would dub "The Great American Desert" just as important in avoiding the southern plains as they did the forbidding presence of the Comanche. In the final analysis, it is crucial to keep this in mind when evaluating Zebulon Pike: he was not the first explorer who did not know where he was, ran into trouble with authorities and was arrested, involved himself in conspiracies, and still left his tracks on the map. The name of Christopher Columbus comes immediately to mind.

## NOTES

1. See Donald Jackson, *Thomas Jefferson and the Stony Mountains* (Urbana: University of Illinois Press, 1981), 103–104; see also Thomas Jefferson to James Madison, April 19, 1804, Papers of Thomas Jefferson, Library of Congress.

2. Jefferson to Madison, April 19, 1804, Papers of Thomas Jefferson, Library of Congress.

3. The best source on von Humboldt's travels in South and Middle America is his own book *Cosmos;* for an excellent modern translation and interpretation, see Helferich, *Humboldt's Cosmos.*

4. Jackson, *Jefferson and the Stony Mountains,* 103–104.

5. See Wheat, *Mapping the Trans-Mississippi West,* 1:132–38. Relevant portions are also found in Jackson, *Jefferson and the Stony Mountains.*

6. See Wheat, *Mapping the Trans-Mississippi West,* 1:100–16.

7. Ibid., 1:137n22. Jackson also gives a good description of the Nau/von Humboldt map in *Journals of Pike* (1:453–57).

8. Jefferson to Alexander von Humboldt, December 6, 1813, Papers of Thomas Jefferson, Library of Congress; reprinted in Jackson, *Journals of Pike,* 2:387–88.

9. For this point, see David D. Hall, *Worlds of Wonder, Days of Judgment: Popular Religious Belief in Early New England* (Cambridge, Mass.: Harvard University Press, 1990).

10. A good exposition of this topic is James Delbourgo, *A Most Amazing Scene of Wonders: Electricity and Enlightenment in Early America* (Cambridge, Mass.: Harvard University Press, 2006).

11. This period of North American exploration is covered extensively in volumes 2 and 3 of John L. Allen, ed., *North American Exploration* (Lincoln: University of Nebraska Press, 1997).

12. See Helferich, *Humboldt's Cosmos.*

13. John L. Allen, *Lewis and Clark and the Image of the American Northwest,* 2nd ed. (New York: Dover Publications, 1991); Jackson, *Journals of Pike;* Gary Moulton, ed., *The Journals of the Lewis and Clark Expedition,* 13 vols. (Lincoln: University of Nebraska Press, 1983–2003).

14. See James Ronda, "Exploring the American West in the Age of Jefferson," in Allen, *North American Exploration,* 3:40–46.

15. The American Philosophical Society, the oldest society in America, was formed on January 2, 1769, with Benjamin Franklin as its first president. For more about its function and purpose, see Carl Van Doren, *Benjamin Franklin* (New York: Viking Press, 1952).

16. There is still no good scholarly bibliography on Wilkinson, despite his significance in the American West in the early nineteenth century. The best popular biography available is Hay and Werner, *Admirable Trumpeter.*

17. Ronda, "Exploring the American West," 3:41; and Jackson, *Jefferson and the Stony Mountains,* 244.

18. See Jackson, *Journals of Pike,* 2:370n4; Wilkinson to Jefferson, June 11, 1804, Thomas Jefferson Papers, Library of Congress.

19. The Wilkinson-Burr "conspiracy" is best articulated in the documents and editorial notes in Kline, *Political Correspondence of Burr,* but also useful is Isenberg's *Fallen Founder,* 272, 288, 299–301, 306–309. An older version of the Wilkinson-Burr connection is Abernethy, *Burr Conspiracy.*

20. See Jackson, *Journals of Pike,* 1:452–62. Even Jackson is not able to determine definitively that Nau was the cartographer who copied von Humboldt's map. But the

circumstantial evidence is very strong. Carl Irving Wheat, the greatest scholar of the cartography of the trans-Mississippi West between the sixteenth and late nineteenth centuries, seemed to have missed this connection altogether, with exception of his footnote 22 on page 137 of vol. 1; even there, he does not seem to have made the Nau connection.

21. *Medical Repository*, 2nd hexade, 4 (1804): 409–11; reprinted in Jackson, *Journals of Pike*, 1:228.

22. "Pike's Memorandum on Louisiana," August 1803, in Jackson, *Journals of Zebulon Pike*, 1:226–28.

23. Ibid., 1:227–28.

24. See ibid. See also Allen, "Garden-Desert Continuum."

25. See Ronda, "Exploring the American West," 3:41–42.

26. Wilkinson to Henry Dearborn, July 27, 1805, in Jackson, *Journals of Pike*, 1:229.

27. The journal of Pike's Mississippi River exploration is found in Jackson, *Journals of Pike*, 1:3–225. This section is complete with Jackson's footnotes and two of Pike's maps (which, though he disparaged, were actually quite good).

28. Quoted in Jackson, *Journals of Pike*, 1:285–88.

29. Ibid., 1:286.

30. Ibid.

31. The most complete discussion of the "height-of-land" concept may be found throughout Allen, *Lewis and Clark*. A more succinct version may be found in John L. Allen, "Pyramidal Height-of-Land: A Persistent Myth in the Exploration of Western Anglo-America," *International Geography* 1 (1972): 395–96.

32. The most readily available copy of this map is found in Wheat, *Mapping the Trans-Mississippi West*, vol. 1, between pages 134 and 135.

33. See Dan Flores, ed., *Jefferson and Southwestern Exploration: The Freeman and Custis Accounts of the Red River Expeditions of 1806* (Norman: University of Oklahoma Press, 1984) for the best available accounts and journal reproductions of the southwestern expedition specifically sanctioned by Jefferson. The accounts of the Pike expedition are notably missing from these accounts, reinforcing the notion that Wilkinson, rather than Jefferson, was the prime mover in Pike's expedition into the southwestern plains.

34. Wheat, *Mapping the Trans-Mississippi West*, 1:132–34, is more charitable in his descriptions of von Humboldt's maps.

35. See Allen, *Lewis and Clark*, 26–28.

36. Wilkinson to Pike, June 24, 1806, in Jackson, *Journals of Pike*, 1:286.

37. See John L. Allen, "Geographical Knowledge and American Images of Louisiana Territory," *Western Historical Quarterly* 2 (1971):151–70. See also Peter S. Onuf, *The Mind of Thomas Jefferson* (Charlottesville: University of Virginia Press, 2007), 109–11; and Jefferson's *Notes on the State of Virginia*, in *The Life and Selected Writings of Thomas Jefferson*, ed. Adrienne Koch and William Peden (New York: Modern Library, 1993).

38. Jackson, *Journals of Pike*, 2:26–27. Pike's description of the "great south western branch of the Missouri" is his way of describing the Yellowstone. The Yellowstone River is much more clearly defined on the published versions of Pike's maps.

39. Jackson, ed., *Journals of Zebulon Pike*, 1:384.

40. Pike's account was published in 1810; the Biddle *History of the Expedition under the Command of Captains Lewis and Clarke* [sic] would not be published until 1814. For a recent reprinting of Pike's southwestern journals, see Hart and Hulbert, *Southwestern Journals of Pike*.

41. Jackson, *Journals of Pike*, 1:vii.

42. Ibid., 1:228, 2:27–28.

43. Ibid., 2:27–28. Jackson's footnotes for this section are instructive. There are some Pike scholars who believe that Pike, in his description of "the tracts of many leagues . . . on which not a speck of vegetable matter existed" was describing only the area of the Great Sand Dunes National Park in southern Colorado. See, for example, Hollon, *Lost Pathfinder*, 134. The nature of his language, however, gives me the firm impression that he was describing much of the area east of the Rocky Mountains during a very dry year.

44. See "Pike's Dissertation on Louisiana," in Jackson, *Journals of Pike*, 2:28. As Jackson concludes in his extensive footnote beginning on 2:27, "Here begins that long debate about the Great American Desert which Pike is blamed for starting." See also William H. Goetzmann, *Exploration and Empire: The Explorer and the Scientist in the Winning of the American West* (New York: Alfred A. Knopf, 1967), 51, 62.

45. See map 4, "The Internal Part of Louisiana, Section II," in Jackson, *Journals of Pike*, 1:388.

46. Ibid.

47. See Allen, *Lewis and Clark*, 376.

48. See Jefferson's letter to James Madison, August 30, 1807, in Jackson, *Journals of Pike*, 2:268. Jefferson's denial was somewhat disingenuous. His administration had employed several individuals—including Lewis and Clark, who (technically) were in contested territory once they crossed the Continental Divide at Lemhi Pass—as intelligence gatherers. They, like Pike, were military officers sent into country that according to international law was either disputed or (in the case of the drainage of the Rio Grande) recognized as being the possession of some governmental authority other than that of the United States.

# 4

# Jeffersonian Explorers in the Trans-Mississippi West

## ZEBULON PIKE IN PERSPECTIVE

*Jay H. Buckley*

When Americans contemplate the exploration of the Louisiana Purchase, the names Meriwether Lewis and William Clark quickly come to mind. Their historic journey was well conceived, well executed, and well documented. It was one of the first and longest U.S. government–backed explorations of the American West. The name Zebulon Pike, for some, conjures up notions of a lost explorer who was arrested by the Spanish as an alleged American spy. Fewer still have heard of the names William Dunbar, George Hunter, Thomas Freeman, and Peter Custis. Even those who have heard of these men may be hard-pressed to identify any specifics about their lives or accomplishments. During the five-year period between 1803 and 1807, Thomas Jefferson, third president of the United States, and James Wilkinson, top military general of the U.S. Army, planned half a dozen expeditions to explore the Mississippi, Missouri, Platte, Arkansas, and Red rivers—the major streams of the Louisiana Purchase.[1]

Jefferson and Wilkinson separately authorized, organized, and sponsored expeditions to ascend these principal rivers and intended to use the information the explorers acquired during these journeys of discovery to further their own aims: Jefferson's three expeditions championed scientific inquiry and commercial pursuits as the primary motivational forces, yet the president clearly held imperial ambitions to create an "empire of liberty" extending between the two great oceans; meanwhile, Wilkinson's quest for wealth and power caused him to send out Pike on two military reconnaissances under the guise of national defense. In reality, Wilkinson's communiqués indicate that his intentions were less patriotic, whether to separate the cis-Mississippi region from the United States, to provoke war with Spain, or to feign an American attack and then personally thwart it to have the Spanish compensate him for his services.

As the ink dried on the Louisiana Purchase treaty, signed by U.S. ambassadors Robert Livingston and James Monroe and French politician François de Barbé-Marbois on April 30, 1803, the United States acquired 828,000 square miles from France for the tidy sum of $15 million.[2] Jefferson announced it to the American people on the Fourth of July. In his second inaugural address the following year, Jefferson expressed it this way: "[I]s it not better that the opposite bank of the Mississippi should be settled by our own brethren and children, than by strangers of another family? With which shall we be most likely to live in harmony and friendly intercourse?" As exciting and unprecedented as doubling the nation's size was, Jefferson, Congress, and the citizenry clamored for reliable and up-to-date information regarding the vast Louisiana region.[3] Exploration of Louisiana was necessary because the French, eager not to further alienate their Spanish allies, failed to specify clear boundaries defining the purchase area. President Jefferson and General Wilkinson immediately devised plans to explore the vast Louisiana region, a prospect that placed their exploratory ventures within the larger scope of exploration science, international rivalries, American public policy, and national expansion.

Jefferson had long been interested in acquiring practical and scientific knowledge of the trans-Mississippi region's Native inhabitants, geographical secrets, flora and fauna, and climatic, mineralogical, and other scientific data beneficial to the young American republic. During the 1780s and 1790s, he and members of the American Philosophical Society had championed several expeditions to secure that information, but for one reason or another, the proposed ventures involving George Rogers Clark, André Michaux, and John Ledyard failed to yield the desired results.[4]

While Jefferson still championed the cause of Enlightenment science through scientific inquiry as president, he also emphasized the commercial prospects of the expeditions to garner congressional support and funding.[5] Taken together, science and commerce laid the foundation for Jefferson's imperial vision of a continental empire of independent, self-governing yeoman farmers extending to the Pacific. Agriculture and commerce went hand in hand, and the future prosperity of the nation appeared connected to the expansion of agricultural production. Farmers, spread over thousands of miles, needed rivers to import and export goods, so gaining practical and utilitarian knowledge about the western rivers was essential. Jefferson's notion of an agrarian nation of freedom-loving farmers exercising their natural rights of liberty and equality and governed by republican principles constituted the true strength of the new nation and would presumably yield peace, prosperity, and progress. Moreover, as the chief architect of the United States' western land policy after the original states voluntarily ceded their western lands to federal control in the 1780s, Jefferson devised a mathematical grid pattern to ensure orderly surveying as well as to provide an avenue for new states to join the Union on an equal footing. America's westward expansion may not have been inevitable, but Jefferson's "empire of liberty was illimitable."[6]

The scientific, ethnographic, and geographic data Jefferson requested his explorers to gather served as a double-edged sword he could use to acculturate and subjugate the Native inhabitants and wrest control of furs and other resources from Spanish, British, and Russian competitors. Expansion also served as a defensive response to offset vulnerabilities emanating from international instability and dangerous entanglements. With foreign restrictions of American navigation on the Mississippi removed with the Louisiana Purchase, Jefferson focused his sights on advancing American claims to the Rocky Mountains and the Pacific Northwest. He intended to utilize the Great Plains as an Indian reserve for tribal nations residing along the eastern seaboard who were willing to exchange their eastern homes for lands beyond the Mississippi. For Jefferson, "civilizing" and dispossessing Indians were the only viable alternatives because his conceptualization of America held no place for Indians to remain as Indians.[7] For his exploratory plans, then,

Jefferson adroitly employed commerce as the carrot to get congressional funding, stressed scientific discovery to allay Spanish and British fears of American trespassing, and informed the Native inhabitants that he was their new father figure to whom they should turn for advice and remain loyal and dutiful children.[8]

Understanding the motives and actions of James Wilkinson presents an even greater challenge. Ten years younger than Jefferson, Wilkinson was born in Maryland in 1757 and obtained an education befitting a planter's son. Like Jefferson, Wilkinson lost his father while in his youth, which helps explain the time these leaders devoted to mentoring their respective protégés, Meriwether Lewis and Zebulon Pike. Wilkinson exhibited considerable aptitude in medicine, but following the outbreak of the Revolutionary War, he opted for serving under George Washington, Nathaniel Greene, and Benedict Arnold (a capable general best remembered for defecting from the American to the British side). Perhaps coincidentally, the ambitious Wilkinson repeatedly found himself embroiled in schemes designed to bring down superior military officers, notably George Washington and Anthony Wayne, but he somehow escaped unscathed and ultimately ascended to become the U.S. Army's top-ranking general. Remarkably, all the while, the duplicitous Wilkinson operated as a Spanish confidant, divulging military secrets and swearing an oath of allegiance to Spain in exchange for trading privileges on the Mississippi, land in the Yazoo strip, and monetary considerations. Twice forced to resign his military commission, Wilkinson—never one to let a lost battle or a court-martial depress him—reinvented himself to live another day.

In contrast with Jefferson's imperial vision, Wilkinson's vision for America emanated from his personal ambitions for self-aggrandizement. He schemed to separate the western United States, either to have it join Spain or to become its own country; fostered enmity between Kentuckians and the United States; and chose to follow whatever course seemed most likely to advance his fame and fortune. He convinced Spanish governor Esteban Rodríguez Miró to grant him trading privileges at New Orleans and a hefty pension in exchange for military intelligence and his oath of allegiance to Spain. Between 1789 and 1796, Spanish officials in Louisiana paid Wilkinson, code-named Agent 13, pension payments, loans, and other considerations totaling nearly $30,000. During the following decade, there is plausible evidence suggesting that Wilkinson encouraged and supported a scheme involving Aaron Burr in the land bordered by the Appalachian-Allegheny mountains, the Ohio and Mississippi rivers, and the Gulf of Mexico.[9]

The nefarious Wilkinson understood that to advance his plans he needed to acquire information about the rivers of the West. Acting in his military capacity, he received the keys to the city of New Orleans on behalf of the United States on December 20, 1803, as the French *drapeau tricolore* was lowered and replaced by the American Stars and Stripes. Wilkinson retained his position as commander of the western army when he accepted Jefferson's commission as governor of Upper Louisiana Territory in the spring of 1805. While wearing both civilian and military hats, Wilkinson carefully initiated correspondence with Aaron Burr, a friend who had served with him under Benedict Arnold during the invasion of Canada but also a decided foe of Jefferson's administration. Burr, whose political career was destroyed as a consequence of his duel with Alexander Hamilton, journeyed to the Ohio River valley in April 1805 and raised a regiment of several hundred men, either to lead a filibuster into Spanish territory or, alternatively, to join with Wilkinson's army if war with Spain broke out. Burr met with Wilkinson on several occasions and appears to have conspired to separate the trans-Allegheny area by theft, stratagem, or military might. Wilkinson also carefully laid out his plans for exploring the Mississippi and its southern tributaries.[10]

In the early 1800s, President Jefferson and his subordinate General Wilkinson found themselves embroiled in an intense geopolitical struggle to claim North America's valuable fur resources, an important prelude to acquiring and possessing the region. Between 1790 and 1810, each of the contesting powers dispatched governmental and private expeditions for the purpose of probing the continental interior and searching for routes and furs. For centuries, Spanish and French traders traveled throughout the continent largely unnoticed, and Philip Nolan, Zenon Trudeau, Jacques D'Eglise, Jean Baptiste Truteau, Jacques Clamorgan,

Manuel de Lisa, James Mackay, John Evans, and members of the Chouteau clan continued similar ventures well into the nineteenth century.[11]

Although his expedition to the Pacific via Canada occurred in the 1790s, Nor'wester Alexander Mackenzie's *Voyages from Montreal to the Pacific* was finally published in 1801, serving notice to the world of British designs in North America and detailing a plan for a British monopoly of the North American fur trade. Jefferson read the book with great interest, realizing that American explorers would have to get into the field soon or any pretensions of an American presence in the Pacific Northwest would be lost. Meanwhile, George Vancouver and North West Company men such as Alexander Henry the younger, Simon Frazier, and David Thompson followed Mackenzie's lead by further exploring the Pacific Coast, the Canadian Rockies, and the northern fringes of Louisiana.[12]

The Russians, too, increased their involvement in the scramble for North America. Between 1803 and 1806, Russian captain Ivan Kruzenshtern and naval officer Iurii Lisianski completed their circumnavigation of the globe. In 1799, Tsar Paul I chartered the Russian American Company and gave it monopoly status in Alaska's fur trade. Company leader Aleksandr Baranov established his headquarters in Novoarkhangelsk (New Archangel, now Sitka), and the Russians began eyeing the Pacific Northwest as an agricultural breadbasket for their Alaskan empire.[13]

Hence, Jefferson and Wilkinson found themselves as major players in an international struggle between rival European nations seeking to possess the heart of the continent. Both understood that to stake America's claims in the contested region and protect the young republic's vital economic, commercial, and geopolitical interests, they would have to explore and chronicle the rivers of empire and uncover the geographical secrets of the Great Plains, Rocky Mountains, and Pacific Northwest. With the Spaniards blocking American expansion in the lower Mississippi Valley and the British checking American penetration into the Northwest, Jefferson and Wilkinson sought to overcome these obstacles by acquiring the necessary information regarding Louisiana that would aid the expansion of America's domain.[14]

## JEFFERSONIAN FORAYS INTO THE LOUISIANA PURCHASE

### Lewis and Clark Explore the Missouri

The Lewis and Clark expedition was not the earliest exploratory venture authorized by Jefferson, but it was the first to actually embark. After becoming president, Jefferson asked fellow Virginian Meriwether Lewis to be his private secretary. Lewis's military position as ensign and quartermaster had given him occasion to meet most of the military leaders of the country, and Jefferson wanted to have Lewis help him pare down the nation's officer corps. After the military downsizing was completed, Jefferson mentored his protégé by writing letters of introduction to his associates in Philadelphia, many of them members of the American Philosophical Society, who agreed to tutor Lewis in mathematics, astronomy, and science in preparation for a western reconnaissance. Buried in a confidential message regarding the establishment of government trading houses in late 1802 was a request by Jefferson for Congress to appropriate $2,500 for a military expedition comprising an officer and a dozen soldiers to explore the western rivers to the Pacific to gather information regarding the fur trade even before the acquisition of Louisiana transpired.[15]

After the purchase was finalized, Jefferson expanded his instructions for Lewis (Jefferson considered it the Lewis expedition) to include commercial, geopolitical, and scientific goals: the "object of your mission is to explore the Missouri river, & such principal streams of it, as, by its course and communication with the waters of the Pacific ocean, whether the Columbia, Oregon, Colorado or any other river may offer the most direct & practicable water communication across this continent for the purposes of commerce."[16]

Jefferson told Lewis to avoid the Spanish and to inform British traders that they were no longer welcome in the area now that the United States had purchased it from France. Lewis should learn all he could about the Native inhabitants, including their customs, trading practices, lifestyles, numbers, medicinal practices, and any other useful knowledge. After making contact with Indians, he was to inform them of American

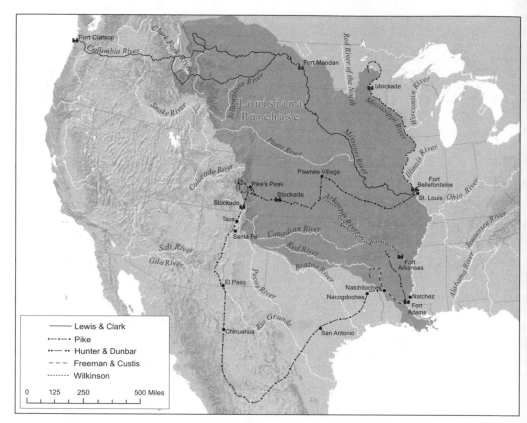

Jeffersonian Explorations, 1804–1807. Map drawn by Chris Madeira and Scot Godfredson.

intentions and distribute emblems of empire such as peace medals with Jefferson's likeness on the front, U.S. flags, and friendship certificates. Above all, he was to seek peace and establish trading alliances and to promise that fur traders would return to their villages. Finally, he was to gather scientific data on geology, geography, zoology, and botany and make celestial observations that would be useful to know about the area.[17]

To accomplish his mission, Lewis invited his former commanding officer and fellow Virginian William Clark to manage the day-to-day operations while he engaged in his scientific inquiries. The expedition set off in a fifty-five-foot keelboat and two pirogues (small boats) on May 14, 1804, with around fifty men, including soldiers, interpreters, civilian hunters, and seven or eight French voyageurs or boatmen. After wintering at Fort Mandan, a small group returned to St. Louis via the keelboat in April 1805. The permanent party—consisting of thirty-three people, including Clark's slave York, Toussaint Charbonneau, and his wife Sa cagawea and son Jean Baptiste—continued toward the headwaters of the Missouri. After several crossings of the Continental Divide, they finally descended the tributaries of the Columbia and in November arrived at the Pacific Ocean, where they erected Fort Clatsop during the winter of 1805–1806. By establishing a military post, flying the flag, and exploring and mapping the region, they strengthened America's claims to the Pacific Northwest under the Discovery Doctrine.[18]

The commercial route via the Missouri and Columbia rivers required a much longer and more difficult portage than they had hoped. It necessitated a strong bond with the Nez Percé and Flathead (Salish) Indians because they occupied the region and possessed large horse herds that made mountain portages possible. The majority of the tribes they met welcomed American trade. Two powerful middlemen who already had access to British goods—the Lakota Confederacy and the Blackfoot Confederacy—were not happy about the possibility that their traditional tribal enemies might gain access to American goods and armament, however, and took measures to waylay the explorers.[19]

On their return journey, the party retraced their route to the Continental Divide, where they divided their forces. Lewis and four men explored the headwaters of the Marias River, while Clark took a group and descended the Yellowstone River. Meanwhile, other groups traveled down the Missouri and dug up supplies cached on the outbound journey. All of the groups rendezvoused near the confluence of the Missouri and Yellowstone rivers in August before continuing to St. Louis, arriving on September 23, 1806.[20]

### Hunter and Dunbar Explore the Ouachita Tributary of the Red

With Lewis and Clark under way on the Missouri exploring the northern and western boundaries of the Purchase, Jefferson selected Scottish-born scientist Sir William Dunbar and Philadelphia chemist George

Hunter to explore the Purchase's southern boundary in present-day Louisiana and Texas. The proposed Grand Expedition or Excursion into the Southwest was an ambitious undertaking on a scale similar to Lewis and Clark's trip up the Missouri. The president tasked Dunbar and Hunter with exploring the headwaters and courses of the Red and Arkansas rivers by ascending the Red, portaging across the mountains, and descending the Arkansas.

Dunbar, owner of The Forest plantation nine miles south of Natchez, was an experienced surveyor who had traded with Indians and had surveyed the Spanish-U.S. border and lower Mississippi Valley in 1798. After becoming a U.S. citizen, he received the honor of being named surveyor general of Mississippi and made meteorological observations of the region. An acquaintance of Jefferson through the American Philosophical Society, Dunbar constructed an observatory at his plantation equipped with the best astronomical instruments available. He also conducted extensive scientific research on chemically treating soils, increasing crop yields, and developing and improving agricultural machinery such as the cotton baler. He was also skilled in mathematics, botany, zoology, ethnology, meteorology, and other sciences.[21]

George Hunter, like Dunbar born in Scotland, was one of the finest chemists in early American history. He journeyed west in 1796 and 1802 to explore the Ohio and Mississippi valleys; his trips provided opportunities for him to visit mining operations, salt licks, and other interesting phenomena before he returned to Philadelphia, where he worked as a druggist and doctor. After the purchase, Hunter expressed an interest, and Jefferson appointed him co-leader of the Red River expedition. Subsequently, his widely circulated accounts of the southern portions of the Louisiana Purchase gained general acceptance.[22]

Hunter arrived at Dunbar's plantation in late July 1804. Jefferson initially wanted to dispatch the expedition earlier, but Spain's unwillingness to issue passports and Osage Chief Great Track's threat to kill American interlopers forced them to reconsider their plans. Jefferson, who had requested and received a three-thousand-dollar appropriation for the venture, thought it best to exercise caution. To avoid possible trouble with the Osages and Spaniards, Dunbar suggested that they pursue an alternative reconnaissance up the Ouachita River, one of the major tributaries along the lower Red, pointing out that there were many "curiosities" along that route; Jefferson consented to the change.[23]

On October 16, 1804, Hunter and his teenage son, along with Dunbar, his two slaves and a servant, and thirteen soldiers, set out from St. Catherine's landing on the Mississippi River. During the autumn and winter of 1804, they ascended the Ouachita. Hunter's and Dunbar's journals contain excellent descriptions of flora, fauna, and soils, as well as accurate thermometer readings and astronomical tabulations. Dunbar utilized a pocket chronometer, a circle of reflection, a compass, and an artificial horizon to take latitudinal and longitudinal readings to make as accurate a map as possible.

Unfortunately, the boat that Hunter had designed and brought down from Pittsburgh did not work as well in inland waterways because its draft was too deep. At Fort Miro (renamed Ouachita Post, now Monroe, Louisiana), Dunbar employed guide Samuel Blazier and, to proceed onward, secured a flatboat with a cabin on deck. On November 22, while cleaning his gun, Hunter accidentally shot himself, wounding his hand and his head, and burning his eyes. Despite the mishap, they proceeded on their journey, strenuously working up the rapids, or "chutes," caused by the Ozark Mountains before arriving in the hot springs area of present-day Arkansas. They spent nearly a month studying the 150-degree water, geological features, and plant and animal life of the area before continuing on their journey. By January 8, cold temperatures and shallow water had turned them back, and while floating downstream they encountered an entourage of Quapaw Indians, who provided them with valuable geographical information. After stopping briefly at Fort Miro, they arrived in Natchez on January 27, 1805.[24]

Both men presumed that their follow-up excursion up the Red would occur in 1805, but personal circumstances, advancing age (both men were in their fifties), new congressional and War Department directives, and the difficulties of their winter journey up the Ouachita persuaded them not to volunteer for the potentially more hazardous Grand Excursion up the Red River. Continued Osage resistance toward American interlopers along the Arkansas and the expected difficulties of a mountain portage further compromised Jefferson's proposal for a team to ascend the Red and cross over and descend the Arkansas. The duo recommended instead that the next expedition should focus solely on the Red, and Jefferson concurred in May 1805. With the new plan in place, Jefferson continued corresponding with Dunbar, who, along with Hunter, began recruiting replacements to lead a party up the Red.[25]

## Pike Explores the Mississippi

While Jefferson dispatched his personal secretary Lewis to explore the Missouri and his scientist friend Dunbar to explore the Ouachita, General Wilkinson formulated exploration plans of his own, turning to Zebulon Montgomery Pike—a New Jersey soldier raised as an army brat and Wilkinson's protégé. Pike enlisted in the army at age fifteen and by 1799 had risen to the rank of first lieutenant and was stationed at Fort Kaskaskia, located on the Mississippi River some fifty miles south of St. Louis, where he served under Wilkinson. Pike was there during the first week of December in 1803 when Lewis and Clark came to the fort to recruit a dozen soldiers for their expedition. Because they were not seeking officers, however, he was not a candidate to accompany them.

Unlike Jefferson, Wilkinson did not solicit congressional approval or funding prior to sending forth his own expedition. Acting under his own prerogative as military commander, he conveyed army merchandise and supplies to Pike to cover the expedition's expenses. Wilkinson's instructions to Pike, issued in St. Louis, directed him to proceed "up the Mississippi with all possible diligence . . . until you reach the source of it" while charting the river's course, soil types, and climatic information. Wilkinson told him to seek out the Indians, noting populations, fur-trading preferences, tribal territory, and information on their neighbors—vital information that could be used to the United States' advantage in controlling and occupying the region. The winter expedition was also an excellent time to check on the fur trade and warn British traders that they were trespassing on U.S. soil. Finally, Wilkinson admonished Pike to keep a diary of all of his observations.[26]

Pike set out from Fort Bellefontaine on August 9, 1805, with twenty enlisted men in a seventy-foot keelboat. They proceeded upriver while Pike made scientific observations, recorded journal entries, and compiled maps. After they reached present-day Minnesota, shallow water forced them to use smaller boats. Establishing winter quarters and leaving Sergeant Kennerman in charge, Pike set out on December 10 with eleven others pulling two sleds and two canoes across the snow and ice. On February 1, 1806, Pike incorrectly identified Leech Lake (instead of Lake Itasca, some 25 miles distant) as the source of the Mississippi, a distance of 2,320 miles from New Orleans.

Pike met with Hugh McGillis of the British North West Fur Company, who treated him with great hospitality and a veritable feast. To McGillis's dismay, Pike told him to lower the Union Jack and replace it with the Stars and Stripes, asserting U.S. sovereignty. Pike tried, unsuccessfully, to have an Indian delegation return home with him. He was, however, able to parley with a party of Sioux, offering them two thousand dollars in wares for a nine-mile tract of land to be used for a U.S. military post (at the site of future Fort Snelling). Upon returning to his winter camp, he found that Sergeant Kennerman had presumed the worst and had rifled through Pike's personal belongings, emptied the larder, and consumed all the whiskey. Instead of shooting him, Pike demoted him to a private, and in late February, the party began its homeward journey. After traveling nearly five thousand miles in nine months, Pike arrived back in St. Louis on April 30, 1806. He immediately went to work to compile his reports, observations, and journals.[27]

## Freeman and Custis Explore the Red

Dunbar and Hunter were the first American-launched expedition to report on Louisiana. Their personal journals informed Jefferson about the southern fringe of the purchase, and a condensed report found its way into official congressional minutes and ran as a serial feature in the *National Intelligencer*. Their report only whetted Jefferson's appetite for more knowledge about Louisiana's southern fringe, but their four-month journey was sufficient for Congress to authorize an additional five-thousand-dollar appropriation (twice the amount provided for Lewis and Clark) to fund a follow-up venture.[28]

Jefferson focused his attention on a reconnaissance along the Red River, which he hoped would become the boundary line of the purchase, but Spanish officials insisted that Louisiana did not extend beyond New

Orleans. His instructions for the Red River Expedition called for finding the headwaters of the Red, negotiating a peace and opening trade with Indian nations, and conducting scientific inquiry into plant and animal life, geography, and the natural world, which made it a virtual southern counterpart to the Lewis and Clark expedition.[29]

Jefferson, Hunter, and Dunbar had some difficulty finding a replacement explorer to lead the Red River excursion, but with their sixth candidate, they finally found their man. Irishman Thomas Freeman immigrated to America in 1784 and worked as a civil engineer, helping lay out the grid system for Washington City. An experienced astronomer and surveyor, Freeman surveyed the boundary between Spain and the United States in 1796, but a misunderstanding with his partner Andrew Ellicott prevented him from completing his assignment. Once Freeman had been cleared of any wrongdoing, Philadelphia mathematician Robert Patterson (who had recently tutored Meriwether Lewis for his expedition) recommended that the Irishman be assigned to conduct the southwestern expedition. Following a mid-November dinner at the White House, Jefferson tapped Freeman to lead his "Grand Excursion" in the Southwest.

Peter Custis, a medical student from Virginia who studied natural history at the University of Pennsylvania with the acclaimed naturalist Benjamin Smith Barton, was picked to join Freeman once more-prominent candidates, including Alexander Wilson, William Bartram, and Constantine Samuel Rafinesque, ruled themselves out. Custis was strong in academic book learning but light on field experience. Nevertheless, Jefferson had selected the first scientifically trained naturalist and ethnographer to accompany an American exploring expedition. Custis received his appointment from Secretary of War Henry Dearborn in February 1806 and agreed to the terms of three dollars a day plus expenses.

Freeman and Custis, Captain Richard Sparks, Lieutenant Enoch Humphreys, thirty-three soldiers, and one slave embarked from Fort Adams on the Mississippi River in two specially constructed flatboats on May 2, 1806, with plans to be away for about one year. Freeman was the designated leader, and Captain Sparks (a Virginian) served as the ranking military officer. Because Freeman and Custis both kept journals, the venture has typically been called the Freeman and Custis expedition. With instructions in hand, the civilian scientists ventured forth in search of a commercial water route to Santa Fe and to establish friendly tribal relations.[30]

After arriving in Natchitoches, Louisiana, on June 2 they had the good fortune to meet Indian agent Dr. John Sibley, who outfitted the expedition with additional trade goods to supply Indian nations upstream. The addition of another dozen military men, along with some French and Caddo guides, rounded the party out to around fifty persons. After leaving the last American settlement on the river, they continued their scientific survey along the Red River in present-day Louisiana, Arkansas, and Texas, making extensive notations of flora, fauna, minerals, and meteorological observations. They met with Caddos, Wichitas, Comanches, and Kiowas, promising friendship and seeking to establish commercial ties that might lure the Indians away from Spanish traders in Santa Fe and San Antonio. They kept detailed records of Indian languages and other ethnographic data and distributed trade items and American tokens of sovereignty. They also carried state-of-the-art scientific equipment (telescopes, chronometers, sextants) and made good use of these instruments in recording daily air and water temperatures, noting latitude and longitude, and collecting plant and animal specimens.

Wilkinson's tantalizing letters to Jefferson—replete with references to mountains of silver, salt licks, and mysterious unicorn-like animals—encouraged the president to proceed with the expedition. Concurrently, the double-dealing general warned Spanish officials such as Nemesio Salcedo (commandant general of the Internal Provinces) of the impending American trespassing. The Spaniards refused to grant passports for expedition members and took the added step of sending Spanish forces to intercept the Americans and prevent them from initiating contact with the Comanches. Freeman and Custis had traveled about 615 miles up the Red River when Francisco Viana's force of 212 Spanish dragoons compelled them to stop near present-day Spanish Bluff, Bowie County, Texas, on July 29. Jefferson had instructed Freeman that if confronted by an opposing military force, he should not risk his life but turn back to preserve the information he had gathered.[31]

Outnumbered four to one, the Americans parleyed for two days but eventually agreed to abandon their trek. The trip downstream took nearly a month. On their outbound journey, Freeman and Custis endured nearly three weeks of backbreaking work negotiating their seven boats through the Great Raft, a hundred mile logjam that created what was known as the Great Swamp, before the Red River resumed its course. On the return trip, they borrowed some Indian horses to skirt around the swamp, arriving back at Natchitoches, where they resumed traveling by water to Fort Adams, which they reached on September 8, 1806.

Their four-month journey failed to reveal whether the Red provided a commercially viable water route to Santa Fe, but it did demonstrate Spain's determination to prevent American penetration into the region.[32] Wilkinson was disappointed that the confrontation had not induced the international incident he and Burr had hoped would lead to war and provide them with legal cover for leading a filibustering expedition into the region. In late October, Burr told Wilkinson he was ready to take action against Spain. Wilkinson decided that the plan was not going to work, so he revealed Burr's "deep, dark, wicked, and widespread conspiracy . . . to seize New Orleans, revolutionize the territory, and carry an expedition against Mexico" in a letter to Jefferson. When word reached Burr that Jefferson was determined to arrest him for treason, Burr fled to Alabama, where federal officials arrested him on February 19, 1807. The "Burr Conspiracy" was a political embarrassment to Jefferson and a political fiasco that precluded him from sending a proposed expedition up the Arkansas River in 1807. Nevertheless, the uproar did cause the Spaniards to accept the 1806 Neutral Ground Agreement, a modest concession that permitted limited American trading enterprises along the border.[33]

### Pike Explores the Southwestern Boundary and Beyond

Several months before the Burr conspiracy imploded, Wilkinson embarked upon another one of his schemes while two of Jefferson's exploring teams remained in the field: Freeman and Custis were on their way up the Red River about to be turned back by the Spanish; Lewis and Clark were in Montana on their return journey. It was time for Wilkinson to act. During the spring and summer, Burr assembled his private army for a filibuster while the general gathered military intelligence and sought ways to provoke the Spanish to declare war. Pike, who was not privy to Burr and Wilkinson's intrigues, received word that Wilkinson had given him a new assignment—to explore the central and southern Great Plains to the Continental Divide to help define the southern limits of the Louisiana Purchase boundary between the United States and Spain.[34]

For this expedition, Wilkinson instructed Pike to perform several tasks. First, as his primary objective, he was to deliver fifty-one Osage men, women, and children back to their village. Then he was to broker peace between the Kansa and Osage nations and to meet with other tribes such as the Pawnees and, especially, the Comanches, to open up discourse and trade with them. Because Pike's journeys would likely take him to "the Head Branches of the Arkansaw, and Red Rivers" near the "settlements of New Mexico," Wilkinson cautioned him to avoid Spanish contact to "prevent alarm or offence." Finally, in his spare time, Pike was to collect geographical and scientific information and to ascertain the navigability of the Arkansas and Red rivers.[35]

In a follow-up letter, Wilkinson authorized Pike to arrest "any unlicensed traders in your route . . . without a proper licence or passport" and to confiscate their property. On July 15, 1806, just six weeks after returning from exploring the Mississippi, Lieutenant Pike (whom Jefferson promoted to captain a few months later while Pike was on his Southwestern expedition) left Fort Bellefontaine in two river boats, escorted by twenty soldiers, interpreter Antoine Baronet Vasquez, surgeon John Robertson, and the general's son, Lieutenant James Biddle Wilkinson. Most of the men with him, a group Pike once referred to as a "Dam'd set of Rascals," had accompanied him up the Mississippi.[36]

After dropping off the Osages in present-day Kansas, Pike continued on to the Pawnee villages, convincing them to take down their Spanish flag and erect an American one. Pike's party then turned south, traveling via horseback to the Arkansas. The party divided; Lieutenant Wilkinson took five men and descended the Arkansas River, while Pike and fifteen others ascended the Arkansas to the Colorado Front Range of the Rocky Mountains. Leaving his men in base camp in late November, Pike and three others attempted to climb Pike's Peak, but they were unable to do so because of the wintery conditions and deep snow. Pike contented himself with exploring the headwaters of the South Platte and Arkansas rivers. With a dozen of his men suffering from frostbite, on January 14, 1807, Pike set out with those who could travel and, seeking the headwaters of the Red, crossed the Sangre de Cristo Mountains through a terrible blizzard and waist-deep snow. Pike built a small stockade on the Conejos River (a tributary of the Rio Grande near present-day Alamosa, Colorado), which he may have mistakenly thought was the Red. He granted permission for Dr. John Robinson to travel to the Spanish settlements. Alerted to the Americans' presence by the arrival of Robinson, a Spanish patrol set out and arrested Pike on February 28, 1807, and escorted his entourage to Santa Fe, where officials confiscated his papers.[37]

The Spanish treated Pike relatively well and marched him and his men to Chihuahua for questioning by General Antonio de Salcedo. Then, traveling along the Old San Antonio Road through Coahuila, Pike finally arrived at Natchitoches on July 1, 1807. Whether or not Wilkinson actually intended for Pike to spy on the Spanish, his tour of the Spanish provinces in northern Mexico provided Wilkinson with important details about the towns and their defenses. Although Jefferson and the War Department approved Pike's exploration retroactively, to Pike's great disappointment, he did not receive the hero's welcome accorded Lewis and Clark, and neither he nor the members of his expedition received extra pay or land as rewards for their efforts, because Congress suspected his complicity with Wilkinson and Burr.[38]

## Aborted and Obscure Expeditions

Jefferson and Wilkinson both planned other expeditions that left few sources to document their purposes or their outcomes. While Jefferson was corresponding with Dunbar regarding the Hunter-Dunbar expedition on the Red, he confided to Dunbar that he expected Congress to authorize his other proposed explorations of western rivers: "[O]ne party up the Panis river [Platte and North Platte], thence along the highlands to the source of the Padoucass river [South Platte] and down to its mouth. Another party up the Arcansa [Arkansas] to its source, thence along the highlands to the source of the Red river, & down that to its mouth." Jefferson concluded by telling Dunbar he was confident that these surveys would "enable us to prepare a map of La. which in its contour and main waters will be perfectly correct."[39]

Fear of Spanish opposition and the distractions occasioned by the Burr conspiracy apparently scuttled any such ventures. Jefferson acknowledged as much in an 1808 letter to adventurer Anthony Bettay of Vincennes. Bettay's claim that he had found a silver mine 1,700 miles up the Platte had prompted Jefferson to inquire about Bettay's travels. "I should be glad of a copy of any sketch or account you have made of the river Platte," Jefferson wrote. He indicated that Bettay's journey was probably among "the first exploring journeys" undertaken after the settlement with Spain and could prove useful since "we wish to become acquainted with all the advantageous water connections across our Continent."[40]

Meanwhile, Wilkinson apparently sent soldier-turned-trader John McClallen westward in the summer of 1806. Captain McClallen resigned his commission and, with Wilkinson's support and encouragement, outfitted a commercial trading venture destined for Santa Fe. McClallen carried a message to the Indians written by Wilkinson, along with presents designed to secure the protection of his party and support for his trading mission with the "Spanish Settlements within the Louisiana Territory." Instead of following Pike's route as he originally planned, McClallen altered his course and ascended the Missouri River, following Lewis and Clark's route. On September 17, 1806, he met the captains as they descended the river on their way back to St. Louis. Clark recorded that "at 11 A.M. we met Captain McClellin late a Capt. of Artily [Artillery] of the U States Army assending in a large boat." Lewis knew McClallen, who seemed astonished and overjoyed to meet them. McClallen informed the captains that the people of the country had given up on them and even the president was worried. After exchanging information until midnight, McClallen told them he was on "a speculative expedition to the confines of New Spain" and his plan was to proceed up to the mouth of the Platte to trade with the Pawnees and Otoes before continuing on to Santa Fe. McClallen continued up the Missouri to western Montana, apparently discovering a route connecting the upper Missouri with the Columbia superior to the one Lewis and Clark had followed.[41]

## REPORTING AND PUBLISHING THE RESULTS

Simply conducting expeditions was not sufficient. To be useful, the knowledge of Louisiana that Jefferson's and Wilkinson's soldiers and scientists gained from observation and inquiry needed to be interpreted and published. Jefferson's "Message from the President" delivered to Congress on February 19, 1806, made some of their findings available to the public for the first time.[42] His report informed the world that the Lewis and Clark and Hunter-Dunbar expeditions had collected a wealth of scientific information. It contained Lewis and Clark's interim report written during the winter of 1804–1805, information documenting Hunter and Dunbar's 1804–1805 exploration of the Ouachita, and physician John Sibley's reflections on the Red River country, along with several maps of the areas by Nicholas King, based on the explorers' field maps.[43]

Though the Hunter and Dunbar journey was relatively short, their journals and maps provided detailed scientific observations and data on the region's plant and animal life and its resources. They described an active trade between trappers and Indians along the Red, Black, and Ouachita rivers and chronicled the locations of hot springs that later attracted hosts of individuals seeking relief from their ailments by soaking in the hot mineral water. Their findings brought them recognition and acclaim following their return. Dunbar resumed plantation oversight and continued his scientific observation and writing, providing one of the first topographical and scientific descriptions of the Mississippi Valley. He likewise published a dozen papers on Indian sign language, natural history, and astronomy in the American Philosophical Society's journal before his death in 1810. Hunter moved his family to Louisiana in 1815 and operated a steam distillery. He was known as a Jeffersonian explorer until his death in New Orleans in 1823.[44]

Thomas Freeman's exploration led to an accurate mapping of the lower Red and a better understanding of the southwestern border between the United States and Spain. Freeman's journal and map, in addition to Custis's natural history catalogues, provided good information on the ecology of the Red River. Custis's descriptions of the 267 plants and animals he identified during his four-and-a-half-month expedition allow modern readers to visualize what the Red River was like in 1806. Tragically, in an attempt to get Custis's work into print, Nicholas King undertook the task to rewrite the journals. Untrained in scientific terminology, King mangled Custis's careful annotations beyond recognition in the 1806 published account.[45] Although Freeman's projected 1807 expedition up the Arkansas never materialized, Jefferson appointed him to survey and map the Tennessee-Alabama border in the years before his death in Huntsville, Alabama, in 1821. Meanwhile, Peter Custis finished his medical degree at the University of Pennsylvania, married, and practiced medicine in North Carolina until his death in 1842.

Pike was exonerated of all charges of complicity in the Burr conspiracy and, more important, re-created an informative and detailed report from memory and published his journals and maps in 1810. Like Lewis and Clark, he provided information on flora and fauna and discovered several new species, but in contrast to the illustrious duo, Pike's southern exploration paved the way for a viable route linking the United States and Santa Fe.[46] While some criticize errors in his maps and journals and his limitations in scientific inquiry, Pike's materials made an important contribution to understanding the Mississippi, its tributaries, and the geography of the southern plains. Their publication contributed to the development of the Santa Fe trade and American expansion into the Southwest. Pike continued serving under Wilkinson and secured Mississippi governor William C. C. Claiborne's recommendation that he be appointed governor of Florida if the United States annexed it. Colonel Pike commanded troops in West Florida stationed at Baton Rouge and was called upon to remove intruders in the neutral territory between the Arroyo Hondo and the Sabine River in 1812. After the United States declared war on Great Britain, Brigadier General Pike led a successful attack on York (Toronto), the capitol of Upper Canada in 1813, only to be fatally wounded by flying debris when a powder magazine exploded during that engagement. His life is immortalized in the name Pikes Peak.[47]

Unlike Pike, Lewis and Clark are well remembered, notwithstanding the lengthy hiatus before the publication of their journals. The Corps of Discovery conducted numerous scientific observations and gathered a wealth of geographic and ethnographic information. They scientifically classified 178 plants and 122 animals new to science. Clark's beautiful maps corrected and filled in the canvas and are remarkably accurate, especially in areas they traveled. The journals that Lewis, Clark, and half a dozen others kept are rich in content, constituting a national treasure.[48] Jefferson appointed Lewis as territorial governor of Upper Louisiana and Clark as principal Indian agent for the western tribes. Lewis, assigned the task of publishing the expedition's record, purchased some of the other expedition accounts to forestall competing works. Robert Frazier attempted to publish his on his own, but never did. To Lewis's dismay, Patrick Gass beat Lewis to the punch and published his journal. Lewis never completed the task before his untimely death in October 1809.[49] Following his passing, Benjamin Smith Barton agreed to write a detailed, scientific volume but failed to do so before his death, prompting the scientific community to underestimate the value and importance of Lewis and Clark's scientific findings. Nicholas Biddle, meanwhile, consented to provide a two-volume narrative. Clark, who promised to provide a map, sought out several publishers. Unfortunately, the Philadelphia publisher C. and A. Conrad, who had published the Pike volumes, went out of business in 1812, and Biddle's two-volume narrative did not appear in print until 1814.[50] Clark became Missouri territorial governor in 1813 and held that office until statehood in 1820, after which time he became superintendent of Indian affairs for the western tribes.[51]

Because of the vague boundary lines of the Louisiana Purchase, Jefferson and Wilkinson had made a special effort to learn as much geographical information as possible about the United States' northern border with Britain and southern border with Spain in addition to filling in details for the region between. Their men provided materials on the Missouri, Columbia, Ouachita, Red, Arkansas, and Rio Grande. Freeman's map of the lower Red River, limited because of his expedition's short duration, provided little new geographical information. Clark gathered additional information from former expedition members turned fur traders George Drouillard and John Colter regarding the Yellowstone basin and incorporated this, along with the geographical information from Pike's foray into the southern Rockies, James B. Wilkinson's expedition on the Arkansas, Dunbar's exploration of the Ouachita, Freeman's Red River Expedition, and other similar sources, into his masterful 1810–12 manuscript map of the West. It is a fairly accurate depiction of the Missouri and Columbia river basins, and its complex rendering of the multiple ranges constituting the Rocky Mountains made it superior to its predecessors and finally helped extinguish the long-held notion of a Northwest Passage through North America. It remained, during his lifetime, the best cartographic representation of the American West [52]

The exploration notes and maps of Dunbar, Pike, Freeman, and Clark (and their subsequent engravings by Nicholas King and Samuel Lewis) were used by cartographers to compile some of the earliest American maps of the continent. Mapmaker John Melish used geographic information from their expedition maps to inform his series of American maps, such as his 1816 *Map of the United States with the Contiguous British and Spanish Possessions* (published in Philadelphia) and his 1820 large-scale map of the United States.[53]

Some of the explorers' records—including some of Pike's confiscated notes, diaries and maps, Freeman's detailed journal, and Frazier's record of the Lewis and Clark expedition—were lost or later destroyed. Much of Lewis and Clark's extensive and detailed ethnographic records of Indian life on the northern Great Plains and in the Northwest was destroyed when a trunk of expedition papers that Jefferson was shipping to Monticello was vandalized and the contents thrown into the Chesapeake. Because of the dispersal of the information these explorers brought back, tapping into the vast database these explorers had compiled was difficult.[54]

Until the founding of the Smithsonian Institution in 1846, there was no centralized repository for objects and reports from government-sponsored scientific expeditions. Journals and artifacts remained in private hands or were misplaced or destroyed. Some of the Lewis and Clark materials sent to Benjamin Smith Barton for preparation of a scientific volume of the expedition disappeared after Barton's untimely death prevented him from completing the volume. Documents, objects, plant cuttings, animal artifacts, and material culture gathered by Custis, Hunter,

Dunbar, and Pike were also scattered or lost. Fortunately, some remain. Elk antlers collected by Lewis and Clark hang in Monticello. Clark kept some artifacts and gave others to friends. Lewis's plant cuttings were scattered from the American Philosophical Society to the Academy of Natural Sciences to Kew Gardens in England. Pike sent Jefferson two grizzly bear cubs, which, along with other objects, eventually ended up at Charles Willson Peale's museum in Baltimore.[55]

Had the Spanish not arrested Pike, he would be remembered in popular memory for his considerable exploratory accomplishments and not for getting lost or spying. If the Spanish had not stopped Freeman and Custis, their efforts might be viewed by the country as one of its great expeditions: better funded, prepared, staffed, and equipped than that of Lewis and Clark. Interestingly, Lewis and Clark nearly suffered the same fate that Hunter and Dunbar feared and Pike, Freeman, and Custis endured—Spanish arrest for trespassing. Wilkinson informed the Spanish regarding the Lewis and Clark expedition, and the Spanish made at least four attempts to apprehend them. Pedro Vial's party arrived at the Missouri in modern-day Nebraska in September 1804, just missing the captains on their outbound journey. Spanish groups sent out in November 1805, May 1806, and the fall of 1806 also failed to capture Lewis and Clark.[56]

Despite these shortcomings, Jeffersonian explorers provided the American people with current and accurate information about Louisiana, and their reports and maps unleashed a wave of American traders and explorers who followed in their wake. Although the scientific findings did not immediately receive the notoriety and recognition they deserved, the expeditions certainly expanded America's commercial endeavors and abetted America's expansionist impulse. Less than six months after Lewis and Clark returned to St. Louis, Manuel de Lisa, the Missouri Fur Company, and other fur-trading ventures traveled to the upper Missouri and Yellowstone rivers in pursuit of beaver. At least a dozen expedition members joined these ventures and entered the fur trade. At the same time, John Lewis, William Alexander, and other American traders slipped past the Spanish patrols on the Red to enter trade with the Taovayas and Comanches, and other traders followed.

MISSOURI BEAR.
Ursus horribilis Ord.

Titian Ramsay Peale, *Missouri Bear, Ursus horribilis,* ca. 1822. Courtesy of the American Philosophical Society. Zebulon Pike presented these two grizzly bear cubs to Thomas Jefferson, who regifted them to Charles Willson Peale, the famous artist-scientist and museum proprietor in Philadelphia, who had them stuffed and placed in his museum, after which his son painted them.

The first documented U.S. military and scientific exploration of the Platte River had to wait until the following decade, when Stephen H. Long ventured west. Long successfully completed an excursion up the Mississippi River to the Falls of St. Anthony in 1817 that resulted in the establishment of Fort Snelling on the nine miles of land Pike had purchased from the Sioux in 1805. In 1819, Long and his entourage, which included several scientists, joined General Henry Atkinson's Yellowstone Expedition bound from St. Louis to the Rockies aboard the *Western Engineer,* perhaps the first steamboat to penetrate the Missouri River into the Louisiana Purchase territory. They spent the winter near present-day Council Bluffs, Iowa, before returning east. By the summer of 1820, however, Long and nineteen men had returned to explore the

Two pages from Zebulon Pike's "Notebook of Maps, Traverse Tables, and Meteorological Observations." Record Group 94, Records of the Adjutant General's Office, 1780s–1917. National Archives and Records Administration, Washington, D.C.

| Islands | | | Rapids | | Remarks on rivers, quarries, timber, |
|---|---|---|---|---|---|
| Description | Channel on which Shore | Length | Channel | | Barrs, creeks, shoals &c &c. |
| 1½ | low | W | | | A barr extends from below to Prairie to about ½ nearly in ye middle. ye channel on ye W side runs to ye barr. The sand makes faster on W. of barr & head of ye island |
| 3¾ | do | W W F F | | | |
| | | | | Nispauis | Falls in by two mouths. the upper one which is the channel was in low water about 1500 wide and from the Nispis. bears S. 30 W |
| 2 | | | | | river mild |
| 2 small over on the W side | | | | | Sand barrs. |
| 2 small on the W shore | | | | | Sand barrs in the middle |
| | | | | | Illinois at the upper point of this course and must easily be run by a steamer for part of the Mississippi |
| | | | | | Buffaloe on river ~~~~~~~~~ |
| | | | | | Buffaloe or river farther comes in at the upper end of this course on the W side and bears S. 30 W |
| | | | | | A remarkable place for heads which curve each of two turns deep on the W shore |
| | | | | | |
| | | | | | |
| is new | | | | | |
| is Barr river | | | | | |
| | | | quite a | considerable stream | called by the French Outahele |
| | | | la Moine 11 m long extends ↗ | | |

headwaters of the Platte, Arkansas, and Red rivers. While on the Platte, he met with Pawnee, Oto, Missouria, and Omaha Indian representatives. Long continued up the South Platte and then ventured onto the Arkansas River before dividing his party—conceivably to return down that river while he searched for the Red River. He miscalculated, however, and came down the Canadian instead. Nevertheless, Long's notes chronicling the central plains filled in the gaps left from the Jeffersonian explorers and provided important contributions on ethnology and geography, and his map is legendary because it labeled the Great Plains as the "Great American Desert."[57]

Considering all of the expeditions that Jefferson and Wilkinson sent out between 1804 and 1807 together helps paint a more complex picture of Jefferson and Wilkinson's meticulous quest to explore Louisiana. The efforts of Hunter and Dunbar, Lewis and Clark, Freeman and Custis, Pike, and others launched America's westward-looking expansion in the coming years. In 1800, the Potomac was the site of the new national capitol, and beyond it was the back country. When Jefferson left office in 1808, the Potomac was a regional river on the Atlantic seaboard, and the nation's geographic center had shifted westward to the Mississippi River.

Wilkinson's desire for fame and fortune came to a suitable conclusion when he died in Mexico City on December 28, 1825, while trying to finagle a Texas land grant from the Mexican government. Jefferson passed away on the Fourth of July in 1826, but before he died, his prediction of a transcontinental American empire initiated by his purchase of Louisiana was taking shape. James Monroe had been one of the signers of the Louisiana Purchase treaty in 1803. Now, as president, Monroe had his secretary of state, John Quincy Adams, negotiating transcontinental border treaties with England (1817–18), Spain (1819), and Russia (1824), and he authored the Monroe Doctrine, which cautioned European nations against colonizing or interfering in the Western Hemisphere. Mexican Independence in 1821 opened the way for increased trade between Santa Fe and Missouri along the Santa Fe Trail and instigated the surge of thousands of American settlers into Texas. Meanwhile, American fur-trade enterprises expanded to the Pacific and helped fuel America's market revolution as well as paving the way for increased overland migration and settlement in the coming decades. Some eastern Indians had already voluntarily migrated to the Great Plains, a process that expanded and become more coercive in the 1830s. Six new states bordering the Mississippi and Ohio rivers had joined the Union, and additional territories were in the process of joining them. The Louisiana Purchase and the exploratory expeditions Jefferson and Wilkinson sponsored provided important scientific data, fostered trading networks, established American geopolitical claims, and helped Jefferson's vision of an empire for liberty move toward becoming a reality.

## APPENDIX A. CAST OF CHARACTERS

Aaron Burr, Jr. (February 6, 1756–September 14, 1836): New Jersey, soldier, Revolutionary War veteran, third vice president of the U.S.; raised an army in the West in 1805, either to defect from the U.S. or to invade Spain

William Clark (August 1, 1770–September 1, 1838): Virginian, soldier, Indian agent and superintendent, Missouri territorial governor; explored the Missouri and Columbia rivers 1804–1806

Peter Custis (1781–May 1, 1842): Virginian, naturalist, surveyor; explored the Red and Arkansas rivers in 1806

Sir William Dunbar (1749–October 16, 1810): Scottish-born scientist, surveyor of lower Mississippi Valley, territorial legislature; explored the Ouachita tributary of the Red River in 1804–1805

Thomas Freeman (ca. 1765–November 8, 1821): Irish-born surveyor, civil and topographical engineer, astronomer; mapped Tennessee-Alabama border, explored Red and Arkansas rivers in 1806

George Hunter (1750s–February 23, 1823): Scottish-born chemist, doctor, druggist who lived in Philadelphia; explored the Ouachita tributary of the Red River in 1804–1805

Thomas Jefferson (April 13, 1743–July 4, 1826): Virginian, third president of the U.S.; sent out Lewis and Clark, Hunter and Dunbar, Freeman and Custis, proposed Platte expedition

Meriwether Lewis (August 18, 1774–October 11, 1809): Virginian, soldier, Jefferson's secretary, explorer, Upper Louisiana territorial governor

John McClallen (January 29, 1772– ?): New York, soldier; encouraged
  by Wilkinson to trade in Santa Fe or on upper Missouri in 1806
Zebulon M. Pike (January 5, 1779–April 27, 1813): New Jersey, soldier,
  explorer; explored the headwaters of the Mississippi, Arkansas, Red,
  and Rio Grande in 1805–1807 before being arrested by the Spanish
  for spying
James Wilkinson (March 24, 1757–December 28, 1825): Maryland,
  commander of U.S. Army from 1800–1812, Louisiana territorial
  governor; sent out Zebulon Pike, supported Philip Nolan and John
  McClallen trading ventures


## APPENDIX B: JEFFERSONIAN EXPLORATION CHRONOLOGY (1800–1826)

| | |
|---|---|
| 1800, June 15 | General James Wilkinson takes command of the U.S. Army |
| 1800, October 1 | Secret Treaty of San Ildefonso; Spain retroceded Louisiana to France |
| 1801, March 4 | Inauguration of Thomas Jefferson as third president of the United States |
| 1802 | Spain's King Charles transfers Louisiana to France; New Orleans closed to American shipping |
| 1803, January 18 | Congress approves $2,500 for Lewis and Clark expedition |
| 1803, April 30 | United States purchases Louisiana from France |
| 1803, July 4 | Jefferson announces the treaty to the American people |
| 1803, July | Jefferson suggests removing Indian nations to the west of the Mississippi River; bill passes the Senate but fails in the House of Representatives |
| 1803, August 31 | Meriwether Lewis under way down the Ohio |
| 1803, October 20 | Senate ratifies Louisiana Purchase, 24–7 |
| 1803, December 20 | French turn New Orleans and lower Louisiana over to James Wilkinson |

| | |
|---|---|
| 1804, May 14 | Lewis and William Clark embark from St. Louis with around 50 soldiers, civilians, interpreters, and voyageurs |
| 1804, July 11 | Vice President Aaron Burr fatally wounds Alexander Hamilton in a duel |
| 1804, October 16 | George Hunter and William Dunbar and 17 others embark from Natchez to explore the Ouachita, a tributary of the Red |
| 1805, January 27 | Hunter and Dunbar return to Natchez |
| 1805, April 10 | Burr heads west to create a western empire or to invade Spain |
| 1805, August 9 | Zebulon Pike and 20 soldiers ascend the Mississippi to find its headwaters |
| 1806, April 30 | Pike arrives back in St. Louis |
| 1806, May 2 | Thomas Freeman and Peter Custis, and 33 men, explore the Red |
| 1806, July 15 | Pike, with 25 men, sets out to explore Arkansas and Red rivers |
| 1806, July 29 | Spanish troops intercept Freeman and Custis |
| 1806, August 23 | Lewis and Clark return to St. Louis |
| 1806, September 8 | Freeman and Custis return to Mississippi River |
| 1806, October 11 | Burr indicates to Wilkinson it is time to start a war with Spain |
| 1806, October 21 | Wilkinson informs Jefferson of Burr's conspiracy |
| 1807, February 19 | Burr arrested in Alabama |
| 1807, February 28 | Pike arrested by the Spanish |
| 1807, spring | Fur-trading companies, trappers, and horse traders enter Louisiana |
| 1807, July 1 | Pike returns from Mexico |
| 1807, August 3 | Burr's treason trial begins; he is acquitted September 1 by John Marshall |
| 1809, October 11 | Lewis dies while traveling the Natchez Trace in Tennessee |
| 1810, September 16 | Father Miguel Hidalgo y Costilla begins Mexican Independence |

| | |
|---|---|
| 1810, October 16 | Dunbar dies near Natchez, Mississippi |
| 1811 | Wilson Price Hunt leads overland Astorians to the Pacific |
| 1811, December 25 | Wilkinson's court-martial ends when he is found not guilty |
| 1812 | Robert Stuart guides returning Astorians and discovers South Pass |
| 1813, April 27 | Pike dies during the War of 1812 |
| 1814, December 24 | Treaty of Ghent ends the War of 1812 |
| 1817–20 | Stephen H. Long explores the Mississippi, Missouri, Platte, and Arkansas |
| 1818, October 20 | U.S. and Britain agree to 49th parallel between the Rockies/Great Lakes |
| 1819 | John Quincy Adams–Luis de Onís Treaty between Spain and U.S. |
| 1820 | Missouri Compromise |
| 1821, August 24 | Treaty of Córdoba signed; Mexico gains independence from Spain |
| 1821, November 8 | Freeman dies in Huntsville, Alabama |
| 1823 | Monroe Doctrine |
| 1823, February 23 | Hunter dies in New Orleans |
| 1824 | Russia and United States agree to the 54'40" boundary |
| 1825, December 28 | Wilkinson dies in Mexico City while pursuing a Texas land grant |
| 1826, July 4 | Jefferson dies at Monticello |
| 1836, September 14 | Burr dies in New York |

# ACKNOWLEDGMENTS

The author thanks Julie H. Adams and Loren Smith for their research assistance, the Charles Redd Center for Western Studies (at Brigham Young University, Provo, Utah) for providing funding, and Matthew L. Harris and William E. Foley for their helpful suggestions.

# NOTES

1. See Kukla, *Wilderness So Immense;* and Kastor, *Nation's Crucible.* The best general reference is Junius P. Rodriguez, ed., *The Louisiana Purchase: A Historical and Geographical Encyclopedia* (Santa Barbara: ABC-CLIO, 2002).

2. Although some Federalists opposed the acquisition as unconstitutional and too expensive, the Senate ratified the treaty by a 24–7 vote, and Congress allocated the funding. Twenty-five years later in *American Insurance Company v. Canter* (1828), Chief Justice John Marshall asserted the federal government's legal right to acquire new territory under the treaty-making clause of the Constitution, affirming the constitutionality of Jefferson's purchase. Congress divided the purchase into two territories: north of the 33rd parallel was upper Louisiana Territory; south of the line was Orleans Territory. Thomas Jefferson, "The Limits and Bounds of Louisiana," in *Documents Relating to the Purchase and Exploration of Louisiana* (Boston: Houghton Mifflin, 1904), 1–45.

3. Jefferson's second inaugural address, March 4, 1805, quoted in D. W. Meinig, *Continental America, 1800–1867,* vol. 2 of *The Shaping of America: A Geographical Perspective on 500 Years of History* (New Haven, Conn.: Yale University Press, 1993), 2:14.

4. James P. Ronda, "Exploring the American West in the Age of Jefferson," in *North American Exploration,* vol. 3, *A Continent Comprehended,* ed. John Logan Allen (Lincoln: University of Nebraska Press, 1997), 9–74.

5. Alan Taylor, "Jefferson's Pacific: The Science of Distant Empire, 1767–1811," in *Across the Continent: Lewis and Clark and the Making of America,* ed. Douglas Seefeldt, Jeffrey Hantman, and Peter Onuf (Charlottesville: University Press of Virginia, 2005), 39.

6. Onuf, *Jefferson's Empire,* 1; Goetzmann, *Exploration and Empire.*

7. Wallace, *Jefferson and the Indians.*

8. Peter S. Onuf, *The Mind of Thomas Jefferson* (Charlottesville: University of Virginia Press, 2007); William E. Foley, "Lewis and Clark's American Travels: The View from Britain," *Western Historical Quarterly* 34, no. 3 (Autumn 2003): 301–24.

9. The money trail is briefly chronicled in Jacobs, *Tarnished Warrior,* 152; and Melton, *Aaron Burr: Conspiracy to Treason.* In 1804, the Spanish paid Wilkinson another $12,000 for military intelligence. Isenberg, *Fallen Founder,* 282–83, 288–89.

10. James Wilkinson to James Madison, April 7, 1805, in Carter, *Territorial Papers,* vol. 13, *Louisiana-Missouri, 1803–1806,* 114–15. See Foley, "James A. Wilkinson."

11. W. Raymond Wood, *Prologue to Lewis and Clark: The Mackay and Evans Expedition* (Norman: University of Oklahoma Press, 2003); Abraham Nasatir, ed., *Before Lewis and Clark: Documents Illustrating the History of the Missouri, 1785–1804,* 2 vols. (Lincoln: University of Nebraska Press, 1990); John F. McDermott, ed., *The Spanish in the Mississippi Valley, 1762–1804* (Urbana: University of Illinois Press, 1974).

12. Mackenzie's *Voyages from Montreal on the River St. Lawrence through the Continent of North America, to the Frozen and Pacific Oceans: In the Years 1789 and 1793* has been reprinted numerous times. A useful edition is W. Kaye Lamb, ed., *The Journals and*

*Letters of Sir Alexander Mackenzie* (New York: Cambridge University Press, 1970). Also see D'Arcy Jenish, *Epic Wanderer: David Thompson and the Mapping of the Canadian West* (Lincoln: University of Nebraska Press, 2003); and Richard S. Mackie, *Trading beyond the Mountains: The British Fur Trade on the Pacific, 1793–1843* (Vancouver: University of British Columbia Press, 1997).

13.  In 1806, Baranov sent one of his best officers, Nikolai Rezanov, to negotiate with the Spanish in San Francisco Bay to open trade, and the Russians were on the move. Although the Spanish were reticent and resistant to foreign trade, by 1811 Russian Ivan Kuskov had established Fort Ross on the Russian River and Russians were conducting limited trade with the missions in Alta California. James R. Gibson, *Imperial Russia in Frontier America* (New York: Oxford University Press, 1976); Gibson, *Otter Skins, Boston Ships, and China Goods: The Maritime Fur Trade of the Northwest Coast, 1785–1841* (Seattle: University of Washington Press, 1992); Penny Rennick, ed., "Russian America," special issue, *Alaska Geographic* 26, no. 4 (1999).

14.  Donald Jackson, *Thomas Jefferson and the Stony Mountains: Exploring the West from Monticello* (Norman: University of Oklahoma Press, 1993); Ronda, "Moment in Time."

15.  Jefferson's message to Congress, January 18, 1803, in *Letters of the Lewis and Clark Expedition with Related Documents, 1783–1854*, ed. Donald Jackson, 2nd ed. (Urbana: University of Illinois Press, 1978), 1:10–13. As governmental projects sometimes do, the thirteen-person figure swelled to four dozen, and the congressional allocation of $2,500 soon ran a tab of $38,000. The price tag for Louisiana likewise climbed from $15 million to $23,313,567.73.

16.  Jefferson's instructions to Lewis, June 20, 1803, in Jackson, *Letters of Lewis and Clark,* 1:61–66.

17.  Allen, *Passage through the Garden* (1975), reissued as *Lewis and Clark and the Image of the American Northwest* (New York: Dover, 1991).

18.  Robert J. Miller, *Native America, Discovered and Conquered: Thomas Jefferson, Lewis and Clark, and Manifest Destiny* (2006; repr., Lincoln: University of Nebraska Press, 2008).

19.  James P. Ronda, *Lewis and Clark among the Indians* (Lincoln: University of Nebraska Press, 1984).

20.  Gary E. Moulton, ed., *The Journals of the Lewis and Clark Expedition,* 13 vols. (Lincoln: University of Nebraska Press, 1983–2001).

21.  Arthur H. DeRosier, Jr., *William Dunbar: Scientific Pioneer of the Old Southwest* (Lexington: University Press of Kentucky, 2007).

22.  Hunter kept four extensive journals of his western trips and observations of the Ohio and Mississippi valleys. John F. McDermott, ed., *The Western Journals of Dr. George Hunter, 1796–1805* (Philadelphia: American Philosophical Society, 1963).

23.  For correspondence between Dunbar and Jefferson, see Eron Rowland, comp., *Life, Letters, and Papers of William Dunbar* (Jackson: Press of the Mississippi Historical Society, 1930). Dunbar's journal for the trip up the Ouachita and other correspondence and material are in the William Dunbar Collection, Riley-Hickingbothan

Library, Ouachita Baptiste University, Arkadelphia, Arkansas. The "boiling springs" are present-day Hot Springs National Park. Jefferson had reason to be cautious with exploring Spanish-contested areas. Philip Nolan, a Wilkinson protégé, had tried operating a contraband- and horse-trading network among the Comanches and Taovayas in Spanish Texas. Operating out of Natchez, he explored the Red River country before being captured and killed for spying in central Texas in 1801.

24. Trey Berry, Pam Beasley, and Jeanne Clements, eds., *The Forgotten Expedition: The Louisiana Purchase Journals of Dunbar and Hunter, 1804–1805* (Baton Rouge: Louisiana State University Press, 2006); Trey Berry, "The Expedition of William Dunbar and George Hunter along the Ouachita River, 1804–1805," *Arkansas Historical Quarterly* 62, no. 4 (2003): 386–403.

25. John F. McDermott, ed., "The Western Journals of George Hunter, 1796–1805," special issue, *Proceedings, American Philosophical Society* 103, no. 5 (1959). Reprint, Philadelphia: American Philosophical Society, 1963.

26. Wilkinson to Pike, July 30, 1805, in Jackson, *Journals of Pike*, 1:3–4. Historians estimate the expedition's expenses at around $2,000. Biographies include Hollon, *Lost Pathfinder*; and John Upton Terrell, *Zebulon Pike*.

27. Pike, "Journal of the Mississippi River Expedition," in Jackson, *Journals of Pike*, 1:5–131. In early July, Pike informed Wilkinson that he had completed the task of finishing his reports. Pike to Wilkinson, July 2, 1806, in ibid., 280.

28. The total expenditure for the second Red River Expedition ended up at $8,700. Dan L. Flores, "'A Very Different Story: Exploring the Southwest from Monticello with the Freeman and Custis Expedition of 1806," *Montana: The Magazine of Western History* 50, no. 1 (Spring 2000): 2–17.

29. Dan L. Flores, ed., *Jefferson and Southwestern Exploration: The Freeman and Custis Accounts of the Red River Expedition of 1806* (1984), reissued as *Southern Counterpart to Lewis and Clark: The Freeman and Custis Expedition of 1806* (Norman: University of Oklahoma Press, 2002).

30. Dan L. Flores, "Red River Expedition," *Handbook of Texas Online*, http://www.tshaonline.org/handbook/online/articles/RR/upr2.html.

31. A six-hundred-man force commanded by Lieutenant Facundo Melgares left Santa Fe in case Viana missed Freeman and Custis in Texas.

32. Jefferson insisted that the Rio Grande was the southern boundary; Spain insisted it was the Sabine River, thence north to the Missouri. Not until 1819 did the two nations settle on a transcontinental boundary compromise, along the Red River. With Mexican Independence in 1821, the trickle of American traders venturing to Santa Fe and settlers moving into Texas turned into a stream.

33. Wilkinson to Jefferson, October 21, 1806, in Wilkinson, *Memoirs of My Own Times*, 2:appendix, xcv. Burr's trial ended when John Marshall's court acquitted him. After a short European exile, Burr returned to New York and his law practice before his death on September 14, 1836.

34. It is unclear whether Wilkinson directed Pike to deliberately trespass on Spanish territory in order to be arrested so that Pike could have an opportunity to observe

Spanish military strength. Certainly that would have been critical information for a Wilkinson-Burr plot to invade Spain.

35. Wilkinson to Pike, June 24, 1806, in Jackson, *Journals of Pike*, 1:285–87. The Colorado Springs Pioneer Museum contains many of Donald Jackson's research notes and papers and is especially rich in Lewis and Clark and Pike material. I am grateful to Matt Mayberry, Leah Davis Witherow, and Kelly Murphy for their assistance in accessing the museum's collections. Incidentally, the museum hosted Pike's World: Exploration and Empire in the Greater Southwest, a magnificent Pike Bicentennial exhibit in 2006.

36. Wilkinson to Pike, July 12, 1806, in Jackson, *Journals of Pike*, 1:288–89. Pike's journal of the western expedition commences on page 290 and concludes on page 448.

37. Pike's notes and papers were discovered in the Mexican archives by Herbert Eugene Bolton, who published them in the *American Historical Review* in 1908 (they have since been republished). The Mexican government later relinquished Pike's papers, and they were delivered to the Archives Division of the Adjutant General's Office.

38. Current information (unless new evidence to the contrary surfaces) indicates that Pike did not know of Wilkinson and Burr's plot and remained a loyal American patriot.

39. Jefferson to Dunbar, March 13, 1804, in Jackson, *Jefferson and the Stony Mountains*, 236n1.

40. Jefferson to Bettay, February 18 1808, ibid., 241n28.

41. William Clark, September 17, 1806, in Moulton, ed., *Journals of Lewis and Clark*, 8:362–64. Gary Moulton speculates that Wilkinson may have been a secret backer of his enterprise and that even a few of Lewis and Clark's men quickly returned from St. Louis to join McClallen (364n2). No one knows John McClallen's fate—he simply faded into history. No extant journals or maps are known to exist. John C. Jackson, *By Honor and Right: How One Man Boldly Defined the Destiny of a Nation* (Amherst, N.Y.: Prometheus Books, 2010). See also Harry M. Majors, "John McClellan in the Montana Rockies, 1807," *Northwest Discovery: The Journal of Northwest History and Natural History* 2, no. 9 (November/December 1981): 554–630.

42. Hutchins, LePage du Pratz, Pittman, and others had all published earlier accounts of Louisiana and its people.

43. Originally published as *Messages from the President of the United States, Communicating Discoveries Made in Exploring the Missouri, Red River, and Washita, by Captains Lewis and Clark, Doctor Sibley and Mr. Dunbar, with A Statistical Account of the Countries Adjacent*, a beautiful facsimile of the 1806 Natchez edition has been reissued as *Jefferson's Western Explorations: Discoveries Made in Exploring the Missouri, Red River, and Washita, by Captains Lewis and Clark, Doctor Sibley, and William Dunbar, and Compiled by Thomas Jefferson, a facsimile*, ed. Doug Erickson, Jeremy Skinner, and Paul Merchant (Spokane, Wash.: Arthur H. Clark, 2004). Also see William Dunbar, "Journal of a Voyage," in *Documents Relating to the Purchase and Exploration of Louisiana* (Boston: Houghton Mifflin, 1904).

44. For the Louisiana Purchase journals of Hunter and Dunbar, see Berry, Beasley, and Clements, *Forgotten Expedition*.

45. Thomas Freeman, *An Account of the Red River, in Louisiana, Drawn up from the Returns of Messrs. Freeman and Custis to the War Office of the United States, Who Explored the Same, in the Year 1806* (Washington, D.C.: n.p., 1806/07). See also Thomas Freeman Papers, Peter Force Collection, Library of Congress. For an excellent edited edition with commentary, see Flores, *Jefferson and Southwestern Exploration*. See also Dan L. Flores, "The Ecology of the Red River in 1806: Peter Custis and Early Southwestern Natural History," *Southwestern Historical Quarterly* 88 (July 1984): 1–42.

46. Nicholas King rendered a hastily prepared version of Pike's Mississippi route and maps in late 1806 or early 1807. Jackson, *Journals of Pike*, 1:131–79. Three years later, the official account was published under the title Pike, *Exploratory Travels through the Western Territories of North America*. For useful editions, see Coues, *Expeditions of Pike* (1895); and Hart and Hulbert, *Southwestern Journals of Pike.*

47. Carter, *Territorial Papers*, vol. 9, *Territory of Orleans*, 909, 927–28, 998–1001; Michèle Butts, "Zebulon Montgomery Pike," in *Encyclopedia of the War of 1812*, ed. David S. Heidler and Jeanne T. Heidler, 415–16 (Annapolis, Md.: Naval Institute Press, 2004); and Olsen, "Zebulon Pike." Reaching the summit of Pikes Peak inspired Katharine Lee Bates to pen the lines of her most famous poem, "America the Beautiful."

48. Moulton, *Journals of Lewis and Clark;* Paul R. Cutright, *Lewis and Clark: Pioneering Naturalists* (1969; repr., Lincoln: University of Nebraska Press, 1989).

49. James J. Holmberg, John D. W. Guice, and Jay H. Buckley, *By His Own Hand? The Mysterious Death of Meriwether Lewis* (Norman: University of Oklahoma Press, 2006).

50. Nicholas Biddle and John Allen, eds., *History of the Expedition under the Command of Captains Lewis and Clark, to the Sources of the Missouri, Thence across the Rocky Mountains and down the River Columbia to the Pacific Ocean, Performed during the Years 1804, 1805 and 1806, by Order of the Government of the United States* (Philadelphia: Bradford and Inskeep, 1814); Paul Russell Cutright, *A History of the Lewis and Clark Journals* (Norman: University of Oklahoma Press, 1976); Doug Erickson, Jeremy Skinner, and Paul Merchant, with Stephen Dow Beckham, *The Literature of the Lewis and Clark Expedition: A Bibliography and Essays* (Portland: Lewis and Clark College, 2003).

51. Jay H. Buckley, *William Clark: Indian Diplomat* (Norman: University of Oklahoma Press, 2008).

52. Clark's original master map, on a sheet of paper 32 inches high and 52 inches wide, was recently republished in 2004 by the Beinecke Rare Book and Manuscript Library, William Robertson Coe Collection of Western Americana, Yale University Library. John L. Allen, "The Maps of the Lewis and Clark Expedition," in *Mapping the West: America's Westward Movement, 1524–1890*, ed. Paul E. Cohen (New York: Rizzoli, 2002), 74–96; Gary E. Moulton, ed., *Atlas of the Lewis and Clark Expedition* (Lincoln: University of Nebraska Press, 1983). Before the Louisiana Purchase, one of the most accurate and comprehensive maps of the continent may have been Aaron Arrowsmith's 1802 *Map Exhibiting All the New Discoveries in the Interior Parts of North America*. In 1804, American cartographer Samuel Lewis worked with Arrowsmith to create the first printed map depicting the topography of the Louisiana Purchase, drawn from

information from Pierre Antoine Soulard's 1795 map. Nevertheless, their map contained numerous errors and large gaps requiring accurate information.

53.  John R. Short, *Representing the Republic: Mapping the United States, 1600–1900* (London: Reaktion Books, 2001), 127–37. In 1838, the Army Corps of Topographical Engineers was established to explore and develop the continent. Frémont's expeditions in the 1840s are among the first of this organization to begin fulfilling their charge.

54.  Jefferson was sending the linguistic evidence to Monticello from Washington, D.C. When Lewis heard of the loss, he noted the irony that they "had passed the continent of America and after their exposure to so many casualties and wrisks [they] should have met such destiny in their passage through a small portion only of the Chesapeake." Lewis to Jefferson, June 27, 1807, in Jackson, *Letters of Lewis and Clark,* 2:418.

55.  The fate of the Lewis and Clark objects is chronicled in Carolyn Gilman, "The Journey of Our Objects," in *Lewis and Clark: Across the Divide* (Washington, D.C.: Smithsonian Institution, 2003), 335–90. For plant specimens, see C. V. Morton, "Freeman and Custis' Account of the Red River Expedition of 1806: An Overlooked Publication of Botanical Interest," *Journal of the Arnold Arboretum* 48 (1967): 431–59; and Moulton, *Journals of Lewis and Clark,* vol. 12, *Herbarium.*

56.  Warren L. Cook, *Flood Tide of Empire: Spain and the Pacific Northwest, 1543–1819* (New Haven, Conn.: Yale University Press, 1973); Noel M. Loomis and Abraham P. Nasatir, *Pedro Vial and the Road to Santa Fe* (Norman: University of Oklahoma Press, 1967); John F. McDermott, ed., *The Spanish in the Mississippi Valley, 1762–1804* (Urbana: University of Chicago Press, 1974).

57.  Long kept detailed notes of the expedition, but Edwin James, a botanist and geologist who accompanied him on the expedition, was the one who published *Account of an Expedition from Pittsburgh to the Rocky Mountains: Under the Command of Major Stephen H. Long.* A useful version is contained in Reuben G. Thwaites, ed., *Early Western Travels, 1748–1846,* vols. 14–17 (Cleveland: Arthur H. Clark, 1904–1907).

# 5

# An Empire and Ecology of Liberty

*Jared Orsi*

In early September 1805, two very powerful men were thinking about rivers. Upon their concerns hung the fates of nations. One was Nemesio Salcedo, the highest-ranking Spanish official in northern Mexico. On September 9, from the city of Chihuahua, Salcedo wrote to the governor of New Mexico, alarmed at "the frequency with which the Subjects of the United States of America navigate the Misuri River." The Missouri, he said, was "the Key point to the Internal Country of New Spain," and guarding New Spain required guarding that river. He ordered a party to be sent to the Pawnees, lavishing them with Spanish gifts and asking them to capture Americans and bring them to Santa Fe.[1]

Salcedo had good cause to worry, for unbeknownst to him, another powerful man was thinking about rivers too. Only the day before, from St. Louis, General James Wilkinson, the governor of Upper Louisiana and commander of the U.S. Army, had written to Secretary of War Henry Dearborn proposing to invade New Mexico via the Arkansas River. "Should We be involved in a War," he advised, "it becomes extremely desireable it should be reconnoitred, and this cannot be done, with any prospect of safetey, or Success, before we have brought the . . . Commanchees to a conference, because they reign the uncontrouled Masters of that Country. This I understand may be best accomplished through the Panis [Pawnees]."[2] Like Salcedo, Wilkinson knew that the best way to win the friendship of the "uncontrouled Masters" of the country was to appeal to their material interests, and in a subsequent letter to Dearborn, he urged the secretary to be patient with the expense of plying western Indians with offerings of friendship.[3] Both Wilkinson and Salcedo understood the connections between rivers, states, and material interests in the West.

So too did Thomas Jefferson. We often think of the author of the Declaration of Independence and the third president of the United States as primarily an intellectual founding father, who articulated the ideas of freedom and equality that would animate the nation and its politics for generations. Even one of his grandest material accomplishments, the Louisiana Purchase, is cast by historians as the seed of an idea, the empire of liberty. According to the Jefferson scholar Peter Onuf, for example, Jefferson imagined America as an empire knit together not by a coercive metropolis but by an idea: republicanism. This common ideological commitment had been awakened in Americans by the experience of defending themselves against violations of that principle—first against the British in the American Revolution and then against the Federalists in the revolution of 1800. Jefferson, Onuf argued, believed the nation's strength came from "the loyalty of patriotic citizens who would rise up in defense of their own liberties and their country's independence whenever they were threatened." It was "a union that transcended mere interest. It was also a union of 'heart' and 'mind,' of a people bound by the love that dedication to republican principles made possible." Historians should not forget, however, that Jefferson began the Declaration of Independence by invoking "Nature and Nature's God" and that Jefferson's intellectual life was rooted deeply in nature, which he understood in profoundly material terms. Without a doubt, Jefferson's articulation of the *idea* of America had profound impact, and he expressed that idea unmistakably and repeatedly in visionary speeches, such as the First Inaugural Address, in which he called Americans to "unite with one heart and one mind" and become a "brethren of the same principle."[4] In the practical business of running the nation, however—for example, when working to secure American control of the Mississippi River—he and his administration displayed a keen sense of the material interests that bound Americans to their nation.

In fact, to become a reality, Jefferson's empire of liberty required success in three related material projects. First, to hold the fragile and far-flung republic together at all, the central government in Washington had to appeal to westerners' material interests. This, in turn, required

extending state mastery over distant lands and ecologies. Finally, to accomplish that, Jefferson needed agents in the West—individuals who
could assess the land and its resources, much as he had done in the
only book he ever published, *Notes on the State of Virginia*. These agents
would also enforce the laws of the national state and act to advance its
interests. To do all this, the agents had to succeed in the most basic of
material endeavors: they had to stay alive.

Salcedo's nightmares and Wilkinson's schemes converged with Jefferson's empire of liberty in the journey of Lieutenant Zebulon Pike, who
left St. Louis in July 1806 as the commander of a military expedition
to do exactly what Wilkinson had recommended: map the rivers and
make friends with the Indians.[5] Six and a half brutal months later, Spaniards arrested Pike's party in what is now southern Colorado, taking him
first to Santa Fe and then south to Chihuahua to meet Salcedo, who
denounced Pike as a spy and sent him home under armed escort.

Pike's travels, however, were more than a botched expedition of discovery—they capture in microcosm the three material components of
Jefferson's empire of liberty. Especially among the Pawnees, whom Pike
visited on the Republican River in September and October 1806, Pike
sought to win the loyalty of western peoples by making both cultural and
material appeals, offering both republican principles and gifts and trade.
In doing so, he unmistakably (though perhaps only semiconsciously)
demanded a wholesale reworking of their ecology to make it fit more
compatibly within the nation-state. Pike's reconnaissance instructions
from Wilkinson also represented a quintessentially Jeffersonian attempt
to exert control by collecting data. Although Jefferson's heart sometimes
led him astray, his head told him that to discover the good toward which
humanity's labors should be directed required no more than looking at
nature and gathering its material data. Fixing latitude and longitude,
reporting on minerals, cataloguing species, and describing how Indians lived on the land—these were the kinds of inquiries that had interested Jefferson in *Notes* and that found their way into his instructions
to Lewis and Clark two decades later. Wilkinson likewise sent Pike into
the field as the agent of the nation, to be its eyes, ears, mouth, and hands
in the West, to exercise state control over distant lands and peoples, to
be the vanguard of an empire of liberty. Despite these grand ambitions,

however, Pike's task frequently devolved into the challenge of merely staying alive. Once he was a few days out from St. Louis, Pike could never be sure where to locate and how to secure the food, water, fuel, and shelter necessary to maintain the bodily comfort and safety of his men and animals.

Thus, the empire of liberty was more than an idea. For its very existence, it required the assembling of an elaborate material foundation to support both inhabitants and visitors in the West and to attach them to the nation. In the end, Pike laid only a brick or two of that foundation, but his expedition reveals to us the intersection of the cultural and the material labor that went into laying a lasting groundwork for an empire and nation.

## A NATION OF ONE HEART AND MIND— AND MANY MATERIAL INTERESTS

Shays's Rebellion in western Massachusetts in 1786 and the many other backcountry revolts of the early republic made plain that the nation had loyalty problems on its margins. In addition to the Indian, Spanish, British, French, and mixed-race peoples, who rarely found much incentive to cooperate with the young nation, there were plenty of Americans on the country's frontiers whose loyalty was instrumental—running only as deeply as national allegiance would help them meet and advance their material interests. Traces of the material underpinnings of loyalty in the early republic can be seen in Pike's expedition. Pike's "primary objective," according to his instructions from Wilkinson, was to escort fifty-some Indians to their villages in what is now Missouri and Nebraska.[6] The bulk of this party consisted of Osage men, women, and children who had been captured by the Potawatomis and ransomed by the United States. In response, an angry Jefferson wrote to William Henry Harrison that the Potawatomis must be "strongly reprimanded, and no exertion spared to recover and restore the prisoners. . . . The Indians on this side of the Mississippi must understand that that river is now ours, & is not to be a river of blood."[7]

Along the Mississippi and everywhere Jefferson looked, the politics of holding the nation together was bound up with land and water. Not the least of the material challenges facing the country was the sheer size of the North American continent. Land was something that nearly everyone realized America had in abundance. Even before Jefferson had set his hand to pen the Declaration of Independence, Thomas Paine had argued for America's viability on the basis of its land, which might be sold "not only to the discharge of the present debt, but to the constant support of government. No nation under heaven hath such an advantage as this." Jefferson praised the "immensity of land courting the industry of the husbandman" and seemingly promising that America would be a nation of liberty-loving yeoman farmers.[8] Land abundance, however, was a mixed blessing. After the Revolution, the United States had inherited one of the most vexing among the problems that had caused the British empire in North America to crumble—the West— and there was little to suggest that the young republic would prove any more adept than the British at peopling a vast hinterland while maintaining control over those subjects. The great philosopher of the French Enlightenment, Montesquieu, had warned that no large republic could survive. Distance was too powerful a centrifugal force, he observed; spacious republics would fragment, "ruined by . . . internal imperfection."[9]

Indeed, Shays's Rebellion made inescapably clear that abundance of land was no guarantee that those who settled on it would succeed or that they would be satisfied with their government. The revolt also demonstrated how easily private material failure could translate into grievances against the state and embroil a region in civil war.[10] In the aftermath of Shays's Rebellion, some of America's leading men offered the Constitution as the antidote to the centrifugal tendencies of spacious republics. Alexander Hamilton confronted and refuted Montesquieu's logic in the very first *Federalist Paper,* and John Jay continued that reasoning in the second by maintaining that a providential convergence of cultural and geographical coherence ensured that in America a more perfect union with a strong central government could hold together a republic. *Federalist Papers 6* and *7* argued that the Constitution would bind the regions together, preventing disputed land claims in the West from bringing the states to war with one another. The Constitution was thus as important for eliminating internal borders as it was for protecting external ones.[11] The founders' recognition that a material basis in land was necessary groundwork for a continental nation was thus evident in the Constitution itself.

Its impact was immediate. Like Daniel Shays and many of his followers, Zebulon Pike's father was a Revolutionary War veteran who tried unsuccessfully to become one of those liberty-loving independent yeoman farmers that Jefferson so admired. A series of short tenures on small plots of land took the Pikes steadily westward after the Revolution until they found themselves in western Pennsylvania by the early 1790s, just as the Whiskey Rebellion was breaking out. Neither Pike nor his father joined their neighbors in the Whiskey Rebellion, however. Instead, they joined the more perfect union's army, which proved to be one of the Constitution's more important early accomplishments in securing the loyalty of westerners such as the Pikes. In the mid-1790s, President George Washington deployed the army to crush both Pennsylvania whiskey rebels and Ohio Valley Indians. Thus, instead of fighting the federal government, the Pikes and other struggling westerners fought Indians—and were rewarded with promotions, land grants, and social and political power. After opening the land of the Ohio country for American settlement, the army, with its demand for food, clothing, tools, weapons, alcohol, and other manufactured goods, stimulated the region's economy.[12] Thus, the army not only served as the stick for beating back various kinds of resistance to federalism in the Northwest but also offered a carrot of social advancement and material gain for potentially disgruntled westerners. As a result, as historian Andrew Cayton has argued, with deployment of the federal army over the course of the 1790s, whites in the Northwest increasingly began to equate their interests with those of the nation.[13] This was not true, however, in the Southwest.

If the army mitigated the problem of land and loyalty north of the Ohio, water continued to pose vexing challenges south of it. In April 1802, after Spain had ceded Louisiana to France, an alarmed Jefferson wrote to his diplomat Robert Livingston that whoever owns the port of New Orleans is "our natural and habitual enemy." From the day that

France takes possession of the city, he continued, "we must marry our-selves to the British fleet and nation." Why was New Orleans so impor-tant as to drive even the Francophile Jefferson to contemplate an alliance with Great Britain? In invoking nature, Jefferson hardly meant "natural" as a mere synonym for "inevitable." Rather, like Wilkinson and Salcedo, he was keenly aware of the material impact that the geography of rivers implied. Through New Orleans, at the mouth of the Mississippi River, he wrote, "the produce of three-eighths of our territory must pass to market, and from its fertility it will ere long yield more than half of our whole produce and contain more than half our inhabitants."[14]

More than national profit was at stake, however. Indeed, there was little consensus on whether the Mississippi River had much economic importance to the nation at all. In the aftermath of the Revolution, John Jay and other Federalists had been ready to cede the river's navigation rights to Spain in exchange for favorable trade relations that would head off the threatened secession of New England from the Articles of Confederation (the first of the early republic's outbursts of secessionist sentiment that threatened to prove Montesquieu correct).[15] Thus, not everyone perceived the vital national economic interests in New Or-leans that Jefferson did.

Rather, the national interest in controlling the Mississippi lay in the fact that western loyalty hung in the balance. Concerns about navigation of the Mississippi and the wealth it brought to westerners had underlain both Shays's Rebellion and the Whiskey Rebellion. Moreover, lingering fear that a federal government dominated by Atlantic states could not be trusted to enforce the nation's Mississippi River rights made Kentucky and Tennessee fertile ground for secessionist movements in the 1780s and early 1790s. James Wilkinson, one of the ringleaders of the abor-tive plots, had secretly taken a loyalty oath to the Spanish government, as had Andrew Jackson.[16] This was far from a "union that transcended mere interest." Americans may have been a "brethren of the same prin-ciple," but the loyalties of westerners ran less to the principle embodied in the empire of liberty than to that empire's ability and willingness to protect and advance their material interests.[17] Statehood for Kentucky (1792) and Tennessee (1796) and the 1795 Treaty of San Lorenzo, which secured Spanish assent to American navigation of the Mississippi, had momentarily abated the secessionist agitation, but with a powerful and expansionist Napoleonic France replacing the weaker Spain as the owner of New Orleans, loyalty of the West was once again cast into doubt. As Madison wrote to Robert Livingston and James Monroe, France believed that holding the mouth of the river would enable that nation to "command the interests and attachments of the Western portion of the United States."[18] Thus, if the regional interest in who controlled the river was material, at stake for the nation was the integrity of the union. If the United States was to hold the loyalty of profit-minded westerners, it had to hold New Orleans. Otherwise Montesquieu would be vindicated.

The most ambitious attempt to vindicate Montesquieu was undertaken by Aaron Burr, and it, too, involved New Orleans. His political career in shambles after murdering Alexander Hamilton in a duel, Burr went west in 1804 and began talking to anyone whom he believed had a grievance against the federal government—and of these there were many. His exact intentions remain unclear to this day, but most likely (and widely discussed at the time) he was trying to build support for a plan to capture New Orleans. Once he controlled the Mississippi, he could attempt to take silver-rich provinces in northern New Spain (Salcedo was right—it was all about rivers). Some also speculated that he might try to persuade western states and territories to secede from the United States. To accomplish any of this, however, he needed more than a small private army, which is where James Wilkinson came in. It is certain that the two talked. What they agreed to is less clear, but Wilkinson, as the head of the U.S. Army, appears to have promised Burr some military support, which the general never delivered. Pike's western expedition—launched just as all this was coming to a head and directed right into the territory that Wilkinson and Burr needed reconnoitered to prepare for a filibuster into New Spain—may well have been a part of all this.[19]

Or maybe not. Pike's expedition never provided any help to Burr's conspiracy, which unraveled before Pike returned from the West. The immediate cause of the conspiracy's demise was that Wilkinson ratted on Burr, who was arrested, but the more intriguing question is why Wilkinson betrayed his coconspirator. One possibility is that Wilkinson had never intended to go all the way down the line with Burr in the first place. Wilkinson, who aspired to profit from the St. Louis fur trade, from which he found himself shut out by the Chouteau family and other competitors on the Missouri and Osage rivers, was looking to the Platte and Arkansas rivers as alternative entry points to the fur trade for a latecomer such as himself. In 1805 and 1806, Wilkinson sent two unsuccessful expeditions to the Platte River. Instead of being linked to Burr's intrigue, Pike's expedition to explore the Arkansas may very well have been a quintessentially American attempt on Wilkinson's part to blend private profiteering with public service.[20]

A compatible explanation for why Burr's plot disintegrated is that he overestimated western grievances and failed to gather enough support to convince Wilkinson to stand by him. In the aftermath of the Louisiana Purchase of 1803, which secured American navigation of the Mississippi River, western enthusiasm for secession declined. Burr found plenty of people like Wilkinson and Jackson willing to talk to him, but they were hesitant to cast their lot with filibustering and secession unless success seemed assured. This would not have surprised Secretary of State James Madison. Even before the Louisiana Purchase, Madison believed that western material interests were tilting against secession. It boiled down to the force of the flow of the river. Westerners, he wrote to Livingston in March 1803, were dependent on manufactured goods, which, because of the difficulty of upstream transport on the Mississippi, had to come overland to the interior from American ports on the Atlantic and down the Ohio River. This, along with the French navy's inability to protect Mississippi River commerce in the event of a war between Great Britain and France, led Madison to doubt that France or any other competitors for New Orleans could excite much secessionist sentiment in the West. "The Western people," he wrote, "believe that they have a natural and indefeasible right to trade freely thro' the Mississippi. They are conscious of their power to enforce this right against any Nation."[21]

Thus, even while Indians, Spaniards, French, and Americans with varying degrees of loyalty to their nation all vied with Jefferson for control of the Mississippi, the geography of rivers was what mattered most to western settlers. As Madison wrote to Livingston, westerners were "bound to the union not only by the ties of kindred and affection" but also by other considerations that "flow from clear and essential interests."[22] Those interests flowed downhill, with gravity, following the water itself. Loyalty's material foundation thwarted the designs of Burr and Napoleon and made way for the empire of liberty.

## SEEING FOR THE STATE

Securing the material interests of westerners was largely a problem of integrating them into Atlantic World commerce, and at the base of this commerce lay an ecological relationship between individuals, the state, and nature. Commerce in the Atlantic World dealt largely in commodities: molasses, tea, coffee, cocoa, sugar, tallow, spices, cotton, indigo, tobacco, lead, coal, salt, furs, and, of course, human beings. Each of these captured energy from the sun and stored it in plant, animal, or mineral matter. The market converted this stored energy into capital. Capital then could be invested in machinery, animals, and labor, and it was thus reconverted into energy that could do work to manufacture things or provide services. This transformation back and forth between energy and capital lay at the heart of the Atlantic World economy, and whoever facilitated that transformation could influence who would and who would not profit from it. Brokering the conversion of energy into capital, however, required a lot more information about the vast amounts of energy stored in the West than anyone had—even Jefferson. Gathering and organizing that information helped lay the groundwork for the empire of liberty.

Jefferson had never traveled farther west than a few days' journey from Monticello. Neither he nor most Americans had ever laid eyes on Louisiana. Thus, he had never seen the very lands that he insisted the Potawatomis, Spaniards, and others must acknowledge were now in the control of Americans. In *Seeing Like a State*, James Scott argues that the ability to gather data about remote peoples and places has historically been central to imperial control and thus to the rise of modern nations such as the United States. In addition to collecting information, according to Scott, modern states have standardized, organized, and simplified that data. This is why the Constitution empowered the centralized U.S. government to establish uniform bankruptcy laws, weights and measures, currency, and foreign exchange rates—all of which would convert the messy variability of local commercial customs into a regular national system that could administer the kind of far-flung republic that Montesquieu had doubted could ever be managed without despotism. Land, too, had to be standardized—complex, faraway ecologies had to be reduced to fungible units with fixed boundaries that could be measured, recorded, and administered by men like Jefferson who had never seen the places they were managing. Scott calls this practice of making remote resources uniform and intelligible to central governments "legibility."[23]

In America, Jefferson had long been at the forefront of rendering the West legible. From his supremely rational mind had sprung the system for surveying and gridding land that was adopted as the Land Ordinance of 1785. Under the Land Ordinance and subsequent acts that extended its parameters beyond the Old Northwest, plots of land were surveyed, numbered, mapped, and sold. Ownership, taxation, transactions, inheritance, and subdivision were all easily tracked in eastern records. Boundary disputes were easily adjudicated by courts. Anyone who wanted to buy, sell, seed, harvest, inherit, or subdivide land in the West not only needed protection from the more perfect union's army and access to the rivers the nation had purchased from France but also increasingly depended on the federal land grid, which guaranteed ownership against poachers, squatters, and neighbors who disputed property boundaries. Seeing like a state enables us to understand the kinds of considerations that led westerners to find it so much more advantageous to cooperate with Jefferson than to conspire with Burr.

Jefferson knew, however, that for the grid to do its full work for the state, *somebody* had to see the West. As a man who shared the Enlightenment's love of empiricism, Jefferson was an inveterate collector of data, especially natural data. Wherever he was, he kept daily records of temperature, humidity, and other climatic data, and wherever he wasn't, he encouraged others to gather data for him. The most elaborate manifestation of this empirical impulse was the set of expeditions he sent between 1804 and 1806 to explore western rivers and record geographic, botanic, zoological, climatic, and ethnographic information. The most celebrated of these was Lewis and Clark's Corps of Discovery, but also important in Jefferson's estimation were the pair of Red River expeditions led by George Hunter and William Dunbar (1804) and Thomas Freeman and Peter Custis (1806).

Like these other expeditions, Pike's 1806–1807 journey constituted a first step in gathering and organizing the information necessary for a centralized state to exercise control over remote landscapes and to induce the loyalty of the people who wished to profit from those landscapes. To be sure, Pike's mission was Wilkinson's brainchild, not Jefferson's. It is no accident, however, that Wilkinson chose to cloak his mysterious personal motives in language Jefferson would appreciate—data gathering. The general's instructions ordered Pike to follow the Arkansas River, which Wilkinson had told Dearborn was so strategic, to the far limits of the territory the United States claimed. Along the way, he was to record "the Geographical structure; the Natural History; and population; of the country" and to "collect & preserve, specimens of everything curious in the mineral or botanical Worlds." With this language, Wilkinson directed Pike to gather information valuable both to the general's personal interests and to the nation's goals as articulated through Jefferson's other expeditions.[24] This language proved an effective shield for whatever Wilkinson was up to precisely because data gathering through exploration was an essential government function that advanced the empire of liberty. To borrow Scott's metaphor, Pike's expedition would help the state (and maybe also Wilkinson and Burr) to *see* in the West.

As the state's western eyes, Pike could also help extend the standardization and regulation of commerce that the Constitution called for.[25] If the United States could monopolize the power to license western commerce—that is, to license the conversion of energy into capital—it could encourage anyone who wished to profit from western trade to cooperate with state authority. So in August 1806, when Pike encountered a party of traders in Missouri with a boatful of arms and goods but no license, he detained them and ordered them back to St. Louis to answer to the governor. All this collecting, preserving, and arresting would help render Louisiana legible to the state, the first step in administering the newly acquired territory and ultimately in bringing western energy flows under the influence of the national government.

Here, then, is the march of the empire of liberty well beyond ties of "kindred and affection." Holding the West required the federal government to meet the material interests of westerners more reliably and lucratively than its competitors, and meeting those material interests required enabling westerners to profit from the conversion of nature's energy into the market's capital. To do so required gathering information—about western nature, the people living there, and their methods for profiting from nature. Through exploration, then, along with settling disputed property claims, surveying land and international boundaries, licensing trade, building roads, and a variety of other functions, the state was creating a national ecosystem. That is, it was forming a continental community of living things and their environments through which energy cycled not just according to the laws of nature but also according to the dictates of the state. The state would determine who owned the land that stored the energy, who had the right to transport that stored energy to market, what paths it would take, and where it would all end up. Directing the flow of energy in this manner both invigorated the national economy and consolidated the national state. State formation was ecological. The empire of liberty was thus also an ecology of liberty.

## INCORPORATING THE "UNCONTROULED MASTERS" OF THE COUNTRY

A Spanish flag flew outside the chief's lodge, where some four hundred Pawnees gathered with Pike's party for a "grand council." After guiding the Osage captives home, he had turned north to pay a diplomatic visit to the Pawnees. "My Brothers," Pike began, "here is an American Flag which I will present you—but it must never be hoisted by the side of that Spanish one which I desire in return." The chiefs were silent.[26] Perhaps they understood that more was at stake than a piece of cloth, that Pike was recruiting them and their material world into the national ecosystem, and that to join that ecosystem was to accept the sovereignty of the American state.

Among the Pawnees, Zebulon Pike was the agent of the ecology of liberty. He came to begin the process of extending the mastery of the federal government over ecosystems of the West. He came also to win the cooperation of the Indians, for, as Wilkinson understood, the material of the West could not be incorporated into the nation without the cooperation of the Indians: they were, as he had told Dearborn, the "uncontrouled Masters of that Country." The Pawnees' ecology, however, did not easily fit into the nation-state's. The Pawnees' world was fluid and cyclical. It changed with the seasons and from year to year. Its borders were fuzzy and always shifting. Many owners used each piece of land. The ecology of liberty, in contrast, had a grid. To win control of western resources, therefore, Pike needed to win over the Pawnees, and to win over the Pawnees, he had to persuade them to change their ecology. Along the way, however, he was often reduced merely to learning how to survive in their ecology. This struggle—simultaneously to change and to survive in the Pawnees' ecology—defined the first months of Pike's mission. Nowhere is this seen more clearly than when he tried to negotiate over a flag.

Pike arrived at the Pawnee village during the fall harvest, the climax of an annual subsistence cycle that was organized both temporally and spatially and drew from a diverse resource base. In the spring, women cleared fields and planted corn, beans, squash, melons, sunflowers, and pumpkins.[27] In early summer, once the crops were sufficiently established, the people extended their caloric and nutritional base by moving west to the hunting grounds between the Platte and the Arkansas rivers. There they hunted bison, whose meat enriched the Pawnee diet and whose body provisioned Pawnee material culture. This space was a borderlands, with many peoples—Comanches, Kiowas, Arapahoes, Cheyennes, Wichitas, Kansas, and others—hunting in the area, sometimes harmoniously, sometimes not. In late August, small warrior parties left to trade and to raid the horse herds of Spaniards and Indians to the southwest, while the bulk of the group made its way home to the village to harvest and feast and cache for the winter whatever was not consumed.[28] Finally, between November and March, the Pawnees returned to the west to hunt bison and other animals for their thick and commercially valuable winter hides, which they sold to American,

Spanish, and British traders, and which sometimes found their way as far as Europe.[29] In return, they acquired arms, tools, cooking wares, and other manufactured goods from the Atlantic economies. If the harvest had been bountiful, a little would remain in the caches to tide them over when they returned to their village to plant again in the spring. Thus, the Pawnees' ecosystem ranged far from the village—from the plains of Kansas to the Valley of Mexico to the factories of the early industrial Atlantic seaboard and British Isles (which, in turn, collected resources from around the world). Which flag unfurled at the chief's door mattered little to the Pawnees, as long as this geographically flexible and seasonally renewing ecosystem endured.

To Pike, however, the flag was everything. It was the symbol of the nation-state, the institution that brokered the release of energy. Therefore, the flag Pike offered was an exclusive one. "After next year," he proclaimed to the Pawnees, "we will not permit Spanish officers, or soldiers; to come into this country to present medals or Flags." To do otherwise would have violated the very core of the Enlightenment concept of the nation: sovereignty. To the new nation-states of the Atlantic World, which were scrambling to mark off boundaries and retain exclusive control of territory within them, contested spaces such as the Great Plains hunting grounds that were shared by rival powers, where access to resources was not regulated by a single, sovereign authority, presented an uncomfortable anomaly. Having a portion of the nation's ecosystem tied to both Spain and the United States would not do, any more than it would to have a plot in Jefferson's grid in Ohio managed by two proprietors. Dual sovereignty had been precisely the Mississippi River problem that had provoked so much difficulty, from the Whiskey rebels to Napoleon. "The river is ours now," Jefferson had said indignantly, and Pike had come to show that the rivers of the Great Plains, too, fell under the sovereignty of the United States.[30]

But the chiefs' stony silence at the grand council indicated their hostility to this prospect. So Pike tried again: "My brothers; You cannot have two Fathers—your former Fathers the Spaniards have now no further Authority over you."[31] This was language the Pawnees could understand. Along the march to the village, Pike had labored over his speech by the evening campfires, selecting his words carefully and tediously translating them into French. In this chore, he drew from a wealth of American knowledge about how to talk to Indians.[32] Cultural chasms may have divided Indians and Euro-Americans in some respects, but in others, their outlooks overlapped considerably.[33] Among these was gender. The language of patriarchy held powerful connotations for both cultures, and it provided Pike the linguistic common ground to make his vision of national sovereignty intelligible to the Pawnees. In particular, gender conveyed the complicated relationship between equality and hierarchy that characterized both the Pawnee and postrevolutionary American worlds.[34] Pike called the Pawnees brothers, language both sides would have understood to establish bonds among equals. Jefferson, however, always addressed Indians as children, rhetorically subordinating even chiefs to his authority and to the sovereignty of the United States, and so Pike, too, also invoked the unequal language of parenthood, demanding that the Pawnees choose between Spanish and American fathers and implicitly denying continued autonomy as one of the options. Of course, in Lockean social contract theory and in the ideology of the American Revolution, Pike was Jefferson's son, as well—equal among his citizen brothers, subordinate to Jefferson, the representative of the law of a sovereign state to which they had willingly ceded some of their natural freedom.[35] In invoking both brotherhood and fatherhood, Pike, who had accepted subordination because of the opportunity it gave him to pursue individual life, liberty, and property, invited the Pawnees to join him in brotherly subordination to the state father. Pike had chosen his words well. After a silence of some time, an old man rose. He went to the door of the lodge, took down the Spanish flag, and laid it at Pike's feet.

At this, however, the Pawnees' faces "clouded with sorrow," Pike later wrote, "as if some great national calamity was about to befal them."[36] In the Pawnees' ecology, land could have many owners and people could have many trade partners and many fathers and brothers. In Jefferson's gridded empire of liberty, land could have but one owner, and Indians' allegiance would have to run uniquely to a single nation-state. The bounded, sovereign, regulated, hierarchical national ecosystem that Pike's flag symbolized thus heralded an ecological revolution. In a nation, the state bounded the ecosystem; it brokered the energy transfer by sanctioning licit trade and punishing illicit trade; it subordinated the parts of the system to the whole. The flag that Pike offered to the Pawnees on the Republican River at the end of the harvest season heralded property lines to identify who could farm where. It heralded fixed boundaries among peoples to determine who could hunt where. It heralded taxes and courts. It meant few trading partners instead of many. It meant the end of raiding. It heralded an ecosystem regulated not by seasons but by the state. It signaled an ecology of liberty.

And then Pike retreated. Even without fully grasping the revolutionary ecological implications of his demands, he did at least understand that his own immediate ecological well-being depended on the Pawnees' good will. Despite being the forerunner of the national ecosystem, he was still subject to the grasslands' considerable environmental constraints, including the fact that traveling north–south, perpendicularly to the east-flowing rivers (which, as Wilkinson and Salcedo knew, were the highways of the Great Plains, along which food, fuel, and water could be reliably secured), required tremendous amounts of energy. To get back—south—to the Arkansas River, he needed the Pawnees' fresh horses. Perhaps with horses on his mind, Pike took up the Spanish colors himself and congratulated the Pawnees for showing themselves to be "dutiful children in acknowledging their American father."[37] Returning the Spanish flag to them, he warned that it should never fly in the presence of the Americans. At this the Pawnees burst into cheers and applause.[38]

Even with this gesture, however, the tension did not abate. The next day, the leading Pawnee chief, Sharitarish, informed Pike that he intended to block the Americans' path, with force if necessary. Promptly, the corn and other gifts the villagers had been bestowing upon the hungry American travelers ceased to arrive, and the Pawnees feigned mounted attacks on the Americans' camp almost nightly. Most troublesome of all to Pike, the Pawnees refused to sell him the horses he desperately needed to proceed. After days of haggling, he managed to acquire enough mounts to depart—though Pike's lieutenant called them "miserable horses at the most exorbitant prices."[39] To change the Pawnees' ecosystem, then, Pike found that he first had to accommodate himself to it.

## LEGACIES IN THE NEBRASKA MUD

Despite the stumbling getaway, Pike had, in very small but telling ways, indeed helped advance the empire of liberty. For even in besting Pike, the Pawnees inched further into participation in the national ecosystem. In horses, they supplied Pike the energy he needed to travel overland, away from the rivers. And he gave them notes redeemable only upon presentation to the U.S. government in St. Louis in exchange for goods and cash: capital that belonged to the national treasury, which had generated it by (among other things) taxing the fruits of western trade— that is, the wealth produced by people bringing the stored energy of the West to market. Energy, then, was circulating in a national system: the U.S. government was the broker; Pike was the courier; and the Pawnees and their material world were becoming incorporated into it on a daily basis.

Since then, the empire of liberty has swept over the continent. Two hundred years later, almost to the day, on a wet, crisp October morning, I visit the spot where Pike and the Pawnee elders haggled over a flag. Here, the grid—the empire's imprint on the land from the Ohio River to the Rocky Mountains—is unmistakably visible. Dirt county roads follow the old survey lines and cross at right angles, taking travelers from the state highway to a cornfield on a plateau just above the floodplain of the Republican River. Straight rows of corn furrow the soil where Sharitarish's lodge once stood. Barbed wire and "no trespassing" signs mark the boundaries of the property rights that define the empire of liberty, while a national historic landmark plaque bestows on visitors a community right to view the plot and appreciate its national significance. This mix of private property and civic cultural commons might have pleased Jefferson and appealed to his love for both independence through smallholder landownership and public-spirited expressions of commonwealth. This is indeed what a landscape populated with the civic-minded, culturally refined smallholders whom he extolled in *Notes on the State of Virginia* might look like. The grid of the empire of liberty appears to have triumphed.

And yet not all has been gridded. Hoofprints in the muddy road show that a deer recently bounded across, ignoring the signs and fences, crossing the grid to browse in the field of corn stubble. Sinews of water from last night's rain wend their way across an unplanted field nearby, seeking the lowest path to the river, disrupting the geometric lines of the furrows and reminding me that old, tiny watersheds still work at cross-purposes to the grid. Together, the deer, the streamlets, and the grid coexist. Salcedo, Wilkinson, Burr, and Sharitarish could not have foreseen this intricate landscape made up at once of an idea of a nation, the physical imprint of that nation, and the material that the nation did not come to control. Not even Jefferson did. Clearly, though, they did understand something that we do not fully grasp: the interplay of the land and the nation. They understood that whoever imprinted their culture on the land would leave an enduring legacy. The kindred and affection that bound the brethren of the same principle can be seen in the damp Nebraska soil today, but only because the empire of liberty aspired to become the uncontrolled master of western rivers.

## ACKNOWLEDGMENTS

Jared Orsi thanks Peter Blodgett, Jay Buckley, Mark Fiege, Richard Gould, Matt Harris, Eric Hinderaker, Ann Little, Richard Orsi, James Sherow, Steven Stoll, and the manuscript's anonymous reviewers. Generous funding for this chapter was provided by the Charles Redd Center for Western Studies, Colorado Humanities, Colorado State University, the Huntington Library, Occidental College, and the Santa Fe Trail Association.

## NOTES

1. Salcedo to Alencaster, September 9, 1805, in Jackson, *Journals of Pike,* 2:104–108. Jackson's two-volume edition comprises approximately one thousand pages of documents, including Pike's journals, maps, and reports, as well as extensive correspondence and other documents related to his expeditions of 1805–1807. Additionally, the *National Intelligencer and Washington Advertiser* and manuscript and published primary materials from the Massachusetts Historical Society, the Library of Congress, the National Archives (Denver and Washington, D.C.), the Detroit Public Library, the Denver Public

Library, the Huntington Library, the Missouri Historical Society, the Chicago Historical Society, and the Western Reserve Historical Society that are not cited in this chapter nevertheless inform its ideas.

2. Wilkinson to Dearborn, September 8, 1805, in Jackson, *Journals of Pike*, 2:100–102.

3. Wilkinson to Dearborn, September 22, 1805, Huntington Manuscripts 21264, Huntington Library, San Marino, California.

4. Onuf, *Jefferson's Empire*, 8, 10, 53. For Jefferson's understanding of nature, see Charles A. Miller, *Jefferson and Nature: An Interpretation* (Baltimore: Johns Hopkins University Press, 1988).

5. Unbeknownst to him until he returned, Pike was promoted to captain during the expedition.

6. Wilkinson to Pike, June 24, 1806, in Jackson, *Journals of Pike*, 1:285.

7. Jefferson to Harrison, January 16, 1806, in ibid., 2:287n1.

8. Thomas Paine, *Common Sense* (New York: Penguin, 1986), 107; Thomas Jefferson, *Notes on the State of Virginia* (Gloucester, Mass.: Peter Smith, 1976), 157.

9. Charles de Secondat, baron de Montesquieu, *The Spirit of the Laws*, in *Great Books of the Western World*, ed. Robert Maynard Hutchins (Chicago: Encyclopedia Britannica, 1952), 58. Fear that large republics would fragment was used as an argument against the Constitution in 1787. It was sufficiently potent that Alexander Hamilton felt compelled to confront and refute it in the first *Federalist Paper*: "We already hear it whispered in the private circles of those who oppose the new Constitution, that the thirteen States are of too great extent for any general system, and that we must of necessity resort to separate confederacies of distinct portions of the whole." The *Federalist Papers* can be accessed online at http://thomas.loc.gov/home/histdox/fedpapers.html.

10. *Federalist Paper 6*.

11. For geostrategic implications of land in the Constitution, see Akhil Reed Amar, *America's Constitution: A Biography* (New York: Random House, 2005), 43–53.

12. Richard C. Wade, *The Urban Frontier: The Rise of Western Cities, 1790–1830* (Cambridge, Mass.: Harvard University Press, 1967), 66.

13. Andrew R. L. Cayton, "'Separate Interests' and the Nation State: The Washington Administration and the Origins of Regionalism in the Trans-Appalachian West," *Journal of American History* 79 (June 1992): 67.

14. Thomas Jefferson to Robert R. Livingston, April 18, 1802, in *The Louisiana Purchase: Emergence of an American Nation*, ed. Peter J. Kastor (Washington, D.C.: CQ Press, 2002), 161.

15. Kukla, *Wilderness So Immense*, 67–69.

16. Eliga H. Gould, "Entangled Histories, Entangled Worlds: The English-Speaking Atlantic as a Spanish Periphery," *American Historical Review* 112 (June 2007): 782.

17. Cayton, "Separate Interests," 59; James E. Lewis, Jr., "The Burr Conspiracy and the Problem of Western Loyalty," in Kastor, *Louisiana Purchase*, 64–71.

18. Madison to Livingston and Monroe, March 2, 1803, in Kastor, *Louisiana Purchase*, 174.

19. Lewis, "Burr Conspiracy."

20. Isaac Joslin Cox, "Opening the Santa Fe Trail," *Missouri Historical Review* 25 (October 1930–July 1931): 43–44, 49–50.

21. Madison to Livingston and Monroe, March 2, 1803, in Kastor, *Louisiana Purchase*, 175.

22. Ibid., 174.

23. James C. Scott, *Seeing like a State: How Certain Schemes to Improve the Human Condition Have Failed* (New Haven, Conn.: Yale University Press, 1998); Kate Brown, "Gridded Lives: Why Kazakhstan and Montana Are Nearly the Same Place," *American Historical Review* 106 (February 2001): 17–48; Amar, *America's Constitution*, 108.

24. Wilkinson to Pike, June 24, 1806, in Jackson, *Journals of Pike*, 1:286.

25. Wilkinson to Pike, July 12, 1806, in ibid., 1:288.

26. "Pike's Speech to the Pawnees," September 29, 1806, in ibid., 2:147; "Diary of an Expedition," in ibid., 1:328; Pike to Wilkinson, October 2, 1806, in ibid., 2:150–51; "Lieutenant Wilkinson's Report," in ibid., 2:6–7.

27. Douglas R. Parks, "Pawnee," in *Handbook of North American Indians*, vol. 13, *Plains*, part 1 (Washington, D.C.: Smithsonian Institution, 2001), 525–26. See also George E. Hyde, *The Pawnee Indians*, 2nd ed. (Norman: University of Oklahoma Press, 1974); Waldo R. Wedel, *Central Plains Prehistory: Holocene Environments and Culture Changes in the Republican River Basin* (Lincoln: University of Nebraska Press, 1986); Richard White, *Roots of Dependency: Subsistence, Environment, and Social Change among the Choctaws, Pawnees, and Navajos* (Lincoln: University of Nebraska Press, 1983); and David J. Wishart, *An Unspeakable Sadness: The Dispossession of the Nebraska Indians* (Lincoln: University of Nebraska Press, 1994).

28. Wishart, *Unspeakable Sadness*, 23, 32–35.

29. Pike mentions the winter hunt: "The Pawnees, like the Osage, quit their villages in the winter." Pike, "Dissertation on Louisiana," in Jackson, *Journals of Pike*, 1:36. The international extent of the fur trade is well chronicled in, among other places, the *Papers of the St. Louis Fur Trade*, a multireel microfilm series on the Chouteau fur-trade operations, produced from manuscripts in the Missouri Historical Society. I consulted the edition held by the Denver Public Library.

30. Pike, "Diary of an Expedition," in Jackson, *Journals of Pike*, 1:287. What he found in Louisiana, however, was that American sovereignty was in fact quite weak. The Pawnees, he reported after his expedition, were "decidedly under Spanish influence." The United States could remedy that, he recommended, by withholding arms, ammunition, and clothing for a few years, while also encouraging the Osages and Kansas to harass the Pawnees until they were sufficiently distressed to "feel the necessity of a good understanding with the U.S." Pinching one realm of Pawnee ecology—trade—would, he believed, persuade them to join the national ecosystem and forsake all others. Pike, "Dissertation . . . on Louisiana," January 1808, in ibid., 2:37.

31. "Pike's Speech to the Pawnees," September 29, 1806, in ibid., 2:147.

32. Here, a comparison of the language Pike and Lewis and Clark used to talk to Indians is instructive. In a confrontation subsequent to the flag negotiation, in which

the Pawnee chief Sharitarish threatened to use force to stop Pike and his party from proceeding west, Pike boasted that the "young warriors of his [Sharitarish's] *great American father* were not *women* to be turned back by *words*" and instead "would sell our lives at a dear rate to his nation—that we knew our great father would . . . revenge our deaths on his [Sharitarish's] people" (italics in original). Strikingly, in a very similar situation, with the Teton Sioux threatening to block Lewis and Clark's passage up the Missouri, Clark (according to John Ordway's diary) resorted to almost identical language, telling the chief that "we were not Squaws, but warriers." When the chief responded in similarly gendered terms, insisting that his men, too, were "warriors," Clark continued by saying, "[W]e were Sent by their great father the president of the U. S. and that if they misused us that he [Clark] or Capt. Lewis could by writing to him have them all destroyed." As far as I know, Pike did not, at the time he published his journals, have access to Ordway's diary, so the most likely explanation for the similarity in language is that both Clark and Pike drew from a common font of knowledge about how to talk in language Indians understood (or perhaps that they mistakenly believed Indians understood). For Pike's entry, see "Diary of an Expedition," October 1, 1806, in ibid., 1:329–30. For Ordway's entry of September 25, 1804, see Gary E. Moulton, ed., *The Journals of the Lewis and Clark Expedition*, 13 vols. (Lincoln: University of Nebraska Press, 1983–2001), 3:111–15, 9:67–68.

33. Nancy Shoemaker, *A Strange Likeness: Becoming Red and White in Eighteenth-Century North America* (New York: Oxford University Press, 2004). I am also indebted to my colleague Ann Little, who pointed this out to me in 2001.

34. On Pawnee submission to authority, see Wishart, *Unspeakable Sadness*, 37.

35. The language of fatherhood also crops up regarding Wilkinson. In talking to the Osages, Pike referred to Wilkinson as "your father who is in St. Louis." See "Pike's Speech to the Osages," August 22, 1806, in Jackson, *Journals of Pike*, 2:139. Wilkinson, of course, was also a father figure (even more directly so than Jefferson) to Pike because of the hierarchical army relations that cast Wilkinson as a paternalistic authority figure in Pike's life, dating back to Pike's childhood as the son of a frontier army officer. For example, Pike once referred to Wilkinson not only "as my general, but as a paternal friend." Pike to Wilkinson, August 28, 1806, in ibid., 2:144.

36. Pike, "Diary of an Expedition," September 29, 1806, in ibid., 1:329.

37. Ibid.

38. Ibid.

39. Pike, "Diary of an Expedition," October 3–6, 1806, in ibid., 1:330–31; Wilkinson, "Lieutenant Wilkinson's Report," April 6, 1807, in ibid., 2:7.

# 6

# Enemies and Friends

## PIKE AND MELGARES IN THE COMPETITION

## FOR THE GREAT PLAINS

*Leo E. Oliva*

The story of Lieutenant Zebulon Montgomery Pike's 1806–1807 expedition across the Great Plains to the Rocky Mountains is an outstanding record of exploration for the United States through a portion of the Louisiana Purchase.[1] Pike helped the young nation later claim and, eventually, fulfill that claim to the Southwest (including all or portions of ten states). Just as remarkable and much less known and understood is the expedition of Spanish troops led by Lieutenant Facundo Melgares from New Mexico to the Great Plains just prior to Pike's venture. Pike became aware of the Spanish mission to the Great Plains when he arrived at the Pawnee village on the Republican River (in present-day Nebraska), where Melgares had visited a few weeks before. Pike's party followed the return route of Melgares south to the Arkansas River and along that stream into present-day Colorado to the point where the Spaniards left the river to head back to Santa Fe. Interestingly, almost everything known about Melgares's 1806 trip is obtained from Pike's journal, for the records of that Spanish expedition have not been found (they may have been destroyed by a fire at the archives in Chihuahua City).

The tale of these two expeditions and their respective leaders became more intertwined after the capture of Lieutenant Pike's exploring party near the Rio Grande in present-day southern Colorado and the detention in Santa Fe and Chihuahua, during a portion of which time Lieutenant Melgares was Pike's guard, overseer, and guide. The two enemies—for such they were, as military officers of nations competing for the region through which they both traveled at a time when both nations feared the imminent outbreak of war between them—became friends. Pike learned much about the Great Plains and the provinces of northern New Spain from Melgares, and that information, along with Pike's astute observations of the people and culture of the region, published in his journal of the expedition in 1810, sparked increased interest in the United States to attempt to open trade with New Mexico. Those trading efforts were thwarted so long as Spain retained control of the colony of New Spain (later Mexico) but bore fruitful economic results for both the United States and northern Mexico following Mexican independence from Spanish rule in 1821. It is safe to declare that everyone who ventured forth from the United States to establish contact with northern Mexico after 1811 benefited from Pike's expedition and journal (including information provided by Melgares), either directly or indirectly. Moreover, Pike's erstwhile enemy Facundo Melgares (governor of New Mexico from 1818 to 1822) was the one who later welcomed the first successful U.S. trade expedition to Santa Fe, in 1821.

Both Pike and Melgares were sent by their respective governments with a major purpose of securing friendship, trade relations, and alliances with several Indian tribes of the region, including the Osages, Kansas, Pawnees, and Comanches. Pike was especially directed to open talks with the leaders of the Comanche tribe because they were most closely tied to New Spain. The policy of seeking Indian spheres of influence was not new and had been used by all nations involved in the contest for North America. Indian allies were considered to be the key element to establish effective control and eventual domination of a vast region, including present-day Kansas.

France, which was initially most successful in developing alliances with the Indians of the region (except for the Comanches, who remained in the Spanish sphere of influence), was eliminated as a contender for control of North America at the close of the French and Indian War (known as the Seven Years' War in Europe), concluded by the Treaty of Paris in 1762.[2] Both Britain and Spain competed for favors with the tribes, and the new United States entered the contest after winning independence from Britain by the Treaty of Paris in 1783. England continued to trade with the Plains Indians, but the main contest, after the sale of Louisiana Territory to the United States in 1803, was between the United States and Spain. Immediately the United States increased efforts to establish, gain, and consolidate control over the trade with these various tribes (many of whom were traditional enemies), thereby hoping to establish domination of the tribes and the lands they occupied. On the other side, Spain pursued trade and alliances with Plains tribes and attempted to use them against the United States.[3]

A critical issue in this pursuit of control was the establishment of the boundaries of the Louisiana Purchase. Spain refused to recognize the sale of Louisiana to the United States by France, claimed almost everything west of the Mississippi River, and prohibited U.S. citizens from entering the territory. The United States wished to push that boundary as far west as possible, certainly to the Rocky Mountains and hopefully all the way to the Rio Grande in the Southwest and the Pacific Ocean in the Northwest. The boundary issue was not settled until the Adams-Onís Treaty, also known as the Transcontinental Treaty, of 1819.[4] For all these reasons, the expeditions led by Melgares and Pike constituted an important round of an expanded contest for a huge portion of North America between those two nations. The contest would be quickly won by the United States, thanks especially to Lieutenant Pike but also to Napoleon Bonaparte, who sold Louisiana to the United States and, perhaps more important, occupied Spain from 1808 to 1814, during and after which the Spanish empire in the New World was in rapid decline.[5]

Although they never encountered each other on the Great Plains, the paths of Melgares and Pike met at the village of the Pawnees on the Republican River. Their respective relations with the Indians of the region make up part of this story, along with a brief summary of the two expeditions and the later friendship of these two army officers, which had several ramifications, including much information in Pike's published journal that sparked interest in opening trade between the United States and New Mexico.

Much was at stake for both nations. Although Spanish explorer Francisco Vásquez de Coronado was the first European to explore the Great Plains, Spain was not a major contender in the contest for this region during the era of European colonial competition for control of North America, a contest that involved Spain, France, Britain, and the Netherlands. Spain did explore and lay claim to much of the western portion of North America but did not establish settlements on the plains following Coronado's expedition of 1541 or Don Juan de Oñate's expedition to present-day Kansas in 1601. Instead, the French, with their aggressive policies of expanding trade and influence with tribal Americans, were the first and most successful in winning alliances and trade arrangements with many tribes. They were not successful, however, in winning over the Comanches, with whom, after 1786, Spain held dominion.[6]

Spain continued to consider New Mexico and lands to the north and east as a buffer zone where foreign threats could be countered before they reached more economically important places, such as Chihuahua.[7] Following the removal of France from the competition for the Great Plains at the close of the French and Indian War, Spain acquired French Louisiana and began an effort to become the favored trading partner of those tribes with whom the French had held sway. The major competition faced by Spain was that of Britain and, after 1783, the new United States, which soon developed great interest in the region west of the Mississippi Valley and in opening the Mississippi River to navigation for its citizens. Time and energy were on the side of the young and vigorous United States and against the declining colonial, mercantilist empire of Spain.[8]

Some Spanish officials were concerned about the potential threat posed by the United States. In November 1794, François Hector, baron de Carondelet, governor of Spanish Louisiana, warned his superiors in Madrid that efforts should be made to counteract the trans-Mississippi interests of the United States, warning that if they were not stopped, "in time they will demand the possession of the rich mines of the interior provinces of the very kingdom of Mexico." He declared that the United States was "advancing with an incredible rapidity." Carondelet recognized the importance of keeping the Indian tribes friendly to Spain and in opposition to the United States. He proposed "one hundred thousand pesos increase annually for the Indian department, for the purchase of arms, ammunition, and presents, which are necessary to employ the nations with efficacy." He also outlined a detailed plan for defense of Louisiana from the United States.[9]

In 1794, Carondelet authorized the creation of a new company of merchants in St. Louis (commonly called the Missouri Company) under the leadership of Santiago (Jacques) Clamorgan, to expand trade with Indian tribes and explore along the Missouri Valley to seek a passage to the Pacific (the same mission that would be assigned to Lewis and Clark by President Thomas Jefferson a decade later). Although several attempts were made to find a passage to the Pacific, the company failed.[10]

The United States continued to put pressure on Spain to open the Mississippi River to navigation. Spain, feeling more vulnerable because of changes in the balance of power in Europe and facing possible war with Britain, agreed to the Treaty of Lorenzo el Real (also called the Treaty of Friendship, Boundaries, and Navigation but best known as Pinckney's Treaty) in 1795 and granted concessions to the United States by opening the lower Mississippi to commerce.[11] The following year, Governor Carondelet informed the marquis de Branceforte at New Orleans that this did not stop U.S. citizens from entering lands west of the Mississippi River: "Your Excellency will see himself obliged to take beforehand the most active measures to oppose the introduction of those restless people, who are a sort of determined bandits, armed with carbines, who frequently cross the Mississippi in numbers, with the intention of reconnoitering, of hunting, and if they like the country, of establishing themselves in the *Provincias Internas,* whose Indians they will arm to both further their fur trade and to make the Spaniards uneasy."[12]

A few years later, because of the French Revolution and Napoleon's desire to regain control of Louisiana, Spain realized it could not defend Louisiana if Britain decided to take that territory, so an offer from Napoleon to return Louisiana to France was worked out in 1800, an agreement kept secret for nearly two years. France agreed that Louisiana could never be sold to a third party, only back to Spain.[13]

When Napoleon sold Louisiana to the United States in 1803, Spain refused to recognize the deal because it violated the terms by which the territory had been returned to France. Spanish officials also prepared to resist U.S. expansion into the disputed lands. President Jefferson set the Lewis and Clark expedition into motion prior to the Louisiana Purchase, and Jefferson was determined to explore the West in the face of objections from Spain. Lieutenant Pike's expedition would also be part of that effort, even though he was sent out by General James Wilkinson. Jefferson approved Pike's mission and praised its accomplishments.[14] Spanish officials became fearful of intrusions—and some even expected an actual invasion—from the United States.[15]

Spain continued to see the value of the Indian tribes in the contest for territory, and the trading efforts continued.[16] On May 18, 1804, Sebastián Calvo, marquis de Casa Calvo, informed his superiors that "the Indians all have a decided preference in favor of our nation, from which we can derive advantages if we nurse with tenderness their hatred for the *Guachimangal* (American)."[17] The United States also looked to the Indians for assistance. On May 14, 1804, Louisiana governor William C. Claiborne directed the military commander at the Ouachita Post in the territory, to do everything possible "to maintain the friendship of the Indians. . . . [Y]ou will take care that no violence be offered to unoffending Indians, and that in their trade with the merchants, no injustice be done them. In your conversations with these Indians, you will speak of the friendly disposition of the President of the United States to his *red children,* and his great desire to see them happy. You will add that the Americans are now their brothers and they must live in peace and friendship, as one family."[18]

It should be emphasized again that the boundary of Louisiana was not defined: in fact, the western limits of the territory had never been defined by France or any other nation. Thus, a contest between Spain and the United States to determine that line encouraged exploration and development of better relations with Indians of the region. Spain claimed the Mississippi River was the boundary, while the United States pushed for the Rio Grande. Eventually a compromise was reached in 1819, as noted, but immediately following the Louisiana Purchase in 1803, many efforts were made by both sides to improve their respective claims to portions of the region. Melgares and Pike were both parts of that endeavor.

General James Wilkinson, head of the U.S. Army and also a paid agent for the Spanish government, sent a secret warning to Spanish officials in the late winter of 1804 about the Lewis and Clark expedition and suggested ways that Spain could protect its claims from U.S. intrusions. He wrote that "an express ought immediately to be sent to the governor of Santa Fé, and another to the captain-general of Chihuaga [Chihuahua] in order that they may detach a sufficient body of chasseurs to intercept Captain Lewis and his party who are on the Missouri River, and force them to retire or take them prisoners." Wilkinson emphasized the importance of Spain's "winning the affection" of various Indian tribes and "increasing their jealousy against the United States." By providing arms and ammunition to the Indians, Spain could employ them "not only in checking the extension of American settlements, but also, if necessary, in destroying every settlement located west of the Mississippi." Wilkinson also warned against U.S. incursions in Texas and New Mexico, suggesting that Spain insist that the Mississippi River be the boundary between Spain and the United States.[19]

Wilkinson declared, "It is very probable that the United States will demand possession of one part of the right bank of the Mississippi, in order to check the smuggling that will necessarily prevail if the above-mentioned side belonged to any other nation, and also to favor the collection of its revenues. The true policy of Spain requires obstinate resistance to such a demand by asking [for] the right bank of the Mississippi in its entirety."[20] He even recommended that Spanish troops be sent to destroy Daniel Boone's settlement on the Missouri River. In fact, all American settlers located west of the Mississippi should be destroyed because "if those settlers be allowed to advance, they will very quickly explore the right path which will lead them to the capital of Santa Fé."[21] It is not clear whether Wilkinson was just betraying Lewis and Clark, Jefferson, and the United States or, as Warren Cook has observed, whether "rather than aiding Madrid, he may have been setting the stage for incidents that would provide an excuse to declare war and invade Spanish borderlands."[22]

In response, Spanish troops were sent out to attempt to intercept Lewis and Clark; some of these troops were in present-day Kansas a few weeks ahead of Zebulon M. Pike's expedition in 1806. Unlike Lewis and Clark, who escaped all contact with Spanish troops, Pike (who followed in their footsteps from the Pawnee village in present-day Nebraska to the point where the Spanish troops left the Arkansas River in present-day Colorado) had the misfortune to be detained by Spanish troops and government officials. General Wilkinson undoubtedly contributed to the search for and capture of U.S. explorers—in this case, the very man he sent to find the sources of the Arkansas and Red rivers and to attempt to open friendly relations with several tribes of Indians.

Sebastián Calvo, former military governor of Louisiana and then a member of the Louisiana boundary commission, initially directed Spanish governor Carlos Dehault Delassus at St. Louis, in January 1804, to permit Lewis and Clark to proceed without opposition: "[Y]ou will not put any obstacle to impede Capt. Merry Weather Lewis' entrance in the Missouri whenever he wishes."[23] Calvo changed his mind after hearing from General Wilkinson. Calvo sent an overland express to General Nemesio Salcedo, commandant of the Internal Provinces (located in Chihuahua), with Wilkinson's warnings and declared, "The only means which presents itself is to arrest Captain Merry Weather and his party, which cannot help but pass through the [Indian] nations neighboring New Mexico."[24]

General Salcedo received the message in early May and directed New Mexico governor Fernando de Chacón to seek help from the Indians of the plains in turning back Lewis and Clark and to send Spanish troops to arrest the Corps of Discovery. Governor Chacón was encouraged to solicit Pedro Vial for assistance because Vial had earlier traveled the region.[25] Vial was a native of France who had performed several exploring expeditions on the northern frontier of New Spain, including opening a route between Santa Fe and San Antonio, another route between Santa Fe and Natchitoches, and a route across the Great Plains from Santa Fe to St. Louis and back.[26] Between 1804 and 1806, four expeditions were sent from Santa Fe to try to find and arrest Lewis and Clark, without success. The fourth of those was led by Lieutenant Melgares. In February 1807, another expedition was sent to bring in Pike and his party, which they did.

In August 1804, Pedro Vial, José Jarvet, and fifty men headed north from Santa Fe. Jarvet had earlier served as a translator with the Pawnee Indians.[27] A month later, on the Platte River in present-day Nebraska, they met up with Pawnees, who had earlier become trading partners with New Spain (perhaps in the early 1780s). The Spanish did not find Lewis and Clark but urged the Pawnees not to trade with the United States and to turn back anyone coming from the United States. Pawnee Chief Sharitarish (White Wolf), whom Pike would meet in 1806, welcomed the Spanish and encouraged the trade. A dozen Pawnees, several of whom had been to Santa Fe before, accompanied Vial and party back to Santa Fe, where they arrived in early November.[28] The attempts to bind the Pawnees closer to Spain appeared to be succeeding.

In 1805 a new governor arrived in Santa Fe, Joaquín del Real Alencaster, and he was likewise directed by General Salcedo to send troops to find "Captain Merry" or persuade the Indians to seek out and capture Lewis and Clark. Alencaster was especially charged with seeking better relations with the Indian tribes, particularly the Pawnees, to prevent U.S. intrusions. Vial, Jarvet, and fifty-two men were sent to pursue those missions. Jarvet and Vial were directed to remain with the Pawnees through the coming winter and watch for Lewis and Clark as well as cement relations with the tribes. Jarvet was to accompany the chiefs to Santa Fe in the spring while Vial remained to move closer to the Missouri River, seek information about Lewis and Clark, and arrest them if possible. The party—joined by others, making a total of just over one hundred men (including five recent migrants from the United States who were to proceed to Missouri as spies and later report to Santa Fe)— was attacked by Indians (later confirmed to be Skidi Pawnees) near the junction of the Purgatory and Arkansas rivers. The Spaniards lost most of their supplies and had one man wounded. Unable to continue, the expedition returned to Santa Fe. Vial recommended the establishment of a fort on the Arkansas River.[29]

Spanish officials believed that the United States was winning influence with some of the Plains tribes and had probably encouraged those who attacked Vial's party. The Pawnees did not come to Santa Fe in the autumn of 1805 to trade, as they had done in previous years, and this too was interpreted as the growing influence of the United States. Another expedition from Santa Fe set out under the leadership of Vial and Jarvet in April 1806. Within a month, however, they were back, because many of their troops had deserted; Vial was thereby discredited.[30]

Then another threat from the United States was perceived by Spain. A U.S. expedition planned by William Dunbar and led by Thomas Freeman and Captain Richard Sparks, with twenty-two men, was sent by President Jefferson to explore up the Red River to its source. They carried a Spanish passport issued by Calvo, who insisted that some Spanish subjects accompany them, including a planted spy, Tomás Power. General Salcedo, however, notified Calvo that he would not honor the passport and would not permit the U.S. explorers to enter Spanish territory. Also, orders from Spain reached Salcedo in February 1806, urging him again to stop Lewis and Clark and turn back other attempts to intrude on Spanish territory. This was considered more urgent because of information that U.S. vice president Aaron Burr had designs on Spanish territory. Salcedo notified Governor Alencaster in Santa Fe. Also in February 1806, U.S. troops took possession of the Spanish outpost at Los Adaes in Texas, located only fourteen miles from Natchitoches in Louisiana. This was almost an act of war against Spain by the United States. Clearly, tensions were increasing between the United States and Spain in the region where Zebulon M. Pike would soon venture.[31]

The fourth expedition sent from New Mexico to stop "Captain Merry" was led by Lieutenant Melgares in 1806. It was, according to one historian, "the largest Spanish force ever sent onto the Great Plains."[32] Melgares, with sixty additional soldiers, had been sent by General Salcedo from the presidio of San Fernando de Carrizal some seventy-five miles south of El Paso to Santa Fe, at Governor Alencaster's request, to help deal with the Indians who had stopped Vial and Jarvet from reaching the plains. Melgares carried with him orders to turn back the Freeman-Sparks expedition on the Red River, if that had not already been accomplished by other troops from Texas, and then proceed northward to intercept Lewis and Clark and meet with several Plains tribes (particularly the Pawnees, Omahas, and Kansas) to seek closer ties with them and urge them to reject overtures from the United States. Melgares set out on June 15, 1806, with 105 soldiers, 400 New Mexican militia, 100 Indian allies, and more than 2,000 horses and mules. The size of this force was designed especially to impress the Pawnees, whose loyalty to Spain seemed to be wavering, and secure their cooperation against U.S. citizens.[33]

According to Pike, who later appended information about the Spanish expedition to his journal, Melgares, from an aristocratic family in Spain, was a career army officer and "had distinguished himself in several long expeditions against the Appaches and other Indian nations." Pike additionally described him as "a man of immense fortune, and generous in its disposal, almost to profusion; [who] possessed a liberal education, high sense of honor, and a disposition formed for military enterprise."[34] Melgares was born in 1775 in Villa Carabaca, Murcia, Spain, and received an education and was trained as a military officer.[35] Pike clearly admired him. Pike's background was similar (although lacking the family wealth), for Pike was born the son of a career army officer and likewise became a career officer. Pike mistakenly believed that Melgares had been sent out to search for him rather than Lewis and Clark.[36]

At Santa Fe, the Spanish expedition was provided equipment and supplies for six months. The large force traveled down the Red River but did not meet up with the Freeman-Sparks expedition, which had been turned back by troops from Spanish Nacogdoches, led by garrison commander Francisco Viana, by order of General Salcedo. Melgares did meet some bands of Comanches, who were still aligned with Spain, and held council with them.[37] Melgares then headed northeast, when (according to Pike, who disparaged the Spanish militia by stating, "[I]t is extraordinary with what subordination they act") approximately one-third of his force signed a petition requesting that they proceed no farther and go back home. Melgares reacted quickly and harshly, as Pike reported: "He halted immediately, and caused his dragoons to erect a gallows; then beat to arms. The troops fell in: he separated the *petitioners* from the others, then took the man who had presented the petition, tied him up, and gave him 50 lashes, and threatened to put to death, on the gallows erected, any man who should dare to grumble. This effectually silenced them, and quelled the rising spirit of sedition."[38]

When they reached the Arkansas River, Melgares left 240 of his men with many worn-out horses in a camp southwest of present-day Larned, Kansas. He took the remaining troops and proceeded to the Pawnee village on the Republican River, southwest of present-day Guide Rock, Nebraska, where he met with leaders of the Republican and Grand Pawnees, "held councils with the two nations, and presented them the flags, medals, &c. which were destined for them."[39] Pike saw those gifts when he visited the same village. Melgares, Pike wrote, "did not proceed on to the execution of his mission with the Pawnee Mahaws and Kans, as he represented to me, from the poverty of their horses, and the discontent of his own men, but as I conceive, from the suspicion and discontent which began to arise between the Spaniards and the Indians." The Pawnees opposed Melgares's plans to proceed to the Missouri River, or so Chief Sharitarish (White Wolf) told Pike. The Spanish troops returned to the Arkansas, picked up the remaining soldiers, and continued upstream until they left the river to return to Santa Fe, where they arrived on October 1, 1806.[40]

They brought with them the ten-year-old, half-Pawnee son of José Jarvet along with two Frenchmen (Andrés Sulier and Henrique Visonot) they had met at the Pawnee village. Jarvet's son was sent to live with his father, and the Frenchmen were sent to meet General Salcedo in Chihuahua.[41] The Melgares expedition, as with the three previous attempts to find Lewis and Clark, had failed in that mission. He may not have accomplished his mission to the Indians either. His experiences and observations, however, would prove valuable to Pike and his reports.

Warren Cook, who has written the best account of the Melgares expedition, offers cogently that "the huge Spanish force that advanced northward toward the Missouri ... was hamstrung by horse thieves and stalemated by determined Pawnee opposition." At the same time, Governor "Alencaster wanted to awe the Plains Indians, and Melgares's force was well suited for that purpose." That force, however, "was too unwieldy for a surprise attack on Lewis and Clark. . . . It was overkill, in the modern sense, and that proved a part of Melgares's undoing." As it turned out, "His force was too big to travel swiftly, live off the land, keep from offending Indian allies, and succeed in its hypothetical objective." Cook concluded, "With 240 of his men in one spot and 360 in another, his lines of supply were nonexistent, and it would have been difficult for him to push on to the Missouri, fend off the Pawnee, and remain there for a protracted time until Merry's problematical return. Vial's previous expeditions had not led him to expect Pawnee opposition."[42] How effective Melgares's appeal had been to the Pawnees would be tested a few weeks later by Lieutenant Pike.

The route and experiences of Pike's Southwest Expedition have been covered elsewhere, so only a few episodes are included here before looking more closely at the relationship between Pike and Melgares. Pike fulfilled his assignments regarding Indians with the return of the Osages to their village in western Missouri, arranging a meeting between Osages and Kansas that led to more-peaceful relations between those two tribes, and visiting the Pawnees at their village on the Republican River. The Pawnees were being courted by the Spanish and Anglo-Americans but made no firm commitments to either. Pike faced a tense situation when he requested the Pawnees to lower the Spanish flag recently presented them by Melgares and raise the flag of the United States, but this was done. Pike wisely told the Pawnees to keep the Spanish flag so they could hoist it if Spanish troops returned.[43]

Chief Sharitarish may have prevented Melgares from going farther east to the Missouri River, and he tried to prevent Pike from going farther west into the land of the Comanches, enemies of the Pawnees. Pike threatened to fight to the death if the Pawnees obstructed his party's advance, and he was permitted to push on, following the route of Melgares to the Arkansas River. Pike, it should be noted, was assisted by Indian guides from setting out in Missouri until he reached the Arkansas River. There, near present day Great Bend, Kansas, on October 28, Lieutenant James Wilkinson, son of General Wilkinson (who had sent out the expedition), took five of the soldiers and two Osages and attempted to navigate down the river to Arkansas Post in hastily built skin canoes. They had a very difficult trip. Pike and the remaining fifteen men, including interpreter Antoine François (Baronet) Vasquez (called Barony or Baroney by Pike), Dr. John H. Robinson (a civilian who accompanied the expedition, perhaps at the request of General Wilkinson), and thirteen enlisted men, followed the Spanish trace up the Arkansas. Pike never met up with the Comanches as specifically ordered by General Wilkinson (although he mentioned seeing many Comanche camp sites in his journal), but that may have been fortunate, because they were powerful, had ties to Spain, and were enemies of the Pawnees Pike had visited.

Pike's mission changed as he marched farther up the Arkansas to the mountains. His primary goal was now exploration: seeking the headwaters of the Arkansas and Red rivers, both considered important in settling the boundary of the Louisiana Purchase (as, in fact, they turned out to be in the 1819 Adams-Onís Transcontinental Treaty, which established the boundaries). This assignment seemed fairly easy, since the mouth of each river, where it entered the Mississippi, was well known. It was assumed—mistakenly, as Pike and many other explorers were to learn—that the headwaters of both rivers would be found in the western mountains. What was not understood is that the Red River does not rise in the Rocky Mountains (its sources are on the plains of Texas) and that an attempt to move from the source of the Arkansas south through the mountains would lead not to the Red River but to other tributaries of the Arkansas and, farther south and west, to the drainage of the Rio Grande to the Gulf of Mexico, not to the Mississippi.

Pike kept track of the "Spanish trace" left by Melgares and troops and could easily have followed their tracks to Santa Fe had that been his goal. Actually, Pike carried with him a map showing a route from the Pawnee village to Santa Fe, provided to him soon after he began the expedition by three men at La Charrette village on the Missouri River west of St. Charles.[44] But Santa Fe was not his destination. Pike continued toward the Rocky Mountains, entering present-day Colorado on November 11, 1806, and took time to attempt to climb the mountain he called Grand Peak (later named Pikes Peak in his honor), which he first sighted on November 15, noting that it "appeared like a small blue cloud."[45] Pike tried to ascend the Grand Peak with three companions from November 24 to 27, without success (although they did climb another mountain nearby).

The expedition pushed on. After much struggle in winter weather, Pike and his fourteen companions reached a point near the source of the Arkansas and, while wandering around lost, also found the headwaters of the South Platte River in mid-December. Their suffering intensified as the snow accumulated, and they searched to the south for the source of the Red River. They believed they had found it when they arrived at the Rio Grande on January 30, 1807, and built a small stockade during early February in which to survive the rest of the winter on a tributary, the Conejos River. On February 7, Dr. Robinson left to go to Santa Fe, where his arrival led to the dispatch of troops to bring in Pike and his few soldiers. On February 26, José Jarvet and Pedro Vial, in advance of

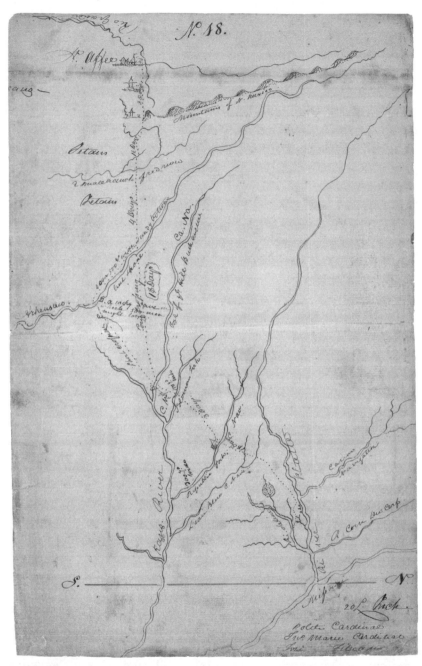

Zebulon Pike's map of the Santa Fe Trail. This sketch (in Pike's own hand) was confiscated by the Spanish after they arrested him on the Conejos River. Record Group
94, Records of the Adjutant General's Office, 1780s–1917. National Archives and Records Administration, Washington, D.C.

a platoon of soldiers, made first contact with Pike at his stockade. They were immediately followed by fifty Spanish dragoons and fifty mounted militiamen, led by Lieutenant Ignatio Saltelo, who took the explorers to Santa Fe to meet Governor Alencaster.[46]

On March 3, Pike was in Santa Fe. After meetings with Governor Alencaster, Pike and seven of his party were escorted on toward Chihuahua and General Salcedo the following day. On March 7, at Albuquerque, Pike was rejoined by Dr. Robinson, who explained that he had recently been placed under the charge of Lieutenant Melgares. Robinson informed Pike that Melgares had led the Spanish troops to the Pawnees. He also told Pike that he would find Melgares to be "a gentleman, a soldier and one of the most gallant men you ever knew."[47] The next day, March 8, they met up with Melgares at the village of San Fernandez. Pike wrote, "[H]e received me with the most manly frankness and the politeness of a man of the world." He continued, "Malgares finding I did not feel myself at ease took every means in his power to banish my reserve, which made it impossible on my part not to endeavor to appear cheerful; we conversed [in French] *as well as we could* and in two hours were as well acquainted as some people would be in the same number of months."[48]

With admiration, Pike further described his new acquaintance: "Malgares possessing none of the haughty Castillian pride, but much of the urbanity of a Frenchman; and I will add my feeble testimony to his loyalty, by declaring that he was one of the few officers or citizens whom I found, who was loyal to their king." Pike was honored when Melgares told him his private possessions, including his papers, would not be confiscated or abused by Melgares or the Spanish troops. Indeed, that evening Lieutenant Melgares hosted a fandango for his new guest at San Fernandez.[49]

From March 9 to 21, on the road to El Paso del Norte, Pike rode daily in company with Melgares, visiting while they traveled and camped each evening. After laying over a day at El Paso, the party, accompanied by an escort of dragoons, continued on to Chihuahua City, arriving there on April 2. There Melgares introduced Pike to General Salcedo, who examined Pike's papers and confiscated some of them. Although Pike remained a guest of the government in Chihuahua until April 28, he had almost daily visits with Melgares, met the lieutenant's wife and her parents (her father, Alberto Maynez, was a captain in the army), visited with several government officials, and continued to gather information that was useful to his reports. Lieutenant Melgares also accompanied Pike when they left Chihuahua to go across Texas and return to the United States at Natchitoches in Louisiana. On May 6, at a point beyond Guajoquilla (now Jiménez), where Captain Mariano Varela replaced Lieutenant Melgares as commander of the party, Pike and Melgares parted. Pike wrote, "Our friend Malgares accompanied us a few miles, to whom we bad[e] an eternal adieu, if war does not bring us together in the field of battle opposed as the most deadly enemies, when our hearts acknowledge the greatest friendship."[50]

The two enemies had truly become friends. At some point they had exchanged gifts: Pike presented Melgares a shotgun, but no record has been found of what Pike received. Pike's party continued across Texas and arrived at Natchitoches on July 1, 1807, completing the Southwest Expedition.[51] His journal of the expedition was first published in 1810, bringing information about the Great Plains and northern New Spain into public view. When the journal was published, Pike attached appendixes that provided detailed reports on the route he traveled, brief summaries of the Indians of the plains, and a lengthy appendix about New Spain.

His report on the plains contained praise for the Arkansas River as a route of travel, with abundant game and only scattered Indian tribes to obstruct passage. He thought this route could become the best overland route to the Pacific Ocean. Yet he compared the Great Plains to a desert, declaring that "these vast plains of the western hemisphere, may become in time equally celebrated as the sandy desarts of Africa," which affected the history of Kansas. Pike said that this inhospitality of the plains might serve "one great advantage to the United States, viz: The restriction of our population to some certain limits, and thereby a continuation of the union." The plains would also be "incapable of cultivation to the wandering and uncivilized aborigines of the country."[52] When these views were reinforced in 1820–21 by the Stephen H. Long expedition, which

*Pike Entering Santa Fe,* a.k.a. *A Spanish Escort,* by Frederic Remington. Published in *Collier's Weekly* on June 16, 1906. Remington destroyed the original oil painting in 1908.

labeled a portion of the plains the "Great American Desert," the U.S. Congress decided to move eastern tribes into present-day Kansas. The lands west of Missouri were not opened to settlement until the passage of the Kansas-Nebraska Act in 1854. For good or ill, Pike was partly responsible for that delay.

Pike's appendix on New Spain was more detailed and, in the long run, more important than what he wrote about the Great Plains. Pike included information about the geography, economy, government, population, society, and culture of the Internal Provinces, especially New Mexico, Biscay (Nueva Vizcaya, now the states of Chihuahua and Durango), and Coahuila. Clearly, much of what Pike wrote about travel across the plains to New Mexico, about the economy of northern Mexico, and about the geography and culture of the region came in large part from his conversations with Melgares, as well as his own observations.

From Melgares, Pike gained information about several Plains tribes, including some that Pike never met, such as the Comanches. He learned much about the military organization of New Spain, and Melgares explained in some detail how he had engaged Indians in battle. They discussed their respective trips across the plains, and Pike gathered geographical information from Melgares about places Pike had not seen. We cannot determine how much of the information Pike presented in his journal and reports was enhanced by his numerous conversations with Melgares, but it appears to be considerable. Because Pike also had opportunities to visit with other army officers and government officials, even he may not have known how much of his report on New Spain came from Melgares.

Pike's observations, plus information gleaned from Melgares, led Pike to point out in his publication of his journals and reports in 1810 that New Mexico was far removed from the source of supplies coming up El Camino Real from Mexico City, and his descriptions of a trip across the plains made clear to enterprising merchants in the United States how close they were to northern New Spain and that profits could be made by taking commodities to New Mexico. Some were willing to risk arrest and confiscation of merchandise—part of Spanish policy to keep outsiders from trading with the empire. The following portion of Pike's report in 1810 inspired enterprising merchants to attempt to open trade between the United States and northern New Spain, especially after the war for Mexico's independence began under Father Miguel Hidalgo y Costilla in 1810, a revolution that Facundo Melgares helped crush the following year as part of the royalist army.[53]

New Mexico carries on a trade direct with Mexico through Biscay, also with Senora and Sinaloa: it sends out about 30,000 sheep annually, tobacco, dressed deer and cabrie [pronghorn] skins, some fur, buffalo robes, salt, and wrought copper vessels of superior quality. It receives in return, from Biscay and Mexico, dry goods, confectionary, arms, iron, steel, ammunition, and some choice European wines and liquors, and from Senora and Sinaloa, gold, silver, and cheese. The following articles sell as stated (in this province), which will shew the cheapness of provisions and the extreme dearness of imported goods:

| | |
|---|---|
| Flour sells, per hundred at | 2 dollars |
| Salt, per mule-load | 5 |
| Sheep, each | 1 |
| Beeves, each | 5 |
| Wine del Passo, per barrel | 15 |
| Horses, each | 11 |
| Mules, each | 30 |
| Superfine cloths, per yard | 25 |
| Fine cloths, per yard | 20 |
| Linen, per yard | 4 |

and all other dry goods in proportion.

The journey with loaded mules from Santa Fe to Mexico, and returning to Santa Fe, takes five months.[54]

That quotation from Pike's report on New Spain was undoubtedly read or known by every trader who set out from the United States to New Mexico, beginning with the Robert McKnight and James Baird party in 1812 through William Becknell's successful trading venture in 1821, and including the fur-trade ventures of Auguste P. Chouteau and Jules de Mun in 1815–1816 and again in 1817, when they were arrested by Spanish troops.[55] Two years later, Luis de Mun (brother of Jules and an officer in the U.S. Army) wrote a detailed report on New Mexico, relying mostly on Pike's publication, with additional information from his brother.[56] He described three possible routes through New Mexico's mountains, including one through San Miguel del Vado and Glorieta Pass, which later became the route of the Santa Fe Trail. David Meriwether reached Santa Fe in 1819. A trading venture led by Thomas James and John McKnight reached Santa Fe a few weeks after Becknell in 1821. The fur-trapping expedition of Hugh Glenn and Jacob Fowler followed the Arkansas into present-day Colorado in 1821, and Glenn entered New Mexico early in 1822. News traveled fast that Mexico was independent and traders were welcome.

It is safe to conclude that everyone who traveled across the Great Plains to the Southwest, including other explorers, such as Stephen

Long, knew of Pike's expedition, whether from reading the reports, talking with someone who had read the reports, or even talking with soldiers who were on that expedition. Pike, with the help of Melgares and others in New Spain, provided the solid information that stimulated attempts to open trade, which became successful when Mexico won independence from Spain in 1821 and the restrictions on trade with foreigners were removed. When Becknell's small party arrived in New Mexico in 1821 with a pack train of trade items, they were welcomed at Santa Fe by Governor Facundo Melgares (who had been a friend to Pike and respected Americans, in part, because of that relationship). Becknell quickly sold his commodities at a great profit and returned to Missouri, where he outfitted the first wagons for a trading trip to Santa Fe in 1822, and Becknell was followed by many others.

The Pike expedition of 1806–1807, the Melgares expedition that preceded it, and Pike's published reports of both helped point the way to the Santa Fe trade. Eventually the many actions set in motion by the two expeditions and Pike's published accounts resulted in the annexation of Texas in 1845 and the war with Mexico, 1846–48, which brought the entire Southwest—more than half of Mexico—into the United States. President Jefferson and General Wilkinson could never have dreamed that the Pike expedition of a few soldiers would bear such fruit for a growing nation. Indeed, Wilkinson considered the expedition a failure because Pike had neither met with the Comanches nor found the source of the Red River. Still today, unfortunately, Zebulon Montgomery Pike does not receive the recognition he deserves (being known primarily for a mountain that bears his name), and very few people have ever heard of Facundo Melgares, two enemies who became friends and altered the course of the history of North America.

## NOTES

1. Pike, of the First U.S. Infantry, was promoted from lieutenant to captain during his expedition, effective August 12, 1806, but did not learn about his promotion until his return to the United States the following year. Thus, he was referred to as "Lieutenant Pike" during his entire expedition. To avoid confusion, that rank is used throughout this chapter.

2. Donald A. Nuttall, "The American Threat to New Mexico, 1804–1821," M.A. thesis, San Diego State College, 1959, 17; see also Henry Folmer, *Franco-Spanish Rivalry in North America, 1524–1763* (Glendale, Calif.: Arthur H. Clark, 1953); and A. P. Nasatir, ed., *Before Lewis and Clark: Documents Illustrating the History of the Missouri, 1785–1804*, 2 vols. (1952; repr., Lincoln: University of Nebraska Press, 1990).

3. See Abraham P. Nasatir, *Borderland in Retreat: From Louisiana to the Far Southwest* (Albuquerque: University of New Mexico Press, 1976); and Charles L. Kenner, *A History of New Mexican–Plains Indian Relations* (Norman: University of Oklahoma Press, 1969), 66–68.

4. Nasatir, *Borderland in Retreat*, 136–37.

5. Warren L. Cook, *Flood Tide of Empire: Spain and the Pacific Northwest, 1543–1819* (New Haven, Conn.: Yale University Press, 1973), 450, 491, 516.

6. Nasatir, *Before Lewis and Clark*, 1:2, 17, 19, 50; Kenner, *History*, 52–58.

7. Nuttall, "American Threat," 12.

8. See Cook, *Flood Tide of Empire*, 255–67.

9. Quoted in James Alexander Robertson, ed., *Louisiana under the Rule of Spain, France, and the United States, 1785–1807*, 2 vols. (Cleveland: Arthur H. Clark, 1911), 1:294, 298, 300, 301–45.

10. Cook, *Flood Tide of Empire*, 435–41.

11. Ibid., 269–70.

12. Quoted in Nasatir, *Before Lewis and Clark*, 2:440.

13. Cook, *Flood Tide of Empire*, 442–44.

14. Jackson, *Journals of Pike*, 2:300–301.

15. Donald Nuttall observed that Spain anticipated "an American invasion of New Mexico. The threat was illusory, but it was very much a reality to the Spaniards, and, as such, exerted considerable influence upon New Mexico in the ensuing years. Reaction to the American menace became, in fact, one of the salient features of the province's existence." Nuttall, "American Threat," v.

16. See Nasatir, *Before Lewis and Clark*, 1:108–13.

17. Quoted in Robertson, *Louisiana*, 2:192.

18. Quoted in ibid., 2:192n. Italics in original.

19. Quoted in ibid., 2:337–42.

20. Ibid., 2:345.

21. Ibid., 2:342–43.

22. Cook, *Flood Tide of Empire*, 453–54.

23. Quoted in Nasatir, *Before Lewis and Clark*, 2:725.

24. Quoted in ibid., 2:731; Cook, *Flood Tide of Empire*, 455.

25. Cook, *Flood Tide of Empire*, 456–58.

26. Noel M. Loomis and Abraham P. Nasatir, *Pedro Vial and the Roads to Santa Fe* (Norman: University of Oklahoma Press, 1966), 262–87, 316–415.

27. Ruth Steinberg, "José Jarvet, Spanish Scout and Historical Enigma," *New Mexico Historical Review* 67 (July 1992): 232.

28. Cook, *Flood Tide of Empire*, 462–65.

29. Ibid., 465–69.

30. Ibid., 470–72.

31. Ibid., 472–76.

32. Ibid., 477.

33. Ibid., 483.

34. Pike, journal entry, September 25, 1806, in Jackson, *Journals of Pike*, 1:324.

35. Arthur Gomez, "Royalist in Transition: Facundo Melgares, the Last Spanish Governor of New Mexico, 1818–1822," *New Mexico Historical Review* 68 (October 1993): 372.

36. Cook, *Flood Tide of Empire*, 479–80.

37. Ibid., 480; Jackson, *Journals of Pike*, 1:323–24.

38. Jackson, *Journals of Pike*, 2:57–58 (italics in original). Pike had a similar experience with one of his soldiers and reacted in a similar fashion. On January 24, 1807, while tramping through heavy snow in the mountains, Private John Brown began to complain: Pike noted that he "presumed to make use of language which was seditious and mutinous." Pike let it pass until they were in camp that evening, when he reprimanded Brown by stating that "it was the height of ingratitude in you, to let an expression escape which was indicative of discontent. . . . But your duty as a soldier called on your obedience to your officer, and a prohibition of such language, which for this time, I will pardon, but assure you, should it ever be repeated, by instant *death*, I will revenge your ingratitude and punish your disobedience." Pike recorded no further disciplinary problems. Ibid., 1:372–73.

39. Ibid., 1:325.

40. Ibid., 1:325, 329.

41. Steinberg, "José Jarvet," 245–46; Loomis and Nasatir, *Pedro Vial*, 455.

42. Cook, *Flood Tide of Empire*, 480–403. Isaac J. Cox wrote of Melgares, "His force was really too large for effective scouting and exploration. Mutiny in the ranks retarded his movements, which were still further hampered by the raids of Indians on his livestock." Cox, "Opening the Santa Fe Trail," *Missouri Historical Review* 25 (October 1930): 52.

43. Jackson, *Journals of Pike*, 1:328–29.

44. Lowell M. Schake, *La Charrette: Village Gateway to the American West* (Lincoln, Neb.: iUniverse, 2003), 23–25.

45. Jackson, *Journals of Pike*, 1:345.

46. For details of the expedition from the Pawnee village to the arrival of the Spanish troops, see ibid., 1:331–85. The identity of Jarvet and Vial is provided by Steinberg, "José Jarvet," 246.

47. Jackson, *Journals of Pike*, 1:404.

48. Ibid., 1:405. Italics in original.

49. Ibid., 1:405–406.

50. Ibid., 1:425.

51. Ibid., 1:447.

52. Ibid., 2:25–28.

53.   Gomez, "Royalist in Transition," 378–79.

54.   Jackson, *Journals of Pike,* 2:50–51.

55.   Frank B. Golley states that their 1812 party used Pike's work "as their guide book." Golley, "James Baird, Early Santa Fe Trader," *Bulletin of the Missouri Historical Society* 15 (April 1959): 179.

56.   Loomis and Nasatir, *Pedro Vial,* 257.

7

# James Wilkinson

PIKE'S MENTOR AND JEFFERSON'S CAPRICIOUS

POINT MAN IN THE WEST

*William E. Foley*

The annals of the early American republic are replete with flawed characters, but few, if any, match the audacity or the mendacity of General James A. Wilkinson. Variously a soldier forced to resign from the Revolutionary Army, an entrepreneur with grand designs and limited successes, a secret agent on imperial Spain's payroll, the commanding general of the U.S. Army, a key implementer of Thomas Jefferson's western policies, a sponsor and mentor for the exploratory ventures of Zebulon Pike, Philip Nolan, and John McClallen, and a collaborator-turned-informant in the alleged Burr conspiracy, Wilkinson had chances aplenty to demonstrate his capricious ways. Taking his measure is no simple task, but self-aggrandizement remained the one discernible constant in his inconstant life.

As unlikely as his selection to serve as President Thomas Jefferson's point man in the West might have seemed, Wilkinson's far-ranging knowledge of the region and its inhabitants, his administrative and command experience, and his political connections persuaded the westward-looking chief executive to ignore his widely reported flaws and look to him for assistance at critical moments. Jefferson decided to retain Wilkinson as the army's top commander, to appoint him governor of Louisiana Territory, and to embrace his rendition of Aaron Burr's intrigues long after the allegations of his clandestine dealings with a foreign power were common knowledge. Had he discovered that his appointee, known to his Spanish handlers as Agent 13, had urged them to intercept and detain the Lewis and Clark expedition, he assuredly would have been less tolerant of his foibles, but at the time even Wilkinson's most ardent critics were unaware of that deceit. The duplicitous and calculating commander found ways to disguise his treachery, accentuate his assets, and make himself useful to his superiors. Valuable as his services sometimes were, Jefferson, and even more so the president's advisers, chose to keep their unpredictable western agent under a watchful eye.

As a Federalist protégé who won over John Adams and found favor with Alexander Hamilton, Wilkinson faced an uncertain future following Jefferson's electoral triumph in 1800.[1] Fortunately for him, he was as practiced in the art of politics as he was in the politics of intrigue. Careful to mute his party preferences, the apolitical Wilkinson transitioned into Republican ranks with barely a backward glance. His readiness to curry Republican favor may have prompted his decision to send Jefferson, a fellow member of the American Philosophical Society, an assortment of petrifactions, Indian knives, meteorological observations, and sketches of the Mississippi Territory, even before the electoral ballots had been tallied.[2]

Reports that the incoming president intended to initiate reforms to ensure the army's loyalty alarmed members of the officer corps and sent their commanding general scurrying to the new Federal City to make himself available for consultation. Brigadier General Wilkinson attended the inauguration and joined Jefferson and his key advisers at a large public gathering in nearby Alexandria, but when planning for the new army's makeup, the president and Secretary of War Henry Dearborn, who remained dubious of the general, elected not to involve him in their deliberations.[3]

Dearborn's doubts, Republican eagerness to purge Federalists from the army's ranks, and renewed warnings detailing Wilkinson's Spanish connections raised enough questions to place the veteran soldier's continued military career at risk, but the beleaguered brigadier was not without defenders. Hugh Henry Brackenridge, a prominent western Pennsylvania Republican, touted him as a popular and knowledgeable western commander ideally equipped to superintend troops and

*James Wilkinson,* by Charles Willson Peale, from life, 1796–97. Courtesy of Independence National Historical Park.

implement the War Department's plans for retrenchment and reform. Favorable notices from a handful of administration loyalists and the absence of a suitable Republican to take his place sealed the deal in favor of Wilkinson's retention. The controversial commander had survived to fight another day.[4]

Eager to polish his new Republican credentials and reassure his doubting benefactors, Wilkinson struck a symbolic blow at aristocratic tradition by directing members of the military to cut their hair short and dispense with the practice of wearing it in a queue. The order produced strong resentment among army old-timers, but the general persisted with the quiet approval of the president, who cut his own hair to encourage compliance.[5] Though safely ensconced in a command post, Wilkinson's extravagant tastes and lavish spending habits placed him in dire need of additional income. His free-spending ways extended to his government accounts, but as with many other things, those excesses did not become public knowledge until late in his career.[6] When his friend Samuel Smith suggested that Jefferson name him to fill the recently vacated governorship in the Mississippi Territory, the chief executive quashed the proposal on dual grounds: the additional appointment would violate the principle against combining military and civilian authority; and the general's residence in Natchez would be incompatible with his superintendence of the military posts under his command.[7]

A disappointed Wilkinson had to be satisfied with the additional sums he received as compensation for his services as an Indian commissioner during 1801 and 1802. The president had designated him, along with Benjamin Hawkins and Andrew Pickens, to negotiate with the tribes south of the Ohio River for the purpose of securing land concessions, arranging for the establishment of a public road linking the Tennessee settlements with Natchez, and providing for Indian trading factories.[8] Their protracted negotiations with the Choctaws, Cherokees, Chickasaws, and Creeks were tiring and kept him on the road and away from his family for a lengthy period, but the resulting treaties addressed the administration's principal concerns and momentarily helped restore a bit of luster to Wilkinson's tarnished image.

Desirous of a more settled existence, the perennially cash-strapped general set his sights on the new surveyor general's position in the Mississippi Territory. At least three influential congressional Republicans wrote the president on his behalf. Samuel Smith, whose earlier request had been rejected, informed Jefferson that Wilkinson was prepared to relinquish his military duties if necessary, but the representative from Maryland counseled that given the recent reports of possible French plans to invade New Orleans, allowing him to step down would be unwise. For his part, Georgia's Senator James Jackson stressed, "He

[Wilkinson] is getting old in the service of his Country—has a Family to support and is by no means in affluent circumstances" and moreover was an "administration supporter." Joseph Anderson, a senator from Tennessee, alluded to Wilkinson's financial problems, lauded his ability "to blend the character of citizen with that of soldier," and attested to his popularity among the citizens of his state.[9] Their ringing endorsements failed to budge the still-skeptical Henry Dearborn, whose scribbled notation at the bottom of Smith's letter read, "Such a situation would enable him to associate with Spanish agents without suspicion."[10] The secretary's stinging rebuke underscored that questions about the loyal ties of the army's senior officer continued to concern officials in the War Department.

Following the 1801 disclosure of Spain's secret retrocession of Louisiana to France, war clouds loomed on the horizon as U.S. officials pondered their next moves. The subsequent withdrawal of the right of deposit at New Orleans amplified the tensions and prompted the president to dispatch James Monroe to France in search of a diplomatic settlement. Meanwhile, the weary General Wilkinson, who claimed he had traveled more than sixteen thousand miles on public business in 1802 and 1803, prepared for any eventuality.[11] He advised Lieutenant Jacob Kingsbury that "if Monroe succeeds all will be well but if he should fail we shall have noise bustle & Bloodshed" and admonished the veteran soldier to keep his sword sharpened and remain quiet for the present.[12]

Monroe's mission succeeded beyond all expectations, and President Jefferson's announcement on July 4, 1803, that France had agreed to sell the vast trans-Mississippi territory to the United States foreshadowed dramatic changes for the young republic and its officials. Welcome as the acquisition of Louisiana was, the road ahead was strewn with pitfalls. Taking control of the volatile and culturally diverse frontier territory would not be easy, especially because the sale angered the Spaniards, who had conveyed Louisiana to France only after receiving assurances that the territory would never be transferred to a third power. It was a situation tailor-made for a double agent with a foot in both the American and the Spanish camp.

Ambitious as always, Wilkinson moved to center stage when the president tasked him and the youthful and inexperienced William C. C.

Claiborne with superintending America's takeover of Louisiana. Not everyone was impressed with Wilkinson and his swagger. The disgruntled French commissioner Pierre Clement Laussat, for example, called him "an illogical fellow, full of queer whims, and often drunk."[13] Claiborne and Wilkinson had entered New Orleans in December 1803 accompanied by five hundred troops, and to everyone's relief, the transfer ceremonies held on December 20 proceeded without a hitch. Laussat presented the brigadier general with keys to the city, and after affixing their signatures to the official documents, the commissioners adjourned to the balcony of the Cabildo to observe the lowering of the French Tricolor and the raising of the American Stars and Stripes.[14] Reassuring as the peaceful character of the proceedings might have been, Louisiana remained a cauldron of dissatisfied factions with competing visions for its future.[15]

Claiborne took up the reins of civil government, and in late April, Wilkinson left New Orleans. Never one to pass on any opportunity, the general had made the most of his four-month stay in the city. Prior to his departure, the double-dealing general labored to demonstrate his worth simultaneously to his American superiors and to the retreating Spanish dons. A February encounter with West Florida's Governor Vicente Folch enabled Wilkinson to revive his moribund Spanish connection and press for renewed compensation from Spain's royal treasury. Fluent in English (Wilkinson did not speak Spanish) and entirely trustworthy, Folch—a nephew of Wilkinson's old friend, the late Manuel Gayoso de Lemos—seemed the perfect conduit for his new initiative.[16] After extracting assurances of absolute secrecy from Folch, Wilkinson shared his thoughts about the steps that Spain needed to take to protect its endangered North American possessions. As with all of Wilkinson's propositions, there was a price tag attached. Folch understood Wilkinson's game, but the American's suggestions proved sufficiently enticing to hold his interest. Once the hook had been set, Wilkinson proceeded to outline his ideas in greater detail.[17]

The American agent complained to Folch that for the past ten years the Spanish authorities had failed to pay the two-thousand-dollar annual pension they had promised him fifteen years earlier. Eager to cast himself as an insider privy to the plans of the U.S. government, Wilkinson suggested that a twenty-thousand-dollar settlement (the amount in arrears) would help finance his pending trip to the U.S. capital for meetings with the president and members of his cabinet. Claiming to know "what was concealed in the heart of the President," Wilkinson offered to provide his Spanish benefactors with a full version of his so-called "Reflections."[18]

It was another risky move on Wilkinson's part, but the lure of money had always emboldened him to take chances. Lacking the requisite funds in his accounts, Folch suggested that the general approach the marques de Casa Calvo, a former governor who was in New Orleans to help settle Louisiana's boundaries. Fearful that Casa Calvo's talkative private secretary might spill the beans to Daniel Clark, the former U.S. consul whom Wilkinson no longer completely trusted, Wilkinson hesitated momentarily, but greed quickly overcame his doubts as he laid out his proposals to the attentive Spanish boundary commissioner. They came to an understanding, and Wilkinson immediately put his pen to paper to provide the information he had promised. The Spanish version of Wilkinson's "Reflections" that Folch prepared for delivery to Casa Calvo caused later researchers to mistakenly identify him as their author. To help safeguard his anonymity, Wilkinson insisted that the Spaniards refer to him as Number 13 in all correspondence.[19] For these latest services, Wilkinson received twelve thousand dollars, an amount that he hoped would be simply a down payment. To disguise their source, he invested the funds in a cargo of sugar, but questions about the transaction, first raised in New Orleans, forced him to fabricate a story that he had acquired the sugar as payment for an earlier tobacco contract with the Spanish government. By now his deceptions had become a well-practiced art.[20]

For their twelve-thousand-dollar investment, Wilkinson cautioned the Spaniards to be wary of the dangers posed by westward-moving Americans (stale news indeed). He urged Spain to solidify its claims to West Florida, strengthen its fortifications there and along the gulf coast, and encourage American efforts to relocate the Creeks, Choctaws, Chickasaws, and Cherokees west of the Mississippi, because any such attempt would turn those tribes against the United States and ally them with Spain in its campaign to halt American expansion. The Spaniards knew that Wilkinson had recently held talks with representatives from those tribes. The American general further suggested that Spain pursue a possible agreement with the United States to exchange its newly acquired territories on the Mississippi's west bank for East and West Florida.[21]

He likewise importuned the Spaniards to halt American expansion up the Missouri. It is well for him that Jefferson was never privy to his recommendation that "a sufficient body of chasseurs intercept Captain Lewis and his party, who are on the Missouri River and force them to retire or take them prisoners." Wilkinson further opined that Spain would be well advised to drive all existing settlers from the Missouri, including a person named Bone (that is, Daniel Boone) who had been among the first Americans to penetrate the wilderness of Kentucky. Left undisturbed, the general warned, the American interlopers would soon make their way to Santa Fe, a prospect guaranteed to alarm Spanish higher-ups.[22]

Having whetted their appetites, the self-serving agent finally got to the heart of the matter: "Since money is the sinew of war, and a powerful agent for negotiation, the commissioner of boundaries and the governor of West Florida should be authorized to apply annually a certain sum of money to be used under their direction for secret services and especially for the favoring of these propositions. At this moment, for the lack of this arrangement, we are losing in the cause which we are discussing, a man of great talent and national influence."[23] None of this would be especially remarkable had it not come from the commanding general of the U.S. Army. In ensuing years, the self-described "man of great talent and national influence" continued to send his Spanish cohorts tidbits of information, but to his consternation they failed to deem the intelligence he provided worthy of additional compensation. He would have to look elsewhere for that.

Watchful of his rear guard and an old hand at playing both ends against the middle, Wilkinson informed Secretary Dearborn that he was collecting valuable topographical information—data that he knew would be useful to U.S. officials then attempting to resolve disputes over Louisiana's boundaries.[24] With reports and drawings in hand, he left New Orleans on April 25, 1804, and set out for the national capital eager

*Aaron Burr,* by John Vanderlyn, 1802, oil on canvas. Accession no. 1931.58. Courtesy of Collection of The New-York Historical Society.

to share his information with those who would appreciate it. While on his way to Washington, Wilkinson secretly conferred with Aaron Burr at his Richmond Hill estate in New York. Their hastily arranged night-time meeting, which took place less than two months before Burr's fatal encounter with Alexander Hamilton, was no mere social call. One can only speculate about what they discussed, but three days later Wilkinson offered to show the vice president his maps, which included one of the Southwest provided by his former clerk, Philip Nolan, a horse trader and filibuster whose travels had taken him deep into Texas and ultimately cost him his life in 1801. Business done, Wilkinson continued on his way to the Federal City.[25]

Once in Washington, he presented Secretary Dearborn a twenty-two-page treatise describing the region between the Mississippi and the Rio Grande along with twenty-eight manuscript maps for the president's perusal. His lengthy account of Texas included valuable geographic detail and estimates of troop strength in the region. He concluded his letter with an apology for sending "these hurried desultory details" and explained that he had done so to safeguard against the possible loss of this information if something happened to him.[26] Coincidentally, at about the same time, Alexander von Humboldt, the acclaimed German naturalist and explorer, showed up in Washington fresh from his travels in Mexico. Jefferson welcomed the baron to the nation's capital and took advantage of his presence to query him at length about southwestern geography. Eager for Wilkinson to compare notes with the distinguished visitor, the chief executive invited them to dine with him at the President's House. Weakened from a bleeding administered by his physician to alleviate a lingering ailment of his head and breast, Wilkinson reluctantly declined the invitation. In conveying his regrets, he took the liberty of enclosing a list of questions for the baron. The answers he hoped would help him authenticate the accuracy of the information he had acquired from Nolan. The baron showed his vaunted maps of Mexico to the president and the secretary of the treasury with a request that they not be copied since he planned to publish them, but Burr surreptitiously managed to gain access to a copy that he shared with Wilkinson.[27]

The new information supplied by Wilkinson and von Humboldt landed on the president's desk at an opportune moment. The United States was preparing for negotiations with Spain to determine Louisiana's boundaries, and Jefferson had little to guide him. These latest geographic representations seemed to bolster his attempt to claim the Rio Grande as Louisiana's southwestern boundary. Eager to add to his store of knowledge, Jefferson dispatched the Hunter-Dunbar expedition to explore the Ouachita, a tributary of the Red River, in the fall of 1804.

According to historian Isaac Cox, the intelligence Wilkinson provided served his purposes in two ways: it enhanced his standing with

the president and inclined U.S. officials to favor a more aggressive pos-
ture in their dealings with Spain. Conversely, he calculated that the U.S.
government's more-assertive demands would make his anxious Spanish
partners more grateful for any information he sent their way and, better
still, more willing to pay for it.[28]

While in the capital city, Wilkinson resumed his discussions with the
vice president, lobbied members of Congress for support, and continued to correspond with Spanish officials. He likely also monitored the
lively ongoing congressional debates about the viability of republican
institutions in the nation's recently acquired, culturally diverse western territories, judged by many to be ill equipped for self-government.
Responding to the widespread dissatisfaction with an initial arrangement that attached Louisiana's upper portions to Indiana Territory for
administrative purposes, the federal legislators created a separate government for the northern region and called it the Territory of Louisiana.
The enabling legislation vested power in a governor and three judges all
appointed by the president, a form originally prescribed for first-class
territories in the Northwest Ordinance of 1787.[29]

Louisiana's new law took effect on March 3, 1805, and barely a week
later, Jefferson announced his choices for its key offices. To the surprise
of many, he named General Wilkinson as Louisiana's territorial governor. In doing so, he ignored his own prohibition against combining
civilian and military authority. His reasons for the controversial appointment were complex. Wilkinson's influential friends, including the
vice president, rallied to support his nomination, but in the end, what
carried the day was the president's conviction that the general's military
experience would equip him to handle the difficult problems of the remote and sparsely populated frontier territory.[30]

When later called to account for his decision to violate the precept
against filling civilian posts with members of the military, Jefferson clar-
ified his reasoning in a letter addressed to Joseph Anderson, the chair
of the Senate committee on nominations. The president explained, "St.
Louis, as the center of our Western operations, whether respecting the
Spaniards, Indians or English, and as the outwork which covers all that
frontier, is too important to be left in a state of anarchy, or placed in
nerveless hands . . . it will be better for the rest of the Union to consider

it as a military post, in which an energetic government may be the most useful."[31]

The gubernatorial appointment came as good news to Wilkinson, who welcomed the added income and the president's vote of confidence. He wasted little time before heading to St. Louis to take up his new duties. During a stopover at Fort Massac,[32] he huddled for four days with Aaron Burr, who was then on his way to New Orleans, actively recruiting volunteers to join the secret enterprise that he and Wilkinson had in the works. Its precise nature remains a subject for debate. Some believe that their plot involved a treasonous scheme to create a new country by separating trans-Appalachian states and territories from the Union, while others contend that their intent was to invade and conquer Mexico.[33] The preponderance of evidence strongly suggests that Wilkinson and Burr were focused on an invasion of Mexico and used the other option primarily as a smokescreen to reassure the wary Spaniards. John Adair, one of their western recruits, said as much when he advised Wilkinson that "Kentuckians as greedy for plunder as the old Romans" were ready for action, adding, "Mexico glitters in our Eyes."[34]

Following their summit, Wilkinson arranged for Burr to continue his trip to New Orleans on a government barge and supplied him with the kind of effusive letters of introduction that only the general could have written.[35] Meanwhile, Louisiana Territory's incoming governor resumed his journey to St. Louis, pondering the grand designs he and Burr expected to set in motion. Wilkinson was already thinking ahead and looking far beyond the "mongrel community" he was assigned to govern. From Fort Massac, he informed Dearborn of his intent to dispatch three or four small expeditions to the Osage towns, the Platte River, Prairie du Chien, and the headwaters of the Mississippi.[36]

Along the way, summer heat, swarming mosquitoes, turbulent river currents, and feuding constituents seeking his favor tested the new governor's patience and tempered his fantasies. In Kaskaskia, Major Seth Hunt, the loquacious military commandant of Ste. Genevieve, filled his ear with tales of intriguing French Creoles eager to plunder the American public domain, and a short time later, St. Louis fur baron and U.S. Indian agent Pierre Chouteau boarded Wilkinson's boat to present the case for the other side. By the time Wilkinson reached St. Louis on July

1, 1805, it was obvious to him that personal animosities were raging almost everywhere, exacerbated, in his judgment, by small cliques of "pettifoggers, renegadoes, and impatient natives."[37]

The volatile conditions he encountered had been building since the Louisiana Purchase, fueled by ill-defined U.S. policies and the demands of a steady stream of ambitious newcomers eager to capitalize on the change in governments. The American influx threatened to erode French Creole power and influence, and the U.S. government's hesitancy to confirm French and Spanish land titles added to the uneasiness of the outnumbered francophones. The stakes were high as the contesting factions maneuvered to win the new governor's confidence. During a welcoming ceremony in St. Louis, Wilkinson called upon his new constituents "to expel the gall of Party spirit" and embrace "an accord in sentiment, a concert in policy, and a cheerful support of the Government."[38]

Subsequent events made it clear that the disagreements were too intense to be stilled by calls for cooperation and unity. The widening controversy over the validity of unconfirmed Spanish land titles and mining concessions lay at the heart of the matter. Each camp had much at stake and justifiable cause for concern. The task of reconciling their differences would have tested the most able of politicians, but Wilkinson's talents were better suited to military command than civil government. His arrogance and pomposity; his determination to exercise complete control, strengthened no doubt by Jefferson's occasional references to the establishment of a military government; his attempts to remove officials who disagreed with him; and his open courtship of the rich and powerful Creole merchants did little to diminish the internecine feuding.

Troublesome though it might have been, Wilkinson refused to allow the factional discord to get in the way of Jefferson's directives or his own ambitious plans. He devoted considerable time and energy to the military and defensive matters that the president viewed as paramount. Needful of a place to garrison his troops, he selected a site on the banks of the Missouri not far from St. Louis for a combined military installation and government-operated Indian trading factory. The establishment, known as Cantonment Bellefontaine, was ready for occupancy before winter set in.[39] Even as Wilkinson watched the structures at the nearby post taking shape, his sights remained fixed on more distant places, notably Mexico. Cognizant that the Comanche Indians had "it in their power to facilitate or impede our march to New Mexico, should such a movement ever become necessary," he set about to broker a peaceful settlement of their hostilities with the neighboring Osages.[40] As a first step, he sent U.S. Indian agent Pierre Chouteau and a military party under the command of Lieutenant George Peter to the Osage towns to initiate talks between the feuding tribes and to seek Osage permission to erect a military post on their lands. In his instructions, he directed Chouteau to acquire information about the routes and distances between the Osage villages and Santa Fe and to collect mineral and natural history specimens.[41]

At the same time, Wilkinson also dispatched a military expedition to explore the upper reaches of the Mississippi under the command of Lieutenant Zebulon M. Pike. Wilkinson's long association with Pike's father, an aging officer whose service dated to the Revolutionary War, may have influenced his decision to select the untutored young officer for the task. Whatever the reason, the assignment rescued the younger Pike from a mundane military career, allowed him to become the general's protégé, and launched him on a course fraught with peril and uncertainty. Pike's instructions called for him to collect geographical information, purchase sites from the Indians for potential military forts, invite select chiefs to visit St. Louis, and show the U.S. flag in the region.[42]

These expeditions marked Wilkinson's formal debut as a sponsor and outfitter of exploratory ventures. Although he sought to emulate the president's example, Wilkinson's objectives were less altruistic and more closely linked to personal profit and ambition. Knowledge of western rivers and the adjacent terrain could help ensure the success of his ventures, whatever their purpose. Because he financed the expeditions with funds from his military budget, Wilkinson failed to seek prior approval from his superiors, but he did alert them to his intent.

Not long after the departures of Chouteau and Pike, Aaron Burr showed up in St. Louis fresh from his trip to New Orleans. He compared notes with Wilkinson, and they renewed their discussions about a filibuster aimed at overthrowing the Mexican government. Their plan, which rested on the likelihood of a war with Spain, proposed to take advantage of any ensuing chaos to launch a two-pronged attack against

Vera Cruz and a second directed at Texas or Santa Fe.[43] Burr's attempts to enlist recruits attracted relatively few takers in St. Louis and further complicated the territory's confused political climate. Rufus Easton, a territorial judge and an emerging critic of Wilkinson, believed that his estrangement from the governor began when he rejected Burr's overtures.[44]

Only days before his meeting with Burr in St. Louis, Wilkinson advised Secretary Dearborn that he had drawn upon his private funds to outfit a trading expedition destined for the Yellowstone River for the purpose of collecting additional information about the region's Native population and its natural products. Commerce was the lifeblood of St. Louis, and notwithstanding his disavowal of "any view of self-interest," Wilkinson was eager to get in on the action. In addition to the possible acquisition of new knowledge, he undoubtedly hoped that the enterprise would facilitate his entry into the fur trade and earn him a profit to boot. As with so many of his private ventures, the enterprise fared poorly and attracted little notice in St. Louis. Francois Rivet and Joseph Grenier traveled as far as the Yellowstone with little to show for their efforts. When they encountered Lewis and Clark on August 21, 1806, they were heading back to St. Louis to advise Wilkinson of their disappointing results.[45]

Wilkinson also kept an eye fixed on the Southwest, where growing tensions between the United States and Spain made some type of intervention seem increasingly feasible. Shortly before his confab with Burr in the fall of 1805, he informed the secretary of war that he planned to dispatch onetime army scout Robert McClellen to Santa Fe for a firsthand look under the cover of a private trading mission, but the venture never materialized. Sensing the potential risks, McClellen had chosen trading with the Omahas over spying.[46] Keeping his options open, Wilkinson continued his juggling act, sending Dearborn alarmist reports about Spain's malevolent intentions even as he continued to caution the Spaniards about dangers of American encroachment into their territories.[47] By the fall of 1806, the general's machinations had persuaded Burr that war with Spain had become a virtual certainty.[48]

The United States faced additional threats along its northern border, and Jefferson also tasked Wilkinson with keeping Canadian-based

British traders out of the trans-Mississippi territories. Toward that end, the governor, in consultation with other territorial officials, issued strict new regulations governing Indian trade in the Missouri Valley. The new rules prohibited foreigners from participating in the trade and required American citizens to secure licenses from the governor. Wilkinson initially proposed to ban the sale of firearms to Indians, but strong protests registered by St. Louis fur merchants Auguste Chouteau, Manuel Lisa, and others persuaded him to drop the prohibition.[49]

During the summer and fall of 1805, the governor also struggled to deal with the intermittent hostilities between the Osages and a confederation of eastern tribes led by the Sacs and Foxes. Wilkinson blamed the troubles on Sac and Fox dissatisfaction with an 1804 treaty forcing them to cede lands to the United States and the bad influence of Canadian-based traders. Talks with the warring tribes produced a momentary ceasefire, but as soon as they left town, many of them cast aside the U.S.-dictated agreement and resumed their warfare. Eager to show firmness in his dealings with the territory's numerous and powerful Indian populace, the governor instigated legal proceedings against two Kickapoos charged with killing whites, but their 1806 trial and executions in St. Louis failed to produce the desired results.[50]

Other matters also competed for his attention. Although the president had retreated from his earlier plans for closing Upper Louisiana to white settlement altogether, he continued to press proposals for removing settlers from the territory's more sparsely inhabited regions to make room for relocated southern tribes. Even the usually aggressive Wilkinson recognized the need for caution, but his attempts to raise the issue further undermined his standing with his local constituents.[51] By October 1805, pro-Wilkinson and anti-Wilkinson factions had begun to choose sides. The governor's supporters included most of the territory's French inhabitants, a select group of American speculators holding Spanish land concessions, and a motley assortment of Burrites and miscellaneous adventurers. Members of the opposition were primarily Americans who arrived in the territory following the Louisiana Purchase eager to get their hands on the territory's lands.[52]

Given the escalating threats on all fronts, Wilkinson doubted that the initiatives he had taken would be sufficient to defend U.S. interests in the region. He lobbied vigorously for the establishment of strategically placed military posts in the nation's interior regions, but the economy-minded Jefferson administration repeatedly vetoed all such plans, insisting that trade was the key to control.[53] Ignoring Dearborn's previous directives, Wilkinson took steps to establish a temporary outpost on the Platte River that he believed would benefit national interests, facilitate his attempts to enter the Indian trade, and help open the road to Santa Fe. He justified his decision on the grounds that it would enable him to return an ailing Arikara tribal leader to his village and also counter the Spanish troops who lately had stirred up trouble at the Platte River Pawnee villages. On October 22, he dispatched twenty-five soldiers—commanded by his son, Lieutenant James Biddle Wilkinson—up the Missouri with instructions for them to escort the visiting chieftain to his home and to erect a strong post on the Platte. He also granted Dr. Andrew Steele permission to accompany the mission and take with him a private store of trade goods. Wilkinson may have had a personal stake in Steele's mercantile enterprise and likely selected him as an alternative after Robert McClellen declined to undertake a risky journey to Santa Fe disguised as a trader.[54]

Not long after the expedition's departure, Wilkinson received a cautionary advisement from Dearborn warning that "no detachment should be made to any distant new post at present."[55] In an attempt to forestall criticism, Wilkinson wasted no time in notifying his superiors that a hostile Kansa party had forced the expedition to return to Cantonment Bellefontaine prior to the initiation of any work at the Platte River site.[56]

The communication arrived too late to spare him from Dearborn's stinging rebuke for having violated his orders. The secretary also admonished him not to use public workmen for private business. The latter almost certainly came in response to Major Seth Hunt's allegations that Wilkinson and his friends had outfitted a private trading expedition at government expense. Though Hunt was embroiled in a dispute with his commanding officer, his charges rang true enough to revive Dearborn's latent suspicions about the money-hungry general.[57]

After receiving Dearborn's reprimand, Wilkinson mounted a vigorous defense of his actions. He ingeniously sought to justify the venture (no doubt to win over the president) by recasting it as an attempt to ensure Captain Lewis's safe return and to portray himself as the hapless victim of false insinuations spread by enemies intent on his destruction.[58] In response to allegations that he paraded about St. Louis in a fine carriage wearing a cocked hat with a sword at his side, Wilkinson assured the secretary that "my general deportment my dress & address are almost as plain as any *Clod-Hopper,* and my Doors are open at all Hours, but those of rest, to all kinds & descriptions of People without exception."[59] His explanations failed to dissuade Dearborn, who nonetheless had closed the books on the failed Missouri River venture.[60]

The year 1806 was a fateful one for Wilkinson. Because the president's initial nominees for posts in Louisiana Territory were recess appointments, he had to resubmit their names to the Senate for confirmation when Congress reconvened. In anticipation of a renewed debate about Wilkinson's fitness to continue as governor, combatants from each side of the territory's factional divide bombarded the nation's capital with letters and petitions supporting and opposing his reappointment. Territorial judge and former member of Congress John B. C. Lucas advised his old friend Treasury Secretary Albert Gallatin that the governor was "vain and excessively fond of pageantry . . . [with an] unbounded Love of Power" and urged that Wilkinson not be reappointed.[61] Another critic, Edward Hempstead, an American newcomer, privately echoed suspicions voiced by many congressional Republicans: "From a Rank federalist to a suspected republican, he became a *Burrite,* and is now a petty Tyrant."[62] On the other side, the territory's influential francophones and their allies remained committed to Wilkinson.[63]

When his nomination came before the Senate committee on presidential appointments, its chair asked Jefferson to explain his reasons for appointing a military man.[64] Many of the committee's Republican members continued to question the wisdom of combining military and civil authority, but the president chose to stand behind his controversial nominee. The Senate narrowly confirmed his appointment, but only with the aid of Federalist votes.[65] In a dramatic gesture designed to reassure his foremost sponsor, Wilkinson offered to step aside with nary a murmur if the president believed that his private interests or national service required it. This offer, he added, was "alas the only poor return I can make you, for continued acts of undeserved kindness." Equally determined not to give the president any reason for accepting his offer, Wilkinson avowed that he had "avoided every species of Interested pursuit" since arriving in the territory.[66]

His supplications came none too soon, for a few short days after the Senate confirmed the nomination, Jefferson received an accusatory letter from Kentuckian Joseph H. Daveiss, warning him that a plot was afoot to separate the Union in favor of Spain, with General Wilkinson as an instigator. He further alleged that Wilkinson "has been for years and now is a pensioner of Spain" and offered to provide proof. The president shared the letter with the members of his cabinet and invited Daveiss to identify other conspirators in the plot.[67] Fortunately for Wilkinson, his accuser's reputation as a Federalist hack and his penchant for targeting prominent Republicans predisposed Jefferson and the cabinet members to give little credence to his charges. Even so, Secretary Gallatin's assessment of Wilkinson was hardly a ringing endorsement:

> Of the General I have no very exalted opinion; he is extravagant and needy, and would not, I think, feel much delicacy in speculating on public money or public land. In both those respects he must be closely watched; and he has now united himself with every man in Louisiana who had received or claims large grants under the Spanish government (Gratiot, the Chouteaus, Soulard, &c.) But tho not perhaps very scrupulous in that respect, and although I fear that he may sacrifice to a certain degree the interests of the United States to his desire of being popular in his government, he is honorable in his private dealings, and of betraying his to a foreign country I believe him altogether incapable.

He did not believe the controversial general was a traitor, but given the charges swirling about Wilkinson, Gallatin obviously saw a need for caution.[68]

The governor's triumph proved to be short lived. The huzzahs of his supporters in St. Louis had barely died down before rumors of his pending replacement reached their disbelieving ears. He immediately turned to the president and his friend Senator Smith for reassurance.[69] The president obliged with a statement that "nothing is in contemplation at this time," but two days later, on May 6, the secretary of war ordered him to take command of military operations in the Territory of Orleans.[70] Coming at a time when sensational newspaper accounts questioned his loyalty and predicted his removal as governor, the orders seemed to confirm his worst fears.[71] Dearborn cited worsening relations between Spain and the United States and the unresolved Louisiana-Texas boundary dispute as reasons for his change of plans. Goaded by Wilkinson's dire predictions of an American onslaught and by the recent intrusions of U.S.-sponsored expeditions, Spanish officials appeared increasingly intent on hostile action. More concerned with saving face than defending borders, the vainglorious governor focused his enmity on the Washington officials who had leaked word of his pending transfer prior to its public disclosure.[72]

Intent on making the best of this unexpected turn of events, Wilkinson advised Smith that he would accede to Dearborn's directives and head downriver in about two weeks to take up his new command, where he hoped to find "fame and Honour." After further reflection, he quietly altered his plans and tarried for another two months in St. Louis, the place Jefferson called "the center of our western operations."[73] The delay gave him time to dispatch Lieutenant Zebulon Pike on a second military reconnaissance, to monitor developments in the fluid and evolving plot he and Burr concocted, to take stock of the changing state of affairs between the United States and Spain, and above all, to ponder his next moves on the western chessboard. His wife's deteriorating health provided a convenient excuse for postponing his departure.

Resilient as ever, he rebounded from disappointment and redirected his energies to preparing for Pike's new mission. Following his return to St. Louis in April with maps and reports from his journey up the Mississippi, the lieutenant found increased favor with his mentor, who tasked him with an even more important assignment. Pike's orders instructed him to escort some recently released Osage captives to their villages, to assist the Kansa Indians in negotiations with the Pawnees, to make overtures to the warlike High Plains Comanches, and to explore the Arkansas and Red rivers without alarming or annoying the Spaniards. Wilkinson named his son, James Biddle, to be second in command and authorized two civilians, interpreter Baronet Vasquez and physician Dr.

John Hamilton Robinson, to accompany Pike's military detachment. All was in order for them to depart on July 15. As they traveled westward across Kansas and stopped at a Pawnee Indian village on the Republican River, Pike learned that a large body of Spanish troops had preceded them a few days earlier, leaving him to conclude erroneously that he had been their target. The Spanish dragoons retreating back to Santa Fe left a convenient trail for him to follow. When he reached the Arkansas River, Pike deployed Lieutenant Wilkinson and a small detachment to descend that stream, possibly to keep the general's son out of harm's way as the main group ventured ever closer to Spanish territory.[74]

Pike and the others trekked on in search of the Rockies. During the course of their ensuing journey, Pike discovered the peak that bears his name but failed to climb it, became lost three times while exploring and mapping in the rugged mountain ranges, and eventually fell into the hands of Spanish officials, who confiscated his papers. After briefly detaining the American lieutenant in Chihuahua, General Nemesio Salcedo allowed him to return to the United States in 1807; there he found himself suspected of complicity in the Burr conspiracy, which had broken into the open during his absence. Pike remained steadfastly loyal to his benefactor, but there is no evidence to suggest that he was knowingly complicit in Wilkinson's intrigues.[75]

Apart from military reconnaissance, Wilkinson's motives for dispatching Pike remain unclear. In many ways, the mission duplicated key aspects of the Freeman-Custis expedition, already on its way to explore the Red River. Some have suspected that Wilkinson intended to provoke the Spaniards and instigate a war that would provide cover for him to invade Mexico, but by the summer of 1806, the general appeared to be having second thoughts about the viability of the proposed filibuster. His long-standing desire to open a road to Santa Fe and tap the Spanish town's lucrative commercial potential figured prominently in his planning for Pike's expedition and perhaps provides the best indicator of his intentions.[76] To that end, Wilkinson had enlisted the services of John McClallen, a recently retired army captain with mercantile experience and access to eastern capital.[77] The governor was not the only one interested in venturing into the southwestern trade. In July 1806, Manuel Lisa and Jacques Clamorgan, prominent members of the St. Louis trading community, laid plans for outfitting an expedition to Santa Fe. When Lisa sought to have Baronet Vasquez detained for nonpayment of a debt, Pike believed that the move was intended to disrupt his expedition. When he found out about Lisa's meddling, Wilkinson posted security for the interpreter and arranged for Vasquez to rejoin Pike. Branding Lisa "a Black Spaniard" whose despicable intrigues endangered U.S. interests (and truth be told, his own), Wilkinson urged Pike to do whatever he could to defeat the plans of Lisa and Clamorgan.[78]

Lisa apparently got the message. By the following summer when the trading venture finally departed for Santa Fe, he uncharacteristically had disassociated himself from the project and redirected his sights to the Upper Missouri trade, no doubt in part because he did not wish to incur the governor's wrath any more than he already had. Clamorgan eventually made it to Chihuahua, where he sought the Spanish governor's permission to trade in Santa Fe, but the delay in his leave-taking had given Pike and McClallen the benefits of a head start.[79]

A few weeks after Pike's departure, McClallen had set out with a large stock of wares specifically selected for the Santa Fe market. Wilkinson had advised and encouraged the former army captain turned merchant to pursue the opportunities for trade in Spain's interior provinces. With Wilkinson's apparent concurrence, McClallen planned to follow Pike to Santa Fe. He had given Pike and his men a month's head start to allow them sufficient time to arrange for his peaceful passage through the region, but while McClallen's party was advancing up the Missouri, a courier from Pike brought news that dashed their prospects for joining forces. Given the amount of capital he had at risk, McClallen opted for an alternative course that eventually took him to the upper reaches of the Missouri, far from his intended destination.[80]

On August 16, 1806, a few short days before the departure of McClallen and company's star-crossed trading expedition, Wilkinson finally packed up and left St. Louis, never to return. His belated leave-taking had become a source of worry for his superiors in Washington. Concerned that a western conspiracy appeared to be afoot, they justifiably wondered what he was doing and why he had gone incommunicado.[81] Secretary Madison was among those who spied catastrophe, fearing that a combination of domestic and international threats might unleash chaos and deprive the United States of its new territory.[82] Tensions increased in July when more than a thousand Spanish troops crossed the Sabine River and moved in the direction of the U.S. outpost at Natchitoches. Wilkinson did not reach Natchez until September 7, fully four months after Dearborn had issued orders for him to report downriver. After a stopover in Natchez, he advanced to Natchitoches accompanied by a contingent of local militia but reassured the president that he would "drain the cup of conciliation to maintain the peace of our country."[83] The American show of force appeared to have some effect when Spain's military commander General Simon de Herrera y Leyva withdrew his forces from the disputed territories east of the Sabine.[84]

Wilkinson's prolonged silence that summer had concerned officials in Washington, but the absence of communication was equally alarming to Burr, who was conducting a second western excursion to recruit enlistees for his expeditionary force. On October 8, Burr's aide Samuel Swartwout finally caught up with Wilkinson at Natchitoches, where he handed the general a communication—written partly in cipher—informing him that their enterprise was already under way. Burr and the additional forces he picked up along the way expected to join Wilkinson in early December. A sentence declaring that Wilkinson would be second in command was probably jarring in two ways: it openly tied him to the plot, but it also consigned him to playing second fiddle. This put Wilkinson on notice that he soon would have to show his hand.[85]

In the nation's capital, the president summoned members of his cabinet to convene on October 22 to consider possible responses to the recent troop deployments along Louisiana's ill-defined borders, to assess reports of the former vice president's machinations to separate western states and territories from the United States, and, last but not least, to evaluate General Wilkinson's aberrant behavior and allegations linking him to Burr's treasonous project.[86] Gideon Granger, long a Wilkinson ally, initiated the discussion when he showed the president documents prepared by William Eaton, formerly a U.S. consul at Tunis, detailing Burr's schemes for revolutionizing the western country, creating an independent nation, and naming Wilkinson as Burr's chief lieutenant.[87] After placing these weighty issues on the table, the cabinet adjourned to reflect on them.

When they reconvened two days later, the president and his advisors were prepared to act. They unanimously agreed to dispatch captains Edward Prebel and Stephen Decatur to New Orleans to take command of the naval forces there, soon to be augmented with the transfer of gunboats from other U.S. ports. They also authorized John Graham, secretary of Orleans Territory, to make a reconnaissance through Kentucky for the purpose of gathering additional information about Burr's activities. They granted him discretionary powers to confer with area governors and to arrest the former vice president if he had made himself liable. Still pondering how to handle Wilkinson, Jefferson and his department heads postponed any decisions affecting the general pending receipt of additional information.[88]

New dispatches from the West proved reassuring. The threat of armed conflict seemed to have diminished, and no tangible evidence had yet surfaced that would sustain formal charges against Burr. These encouraging reports led the president to rescind the planned naval buildup at New Orleans and substitute the deployment of an additional marine detachment to the port city.[89] Notwithstanding the lessening of tensions, the ill-defined border separating Louisiana from Spain's territories to the west remained a potential flash point. As the two nations struggled to come to terms, representatives of the still-powerful indigenous inhabitants made it clear that they, too, had a stake in the game. Acting on his own, Wilkinson launched an initiative designed to avert renewed hostilities in the contested region. He joined Dehahuit, a Caddo chieftain, and Colonel Herrera for talks, and the unlikely trio hammered out an agreement signed on November 5, 1806, that created a buffer zone between Louisiana and Texas known as the Neutral Ground. The accord called for the area's closure to new white settlement and required the United States and Spain to stand down their armed forces in the region pending the negotiation of a final settlement between their respective governments. The unconventional arrangement made war between the United States and Spain far less likely and signaled Wilkinson's intention to part company with Burr.[90]

Unaware of the agreement, the president forwarded new orders on November 8 instructing Wilkinson to avoid hostilities with Spain if at all possible.[91] The general had guessed right, and his recent actions offered a perfect antidote to counter the allegations of his detractors. The accord also allowed the double-dealing agent to claim credit with his Spanish paymasters for having eliminated the likelihood of further intrusions into their domains. Aaron Burr clearly was the big loser, because the success of his filibuster depended on an outbreak of war between the United States and Spain.

While the general's decision to create the Neutral Ground clearly served America's vital national interests, labeling his actions heroic or patriotic would be erroneous. As with most things Wilkinson did, this was a calculated move intended to rescue his fortunes. Unnerved by the rising crescendo of public unease fueled by talk of treason and conspiracy, he sensed that support for a filibustering expedition was eroding. In a candid retrospective assessment, Jefferson advised Madison in 1811 that he had never doubted the course Wilkinson would choose: "Whatever previous communications might have passed between Burr & Wilkinson on the subject of Mexico, I believe, that on the part of the latter it was on the hypothesis of the approbation of the government. I never believed W. would give up a dependance on the government under whom he was the first, to become a secondary & dependant on Burr."[92] In making his bet, the president correctly calculated that the avaricious general was unlikely to forgo the certainty of his government sinecure and command status for the indeterminate rewards of a chancy Mexican filibuster.

Previous to his departure, Wilkinson had seen few indications of strong interest in St. Louis, and notwithstanding his public pronouncements, his private sources led him to believe that Burr was rallying fewer enlistees than first expected. Newspaper reports branding him Burr's coconspirator gave him added cause for concern. The way forward seemed clear—giving up Burr would prove his loyalty, counter accusations of his collusion, and transform him into a conquering hero riding to his country's rescue.

On October 20, he advised the president that a numerous and powerful association planned to take New Orleans with a force of eight or ten thousand followed by an expedition launched against Vera Cruz with British naval support. In an enclosure marked confidential, he feigned ignorance about the identity of the scheme's prime mover (a disclaimer that even the president must have found laughable) or the plotter's objectives, once the invading forces had taken New Orleans and overthrown the Mexican regime.[93]

Three weeks later, he informed Jefferson that he now could affirm that "a deep, dark and wicked conspiracy" threatened to shake the U.S. government's very foundation. He repeated his earlier warning that New Orleans and Vera Cruz were to be the conspirators' initial targets. Given the seriousness of the situation, he requested presidential authorization to place New Orleans under martial law.[94] Two days after receiving Wilkinson's latest warnings, the president issued a proclamation warning Americans not to involve themselves in the unlawful enterprise and cautioning that those who did would be subject to detention and prosecution.[95]

The reduction of tensions along the Sabine enabled General Wilkinson to return to Natchez to attend his ailing wife, but even her sad state could not deter him from one final attempt to extort his Spanish partners. In mid-November, he cautioned Mexico's viceroy, Jose de Iturrigaray, about the dangers of filibustering Americans bent on invading his country and overturning his government. Agent 13 boldly offered to help thwart the conspirators with his private means and without involving the U.S. government. Because he would be risking his life, his good name, and his property, he requested 121,000 Spanish dollars as compensation for his services. To ensure that his dispatches did not fall into the wrong hands, he sent his aide-de-camp Walter Burling to Mexico City to deliver them in person and to gather intelligence.[96]

Iturrigaray declined Wilkinson's offer of assistance and assured him that the Spanish government in Mexico was capable of repelling any such invasion on its own. The viceroy did forward a copy of the proposal to the foreign minister in Madrid, wryly noting that it contained the American agent's predictable request for a payment. Iturrigaray then burned the original. After years of dealing with their avaricious American partner, Spanish officials finally had Agent 13's real number.[97] Remarkably, Wilkinson successfully used Burling's information about conditions in Mexico to persuade U.S. officials to reimburse his expenditures for the mission.[98]

Once he turned on Burr, Wilkinson was left to fend off challenges from the numerous collaborators he had betrayed. In the past, when allegations of treason and money laundering were hurled in his direction, he had shown himself to be a master of evasion, but the current crisis called for more direct action. Upon his return to New Orleans, he trumpeted the imminent dangers posed by conspiratorial hordes about to descend on the city and disloyal elements that threatened New Orleans from within. To counter their threats and to divert attention from his own past indiscretions, Wilkinson instigated what Nancy Isenberg terms "a brief reign of terror," casting aside civil liberties; rounding up, detaining, and prosecuting former Burrite allies and friends; and intimidating members of the opposition press. His exaggerated rhetoric and extremist measures enabled him to discredit and marginalize enemies who might have become sources for his undoing.[99] Even the president considered Wilkinson's dire predictions overblown.[100] As Burr's filibuster slowly unraveled, fears of disloyalty and disunion gradually subsided. In fact, as Peter Kastor has noted, the Burr conspiracy afforded Louisianans and westerners alike with an unexpected opportunity to demonstrate their loyalty to the United States.[101]

Long after placing himself firmly in the camps of Jefferson and the United States, Wilkinson kept the lines of communication with his Spanish friends open. Even as he was ordering a roundup of suspected enemies in New Orleans, he passed along to Vicente Folch and Juan Ventura Morales the same information regarding Burr that he had conveyed previously to the U.S. president.[102] In a second letter, also dated December 6, Wilkinson assured Folch, "on the *honour of a Soldier,* that every arrangement making here is as well to *protect* the *Dominions* of *Spain* as to support the Government of the *United States* against its own *lawless Citizens.*"[103] He enclosed a copy of Jefferson's November 27 proclamation as further evidence of the U.S. government's good faith and his own continuing commitment to Spanish interests.[104] When a complicated set of circumstances landed Folch in New Orleans for a few days in late June, Wilkinson arranged a private meeting. He showed up carrying a bundle of papers carefully chosen to demonstrate his loyalty to both the cause of his country and Spain's true interests.

Still on the defensive against slanderous allegations at home, he asked Folch to help him discredit the persistent, albeit truthful, charges that he had held a commission and drawn a pension from the Spanish government. Eager not to air his nation's dirty linen in public, his friend complied, and the ruse held a bit longer.[105] Fears of exposure and ridicule haunted the image-conscious general to the end of his life, but for the moment he took comfort in knowing that the U.S. president was in his corner. Grateful for his apparent willingness to side with the U.S. government against Burr, the administration was prepared to give the veteran soldier every benefit of the doubt. In his quest to prosecute and exact revenge from his former vice president, Jefferson wedded himself to the dubious explanations of his star witness for better or worse.

Eager to buttress the case against Burr and extricate himself from the tangled web of conspiracy he had helped weave, Wilkinson followed up with the delivery of a doctored version of the July 29 cipher letter. Conveniently altered to disguise Wilkinson's involvement, the communication offered Jefferson and his team what they believed they needed to bring Burr down: its detailed itinerary for action appeared to give them the smoking gun. In the final months of 1806, Burr was a wanted man. Following failed attempts to arraign him in Kentucky and his exoneration by a grand jury in Mississippi Territory, the former vice president slipped away in disguise. Before he could escape unnoticed, someone spotted him and alerted U.S. military authorities, who arrested him near Fort Stoddard in Alabama on February 19, 1807. From there they sent him under military escort to Richmond, Virginia, for arraignment.[106]

Burr arrived in the state capital on March 26; following a preliminary hearing, federal officials summoned a grand jury to hear the evidence against him. The protracted proceedings attracted large crowds, but Wilkinson, the prosecution's star witness, did not show up until June 16. When he made his grand entry into a packed courtroom, attired in full military dress with sword swinging at his side, the writer Washington Irving likened him to a swelled turkey cock. To Wilkinson's chagrin, John Randolph, the brilliant but eccentric grand jury foreman, insisted that he remove his sword in the jury room. During four days of intense interrogation, he was forced to admit that he had altered a crucial piece of evidence—the ciphered letter of July 29. It almost seemed as if Wilkinson were the one on trial, and following the disclosure of his evidence tampering, the grand jurors narrowly rejected (by a vote of 7 to 9) foreman Randolph's motion to indict him for "misprision," that is, concealment, of treason.[107]

Wilkinson came away from his courtroom performance looking both foolish and complicit, but the grand jury found sufficient evidence to indict Burr on counts of treason and organizing a filibuster against Spain in peacetime. Wilkinson was spared the ordeal of testifying during the regular trial when Justice John Marshall ruled that the prosecution had failed to prove an overt act of war and halted its parade of witnesses before he was called to the stand. In conformity with the judge's ruling, the jury found Burr "not guilty" of treason. During a second trial a few days later on the separate misdemeanor count, jurors returned a similar verdict. Following Burr's acquittal, George Hay, the somewhat chastened lead prosecutor, advised the president that "he [Jefferson] had put too much faith in a faithless man," referring to Wilkinson.[108]

After the trial, many in the court of public opinion judged Wilkinson to have been no less guilty than Burr. As a result, Wilkinson was left to face a barrage of new accusations, with John Randolph leading the pack. When the Virginia congressman scorned Wilkinson's challenge to a duel, the irate general posted handbills about town denouncing his chief critic as "a prevaricating, base, calumniating scoundrel."[109] Randolph retaliated by initiating a congressional investigation to determine whether General Wilkinson had been on the payroll of the Spanish government while in the service of the United States. With evidence supplied by Daniel Clark, Jr., Wilkinson's friend turned accuser, Congress authorized the inquiry to proceed, but Wilkinson successfully preempted their efforts by demanding and receiving a military court of inquiry to consider the charges against him.

Fearful that a congressional investigation might become a tool for discrediting his administration, Jefferson sanctioned the court-martial in January 1808. The military proceeding dragged on for five months before the tribunal finally acquitted him; an affidavit from Governor Folch stating that the archives under his control contained no documents to suggest Wilkinson ever received a pension or salary from Spain had turned the tide in his favor. A few months later, Folch confided to

Wilkinson that he had sent all of the incriminating documents to Havana, where they were sure to remain out of reach until long after the principals involved had departed this world. Isaac Cox has suggested that as a quid pro quo Wilkinson had arranged for a shipment of flour to West Florida to offset the hardships caused by the American embargo.[110] Folch's testimony failed to dissuade Clark, however, who early the following year released his *Proofs of the Corruption of General James Wilkinson*. The war of words continued, and in 1811 Wilkinson countered with *Burr's Conspiracy Exposed and General Wilkinson Vindicated against the Slanders of His Enemies on That Important Occasion,* following it up five years later with his self-justifying *Memoirs*.

Wilkinson was in Washington when Zebulon Pike arrived back in Natchitoches on July 1, 1807, and shortly thereafter the returning explorer sent his mentor a lengthy account of his ordeal, along with other crucial information that he had collected during his tour.[111] The general, no doubt, took delight in Pike's report that Antonio Cordero, the governor of Texas, and his old friend General Simon de Herrera had received Pike warmly and offered toasts to Wilkinson. Equally pleasing was Pike's assessment that if Bonaparte occupied Spain both men would draw their swords in support of Mexican independence.[112]

In a shorter dispatch to Secretary Dearborn, Pike likened his surveys to those of Captains Lewis and Clark.[113] The Pacific Expedition's leaders had been making the rounds in Washington following their triumphal tour, and Pike longed for a similar reception. As with so many things, he was destined to be disappointed. His attempts to secure added compensation and land grants for himself and his "damned rascals" came to naught, and President Jefferson accorded him little notice apart from acknowledging the receipt of a pair of grizzly cubs, which Jefferson quickly shipped off to Peale's Museum in Philadelphia. Secretary Dearborn absolved Pike of any involvement in the Burr conspiracy, but otherwise, only the tarnished Wilkinson stood firmly in his corner.[114] Fortunately for Pike, Wilkinson retained sufficient clout to facilitate his advancement within the army's ranks. The War of 1812 offered Pike new opportunities to gain the recognition he coveted. Tragically, not long after his promotion to the rank of brigadier general in 1813, Pike fell in battle while leading an assault against Toronto (then known as York).[115]

The conflict that claimed Pike's life also contributed to the termination of his mentor's military career.

During the final months of the Jefferson administration, the deteriorating international situation placed increased demands on Wilkinson. Fears that the embargo might foment armed resistance along the Canadian border caused the War Department to order militia detachments to rendezvous in the contested zone. By late August 1808, growing complaints and the high costs of those military deployments had forced officials to reassess their decision to rely on militia. In Dearborn's absence, the president ordered Wilkinson to replace the northern militia detachments with three companies of new recruits recently raised in New York.[116] By year's end, the administration had shifted its focus southward and begun sending many of its new recruits to the gulf coast in anticipation of a possible British assault against New Orleans, where once again Wilkinson was placed in charge.

The ambitious general, who could never be satisfied monitoring routine troop deployments, turned his attention to the formulation of grandiose new schemes involving Spanish America. Predicting that Napoleon would soon ravage Spain and force its ancient nobility to flee abroad, he called upon Spain's representatives in the Americas to confer with him about the possible creation of hereditary constitutional monarchies independent of Spain and allied with the United States.[117] Wilkinson first broached the subject with Secretary Dearborn in a long rambling letter suggesting that liberating the American continents from the shackles of European governments would allow nations in the Western Hemisphere to form distinct communities united by bonds of friendship and mutual interests for the purpose of sustaining their common protection, defense, and happiness. To no one's surprise he singled himself out as the individual best qualified to approach hemispheric leaders. Lest his superiors fail to fully appreciate his sterling qualifications, he boasted that he was better known in Spanish America by name and by military character than was any other American, and he noted that his military identification was sure to impress leaders of their despotic governments.[118] Notwithstanding his recent embarrassments, Wilkinson clearly had no intention of retreating into obscurity. His bold plan anticipated some aspects of the Monroe Doctrine by fifteen years, and with the outgoing president's approval he scheduled brief visits in Havana and Pensacola during his return voyage to New Orleans. His well-laid plans for conferring with Spanish leaders came to naught, however, when his esteemed Hispanic acquaintances turned their collective backs on him, put off by his latest audacious proposals. Their displeasure, revealed in private correspondence, became clear to Wilkinson when he stopped in Pensacola to confer with Governor Folch, who chose to absent himself from the city.[119]

Jefferson's retirement to Monticello closed an important chapter in Wilkinson's life. The new president, James Madison, was even less accepting of the controversial general and more disposed to question his motives. With his principal protector now departed, Wilkinson's numerous critics felt emboldened to come after him, especially after his botched handling of the construction and oversight of a new military encampment outside of New Orleans at Terre aux Boeufs. When the installation turned into a death trap for the men stationed there, Wilkinson had to endure two additional congressional investigations and another court-martial. All eventually exonerated him, but pending their final verdicts President Madison temporarily suspended him from his command. The military tribunal rendered its "not guilty" verdict on December 25, 1811, but the president insisted on reviewing the panel's voluminous records and waited until the following February to sign off on the acquittal and restore Wilkinson to full command. Madison felt compelled to uphold the military's decision, but he took the unusual step of publicly stating that he found aspects of the general's conduct objectionable.[120]

Wilkinson resumed command in New Orleans a few short months before the outbreak of the War of 1812. Back in charge, he sparred with Andrew Jackson, commander of the Tennessee volunteers dispatched to supplement regular troops in the region.[121] The two men, who loathed each other, had no way of knowing the divergent paths their careers were about to take.

After receiving orders to take possession of the Spanish outpost at Mobile, Wilkinson and his forces successfully occupied the installation in April. In his lengthy army career, this was the sole military victory for which he could claim direct credit. Anxious not to burn his few remaining bridges with Spanish officials, Wilkinson was quick to notify Mauricio Zuniga, West Florida's last Spanish governor, that he was acting under orders from President Madison and had accomplished the task without "the effusion of a drop of Blood."[122]

Shortly thereafter Secretary of War John Armstrong advanced Wilkinson to the rank of major general and placed him in charge of a campaign on the northern frontier aimed at taking Montreal. The disastrous results in that arena caused him to lose his command post yet again and led to another court-martial. Although his fellow officers acquitted him, his army career was at an end.[123] He settled briefly in New Orleans, where, still seeking vindication, he wrote his *Memoirs*. He eventually took up residence in Mexico, lured by cheap land and an opportunity to reinvent himself one more time. He cast his lot with the supporters of the Emperor Augustin de Iturbide but quickly became disaffected with the inept emperor, whose abdication forced him to begin his quest anew. James Wilkinson died in Mexico City on December 28, 1825, at the age of sixty-eight, still seeking acceptance and absolution from Thomas Jefferson. That was not to be, but the deceased general surely would have taken delight in knowing that the U.S. ambassador and a future president of Mexico were among the mourners who came to pay their respects.[124]

Because Wilkinson was in many ways larger than life, one must guard against the temptation to overstate the significance of his dramatic deeds and misdeeds. He was neither a hero nor his country's savior, as he sometimes fancied himself, but neither was he sufficiently villainous to mastermind the alleged assassination of Meriwether Lewis, as the authors of a recent study of Lewis's death suggest.[125] Sadly, at his core he remained a two-timing scoundrel ready to sacrifice almost anything or anyone for profit and advancement, and even in his waning years, he seldom wandered far from that well-worn path. His decision to oppose Burr was at its root an act of self-preservation; had the deck been stacked differently, he might easily have chosen a different course.

Jefferson's interest in western exploration and Wilkinson's familiarity with the region had forged a curious partnership beneficial to both. That connection explains in part Jefferson's willingness to turn a blind eye to the general's well-documented shortcomings. But even in their collaborative efforts, Jefferson sought to keep his western agent at arm's length. His ambivalence about Wilkinson likely dated from his days as secretary of state when President Washington had characterized the general as "Brave—enterprising to excess, but many unapprovable points in his character."[126]

Jefferson's resolve to bring down Burr drew him closer to Wilkinson, but only temporarily. In retirement the sage of Monticello paid scant heed to communications from the flawed and aging soldier who had served him. That was unusual for someone who spent endless hours drafting replies to correspondents, including many unknown to him. Common courtesy did prompt Jefferson to acknowledge receipt of a copy of Wilkinson's *Memoirs,* but on other occasions he simply filed away the general's plaintive letters unanswered. He did interrupt his silence to seek Wilkinson's assistance in countering allegations contained in the posthumous edition of Alexander Wilson's *Ornithology* suggesting that he had rejected the renowned scientist's request for employment on Zebulon Pike's southwestern expedition. Thrilled to hear from his former benefactor, Wilkinson readily absolved the president of any responsibility for the decision. In a letter laden with effusive praise, he informed the elder statesman, "I perceive with great pleasure, that the chaste harmony which has distinguished your Pen above all others of our Country continues unimpaired; and with equal satisfaction do I receive the testimony of approbation & esteem which it conveys, to an humble but faithful Citizen, who has been illy requited for his toils sufferings & sacrifices in the public Service."[127] His classic over-the-top prose unfortunately failed to rekindle their dormant relationship. A year before his death, Wilkinson wrote Jefferson twice, but the former president chose not to reply.[128]

Declining health was not the sole reason for Jefferson's failure to respond. The ex-president tipped his hand in an 1812 letter he wrote to his friend and neighbor James Monroe when reports reached him that Wilkinson might make an attempt to employ them as witnesses in his ongoing campaign to clear his name. Jefferson candidly acknowledged his reticence to express any opinion about General Wilkinson save on the subject of his actions in the Burr conspiracy. For that alone was he willing to go on the record, declaring that "after he [Wilkinson] had got over his first agitations we believed his decision firm & his conduct zealous for the defeat of the conspiracy." In all other disputations concerning Wilkinson, the sage of Monticello counted himself as neither a friend nor an enemy and opted to leave it to others to make the call. Jefferson's refusal to say more about his controversial western point man even at that late date speaks volumes to the complexities of their relationship.[129]

## ACKNOWLEDGMENTS

I am grateful for the assistance of Jay Buckley, George Ryscamp, Doug Inglis, and Joseph Sanchez for helping secure documents from the Archivo General de Indias in Seville, Spain.

## NOTES

1. In a letter to Louisiana's Spanish governor, the marques de Casa Calvo, Wilkinson advised him, "The changes in the administration of my Country render my future destination uncertain, but be it what or where it may, you will live in my remembrance & share my affections." James Wilkinson to marques de Casa Calvo, June 26, 1800, Archivo General de Indias (hereafter AGI) Papeles Procedentes de Cuba (hereafter PC), legajo 2375, Seville, Spain.

2. James Wilkinson to Thomas Jefferson, November 29, 1800, Thomas Jefferson Papers, Library of Congress (hereafter LC). Two years earlier, Wilkinson and Jefferson had been named as members of a committee on antiquities at the American Philosophical Society. Broadside 207 in APS online Digital Collections, http://cdm.amphilsoc.org/cdm4/browse.php?CISOROOT=/broadsides&CISOSTART=1,41.

3. Theodore J. Crackel, *Mr. Jefferson's Army: Political and Social Reform of the Military Establishment, 1801–1809* (New York: New York University Press, 1987), 14 and 36–43; Francis Peyton to Thomas Jefferson, March 13, 1801, in *The Papers of Thomas Jefferson*, ed. Barbara B. Oberg (Princeton: Princeton University Press, 2006), 33:271.

4. In June 1801, Andrew Ellicott sent the president a letter outlining Wilkinson's Spanish connections, along with supporting documentation. See Linklater, *Artist in Treason*, 193. In the same month, Jefferson received an anonymous letter from "A Kentucky Citizen" that contained a similar warning about Wilkinson. See "From 'A Kentucky Citizen,'" June 1801, and Hugh Henry Brackenridge to Thomas Jefferson, February 17, 1801, both in Oberg, *Papers of Thomas Jefferson*, 33:4–6 and 456. In his biography, Linklater credits Wilkinson with keeping the army under control and saving the young American republic from the ordeal of a military coup. Although Wilkinson was a crucial

figure in shaping the role of the military, Linklater's assertion that "at a crucial moment Wilkinson single-handedly possessed enough power to decide the fate of the nation" seems a bit of an overreach. Linklater, *Artist in Treason,* 194.

5.  Crackel, *Mr. Jefferson's Army,* 92.

6.  *Annals of Congress,* 11th Cong., 2nd sess., 1810, 2348–60.

7.  Jefferson to Samuel Smith, March 24, 1801, in Oberg, *Papers of Thomas Jefferson,* 33:439.

8.  *American State Papers, Indian Affairs,* http://international.loc.gov/ammem/amlaw/lwsplink.html, 1:648–53, 658–63, 669–85, and 690–93.

9.  Samuel Smith to Jefferson, June 21, 1802, Jefferson Papers, LC; James Jackson to Jefferson, January 9, 1803, and Joseph Anderson to Jefferson, January 10, 1803, both in Letters of Application and Recommendation during the Administration of Thomas Jefferson, National Archives, Washington, D.C. (hereafter NA).

10.  Notation on letter from Samuel Smith to Henry Dearborn, May 30, 1802, cited in Jacobs, *Tarnished Warrior,* 199.

11.  James Wilkinson, *Memoirs of My Own Times* (1816; repr., New York: AMS, 1973), 1:vii.

12.  Wilkinson to Jacob Kingsbury, February 27, 1803, cited in Crackel, *Mr. Jefferson's Army,* 102.

13.  Pierre Clement Laussat to duc Denis Decres, April 7, 1804, in Robertson, *Louisiana,* 2:53.

14.  Kukla, *Wilderness So Immense,* 319–22.

15.  For an analysis of the complex circumstances facing American officials in Louisiana following the transfer, see Kastor, *Nation's Crucible.*

16.  Gayoso, a former governor of Louisiana, had been Wilkinson's trusted confidant, and the nephew was well aware of their closeness.

17.  Cox, "General Wilkinson," 795.

18.  Ibid., 795–96.

19.  Ibid., 796–98. According to Austin Travis Wheeler, Wilkinson employed the numeral "73" to identify himself in the cipher he used in his communications with Spanish officials prior to 1800. Readers of his script mistakenly identified the seven as a one, and he came to be known as Agent 13. See Wheeler, "The Scandalous General James Wilkinson and His Connections with the Spanish, Aaron Burr and Daniel Clark," M.A. thesis, Texas Tech University, 2009, 17–20.

20.  Cox, "General Wilkinson," 800.

21.  "Reflections" [February 1804], in Robertson, *Louisiana,* 339–47. Robertson incorrectly attributed the document's authorship to Folch.

22.  Ibid.

23.  Ibid., 343.

24.  Wilkinson to Dearborn, March 30, 1804, Secretary of War, Letters Received, NA.

25.  In seeking the meeting, Wilkinson wrote, "To save time of which I need much and have but little, I propose to take a Bed with you this night, if it may be done without observation or intrusion—Answer me and if in the affirmative I will be with [you] at 30"

after the 8th Hour." Wilkinson to Burr, May 23, 1804, *American Antiquarian Society Proceedings* 29 (1919): 122–23; and Isenberg, *Fallen Founder,* 287. Their friendship predated these clandestine meetings. Ten months later, Burr referred to Wilkinson as "long my intimate friend." Burr to Rufus Easton, March 18, 1805, Rufus Easton Papers, Missouri History Museum Archives (hereafter MHMA), St. Louis.

26. Wilkinson to Dearborn, July 13, 1804, cited in Dan Flores, *Jefferson and Southwestern Exploration: The Freeman and Custis Accounts of the Red River Expedition of 1806* (Norman: University of Oklahoma Press, 1984), 80–81.

27. Jefferson to baron von Humboldt, May 28, 1804; Wilkinson to Jefferson, June 11, 1804; and James Wilkinson's Queries, June 11, 1804, all in Jefferson Papers, LC; Thomas Jefferson to Alexander von Humboldt, June 9, 1804, in *The Writings of Jefferson,* vol. 11, ed. Andrew A. Lipscomb and Albert Ellery Bergh (Washington, D.C.: Thomas Jefferson Memorial Association, 1904–1905), 27; Jackson, *Journals of Pike,* 2:368–69 and 370n1; and Linklater, *Artist in Treason,* 211–12.

28. Cox, "General Wilkinson," 801.

29. For the story of efforts to extend republican government into Upper Louisiana, see William E. Foley, *The Genesis of Missouri: From Wilderness Outpost to Statehood* (Columbia: University of Missouri Press, 1989), 147–58. The Territory of Louisiana encompassed the areas north of the thirty-third parallel. The lower portions were known as the Territory of Orleans.

30. Clarence E. Carter suggested that Jefferson catered to Burr's whims to secure his cooperation in Judge Samuel Chase's pending impeachment trial. Jefferson also appointed Burr's brother-in-law Joseph Browne to serve as Louisiana's territorial secretary. Carter, "Burr-Wilkinson Intrigue," 448. Postmaster Gideon Granger was another Wilkinson backer. In a letter to his friend, Rufus Easton Granger described Wilkinson as "one of the most agreeable, best informed, most genteel, moderate and sensible republicans in the nation." Granger to Easton, March 15, 1805, Easton Papers, MHMA.

31. Jefferson to Joseph Anderson, December 28, 1805, Jefferson Papers, LC.

32. The Ohio River fort was located in Illinois Territory.

33. Thomas P. Abernethy lays out the case for conspiracy in *The Burr Conspiracy,* but in *Fallen Founder* Nancy Isenberg argues convincingly that Burr was not intent on dividing the United States and that his plans for a Mexican filibuster were not treasonous.

34. James Adair to Wilkinson, December 1804, quoted in Cox, "Opening the Santa Fe Trail," 37–38.

35. Jacobs, *Tarnished Warrior,* 217–18.

36. Wilkinson to Dearborn, June 13, 1805, in *Letters of the Lewis and Clark Expedition,* ed. Donald Jackson (Urbana: University of Illinois Press, 1978), 2:690.

37. Wilkinson to Dearborn, June 27, July 27, and September 8, 1805, in Carter, *Territorial Papers,* vol. 13, *Louisiana-Missouri, 1803–1806,* 144–45, 164–65, and 204–205; and William E. Foley and C. David Rice, *The First Chouteaus: River Barons of Early St. Louis* (Urbana: University of Illinois Press, 1983), 116.

38. Wilkinson to Citizens of St. Louis, July 3, 1805, in Carter, *Territorial Papers,* vol. 13, *Louisiana-Missouri, 1803–1806,* 149–51.

39. Wilkinson to Dearborn, July 27, 1805, in ibid., 167–68.

40. Ibid., 169.

41. Wilkinson to Pierre Chouteau, July 30, 1805, in ibid., 184; and Foley and Rice, *First Chouteaus,* 117–18.

42. Wilkinson to Zebulon Pike, July 30, 1805, in Jackson, *Journals of Pike,* 1:3–4.

43. Flores, *Jefferson and Southwestern Exploration,* 79–80.

44. Rufus Easton to [Gideon Granger], February 17 and June 18, 1807, Easton Papers, MHMA.

45. Wilkinson to Dearborn, September 8, 1805, in Carter, *Territorial Papers,* vol. 13, *Louisiana-Missouri, 1803–1806,* 199; Gary Moulton, ed., *The Definitive Journals of Lewis and Clark,* vol. 9, *John Ordway and Charles Floyd* (Lincoln: University of Nebraska Press, 1995), journal of John Ordway, August 21, 1806; and John C. Jackson, *By Honor and Right: How One Man Boldly Defined the Destiny of a Nation* (Amherst, N.Y.: Prometheus Books, 2010), 69, 125, and 296n15.

46. Wilkinson to Dearborn, September 8, 1805, in Carter, *Territorial Papers,* vol. 13, *Louisiana-Missouri, 1803–1806,* 199; and Jackson, *By Honor and Right,* 79–80.

47. Wilkinson to Dearborn, July 27 and October 8, 1805, in Carter, *Territorial Papers,* vol. 13, *Louisiana-Missouri, 1803–1806,* 165–66 and 235–36; and Wilkinson to Dearborn, September 8, 1805, in Jackson, *Journals of Pike,* 2:100–101. For the growing Spanish concerns about U.S. encroachment, see Nemesio Salcedo to Joaquin del Real Alencaster, September 9, 1805, and October 2, 1805, and Nemesio Salcedo to the marques de Casa Calvo, October 8, 1805, in Jackson, *Journals of Pike,* 2:104–108, 110–11, and 111–12.

48. Burr to William H. Harrison, October 24, 1806, quoted in Flores, *Jefferson and Southwestern Exploration,* 81n123.

49. Wilkinson to Dearborn, September 8, 1805; Merchants of St. Louis to Wilkinson, August 24, 1805; and Fur Trade Regulations, August 26, 1805; all in Carter, *Territorial Papers,* vol. 13, *Louisiana-Missouri, 1803–1806,* 196–200 and 202–203.

50. Wilkinson to Dearborn, August 10, September 22, and October 8, 1805, in ibid., 183, 229–30, and 234; *U.S. v. Ouipinicaka* and *U.S. v. Oaubesca,* May Term 1806, Missouri Supreme Court Case Files, Box 48, Folder 1, and Box 8, Folder 15, Missouri State Archives, Jefferson City.

51. Wilkinson to Madison, August 24, 1805, in ibid., 189–90; and Moses Austin to Gallatin [August 1806?], in *The Austin Papers,* ed. Eugene C. Barker, Annual Report of the American Historical Association for the Year 1919, 2 vols. (Washington, D.C.: Government Printing Office, 1924), 1:122.

52. Foley, *Genesis of Missouri,* 165–66.

53. Dearborn to Wilkinson, April 19, 1805, in Carter, *Territorial Papers,* vol. 13, *Louisiana-Missouri, 1803–1806,* 117.

54. Wilkinson to Dearborn, August 10, September 22, October 8, and October 22, 1805, and Wilkinson to Samuel Smith, March 29, 1806, in ibid., 182–83, 229, 234–36, 244, and 466–67.

55. Dearborn to Wilkinson, November 2, 1805, in ibid., 251–52.

56. Wilkinson to Dearborn, December 10, 1805, in ibid., 297–98.

57. Dearborn to Wilkinson, November 21, 1805, in ibid., 290. For Hunt's charges and Wilkinson's defense, see Wilkinson to Samuel Smith, March 29, 1806, in ibid., 466–67.

58. Wilkinson to Dearborn, December 30, 1805, in ibid., 355–59. He specifically asked that his letter be shown to the president.

59. Wilkinson to Dearborn, December 31, 1805, in ibid., 368–70 (emphasis in original).

60. Dearborn to Wilkinson, February 10, 1806, in ibid., 442.

61. Lucas to Gallatin, November 19, 1805, in ibid., 286.

62. Edward Hempstead to Stephen Hempstead, November 30, 1805, in Hempstead Papers, MHMA.

63. Memorial to the President by Citizens of the Territory, December 27, 1805, in Carter, *Territorial Papers*, vol. 13, *Louisiana-Missouri, 1803–1806*, 329–51.

64. Joseph Anderson to Jefferson, December 26, 1805, in Letters of Application and Recommendation during the Jefferson administration, NA.

65. Carter, *Territorial Papers*, vol. 13, *Louisiana-Missouri, 1803 1806*, 421n78. The vote was 17–14.

66. Wilkinson to Jefferson, March 29, 1806, Jefferson Papers, LC.

67. Joseph H. Daveiss to Jefferson, January 10, 1806, and Jefferson to Daveiss, February 15, 1806, ibid.

68. Gallatin to Jefferson, February 12, 1806, ibid.

69. Wilkinson to Jefferson, March 29, 1806, and Wilkinson to Samuel Smith, March 29, 1806, ibid.

70. Jefferson to Samuel Smith, May 4, 1806, and Dearborn to Wilkinson, May 6, 1806, ibid.

71. Many of the stories emanated from the *Western World*, a notorious Kentucky rag.

72. Wilkinson to Dearborn, June 17, 1806, and Wilkinson to Samuel Smith, June 17, 1806, Jefferson Papers, LC. Matthew Lyon, a Kentucky congressman, had suggested military reassignment as a way to remove the controversial territorial governor less than two weeks before Dearborn acted. Lyon to Jefferson, April 22, 1806, ibid.

73. Wilkinson to Samuel Smith, June 17, 1806, ibid. Jefferson's phrase is cited in James P. Ronda, "A Moment in Time: The West—September, 1806," in Ronda, *Finding the West: Explorations with Lewis and Clark* (Albuquerque: University of New Mexico Press, 2001), 79.

74. See Donald Jackson, *Thomas Jefferson and the Stony Mountains: Exploring the West from Monticello* (Urbana: University of Illinois Press, 1981), 250–54; and Jackson, *Journals of Pike*.

75. Jackson, *Thomas Jefferson and the Stony Mountains*, 250–54.

76. Flores, *Jefferson and Southwestern Exploration*, 288–90.

77. Jackson, *By Honor and Right*, 84–96.

78. Richard E. Oglesby, *Manuel Lisa and the Opening of the Missouri Fur Trade* (Norman: University of Oklahoma Press, 1963), 35–37; and Wilkinson to Pike, August 6, 1806, in Jackson, *Journals of Pike*, 2:134.

79. Oglesby, *Manuel Lisa*, 36 and 39. Clamorgan made it to Chihuahua, where he sought permission from the Spanish governor to trade with Santa Fe.

80. See Jackson, *By Honor and Right*.

81. Joseph Browne to Madison, August 26, 1806, in Carter, *Territorial Papers*, vol. 14, *Louisiana-Missouri, 1806–1814,* 3. Dearborn advised the president on August 31 that Wilkinson was still in St. Louis on July 28 even though he had promised to be at Fort Adams no later than July 25; see ibid., 3n1.

82. Kastor, *Nation's Crucible*, 2–3.

83. Wilkinson to Dearborn, September 8, 1806, in Wilkinson, *Memoirs*, vol. 2, appendix doc. 60.

84. Wilkinson to Dearborn, October 4, 1806, cited in Walter F. McCaleb, *The Aaron Burr Conspiracy*, rev. ed. (New York: Wilson-Erickson, 1936), 118.

85. A deciphered version of the July 29 letter to Wilkinson is found in ibid., 68–69. For a discussion of the letter and its authenticity, see Isenberg, *Fallen Founder*, 312–13.

86. Minutes of cabinet meeting, October 22, 1806, in Lipscomb and Berg, *Writings of Thomas Jefferson*, 1:458–61.

87. Louis B. Wright and Julia H. Macleod, "William Eaton's Relations with Aaron Burr," *Mississippi Valley Historical Review* 31 (March 1945): 528.

88. Minutes of cabinet meeting, October 24, 1806, in Lipscomb and Berg, *Writings of Thomas Jefferson*, 1:462.

89. Minutes of cabinet meeting, October 25, 1806, in ibid.

90. Kastor, *Nation's Crucible*, 68–69.

91. Instructions for General Wilkinson, November 8, 1806, Jefferson Papers, LC.

92. Jefferson to Madison, April 7, 1811, in *The Papers of Thomas Jefferson, Retirement Series*, ed. J. Jefferson Looney (Princeton: Princeton University Press, 2006), 3:543.

93. Wilkinson to Jefferson, October 20 and 21, 1806, in Wilkinson, *Memoirs*, vol. 2, appendix doc. 95.

94. Wilkinson to Jefferson, November 12, 1806, in ibid., vol. 2, appendix doc. 100.

95. Presidential Proclamation, November 27, 1806, in ibid., vol. 2, appendix doc. 96.

96. Wilkinson to Iturrigaray, November 17, 1806, reprinted in *The American Historical Review* 9 (April 1940): 533–37.

97. Iturrigaray to Pedro Cevallos, March 12, 1807, in McCaleb, *Aaron Burr Conspiracy*, 144–45.

98. Flores, *Jefferson and Southwestern Exploration*, 287n13.

99. Isenberg, *Fallen Founder*, 313–16.

100. Jefferson to Wilkinson, January 3, 1807, Jefferson Papers, LC.

101. Kastor, *Nation's Crucible*, 137–38.

102. Wilkinson to Folch and Wilkinson to Folch and Morales, December 6, 1806, AGI, PC, legajo 2375.

103. Wilkinson to Folch, December 6, 1806, ibid. (emphasis in original).

104. Wilkinson to Folch, January 3, 5, and March 31, 1807, ibid.

105. Wilkinson to Folch, June 25, 1807, ibid.; and Vicente Folch to marquis de Someruelos, June 25, 1807, reprinted in *American Historical Review* 10 (July 1905): 837–40.

106. Isenberg, *Fallen Founder,* 309–11 and 319–23.

107. Ibid., 347–49.

108. Hay to Jefferson, October 15, 1807, Jefferson Papers, LC.

109. Linklater, *Artist in Treason,* 276.

110. Ibid., 277; and Cox, "General Wilkinson," 807–808.

111. Pike to Wilkinson, July 5, 1807, in Jackson, *Journals of Pike,* 2:238–44.

112. Ibid., 1:438 and 441.

113. Pike to Dearborn, July 15, 1807, in ibid., 2:249–50.

114. Dearborn to Pike, February 24, 1808, in ibid., 2:300–301.

115. Pike to Jefferson, [October 29, 1807], in ibid., 2:275–76; and Jackson, *Thomas Jefferson and the Stony Mountains,* 259–62.

116. Jefferson to Wilkinson, August 30, 1808, Jefferson Papers, LC.

117. Wilkinson to Folch, August 25 and December 30, 1808, AGI, PC, legajo 2375; and Wilkinson to Simon Herrera, October 12, 1808, Jefferson Papers, LC.

118. Wilkinson to Dearborn, October 1, 1808, Jefferson Papers, LC.

119. Linklater, *Artist in Treason,* 283–84; and Wilkinson to Folch, April 9, 1809, AGI, PC, legajo 2375.

120. Madison to Jefferson, February 7, 1812, in Looney, *Papers of Thomas Jefferson,* 4:480 and 481n.

121. Robert Remini, *Andrew Jackson and the Course of American Empire, 1767–1821* (New York: Harper and Row, 1977), 150 and 175–76.

122. Wilkinson to Zuniga, April 13, 1813, AGI, PC, legajo 2375; and David Stephen Heidler and Jeanne T. Heidler, *Encyclopedia of the War of 1812* (ABC-Clio Electronic Resource, 1997), 554–55.

123. Heidler and Heidler, *Encyclopedia,* 554–55.

124. Linklater, *Artist in Treason,* 328.

125. James E. Starrs and Kira Gale, *The Death of Meriwether Lewis: A Historic Crime Scene Investigation* (Omaha, Neb.: River Junction Press, 2009), 353.

126. *Complete Anas of Thomas Jefferson,* ed. Franklin B. Sawvel (New York: Round Table Press, 1903), 61.

127. Jefferson to Wilkinson, June 25, 1818, and Wilkinson to Jefferson, August 4, 1818, in Jackson, *Journals of Pike,* 2:388–89 and 389–91.

128. Wilkinson to Jefferson, March 21, 1824, and July 20, 1824, Jefferson Papers, LC.

129. Jefferson to Monroe, January 11 or 12, 1812, Jefferson Papers, LC.

# Selected Bibliography

## PRIMARY SOURCES

Bolton, Herbert E., ed. "Papers of Zebulon M. Pike, 1806–1807." *American Historical Review* 13 (July 1908): 798–827.

Carpenter, T. *The Trial of Colonel Aaron Burr on an Indictment of Treason.* Washington, D.C.: Westcott, 1808.

Carter, Clarence E., ed. *The Territorial Papers of the United States,* vol. 9, *The Territory of Orleans, 1803 1811.* Washington, D.C.: Government Printing Office, 1940.

———. *The Territorial Papers of the United States,* vol. 13, *The Territory of Louisiana-Missouri, 1803–1806.* Washington, D.C.: Government Printing Office, 1948.

———. *The Territorial Papers of the United States,* vol. 14, *The Territory of Louisiana-Missouri, 1806–1814.* Washington, D.C.: Government Printing Office, 1949.

Clark, Daniel. *Proofs of the Corruption of Gen. James Wilkinson, and of His Connexion with Aaron Burr, with a Full Refutation of His Slanderous Allegations in Relation to the Character of the Principal Witness against Him.* Philadelphia: William Hall, Jr., and George W. Pierre, 1809.

Coues, Elliot, ed. *The Expeditions of Zebulon Montgomery Pike, to Headwaters of the Mississippi River, through Louisiana Territory, and in New Spain, during the Years 1805-6-7.* 3 vols. New York: Francis P. Harper, 1895.

Davis, Matthew L., comp. *Memoirs of Aaron Burr.* 2 vols. New York: Harper and Brothers, 1807.

Fitch, Raymond E., ed. *Breaking with Burr: Harman Blennerhassett's Journal, 1807.* Athens: Ohio University Press, 1988.

Hart, Stephen Harding, and Archer Butler Hulbert, eds. *The Southwestern Journals of Zebulon Pike, 1806–1807.* 1932. Reprint, with introduction by Mark L. Gardiner, Albuquerque: University of New Mexico Press, 2006.

Holton, Amos. *The Case of Mrs. Clara H. Pike, Widow of Gen. Z. Montgomery Pike: Now Pending before the U.S. Congress, with Some Extracts from Her Letters, Pertaining . . . of Louisiana, in the Years 1805, '6 and '7.* Washington, D.C.: T. Barnard Printer, 1846.

Jackson, Donald, ed. *The Journals of Zebulon Montgomery Pike, with Letters and Related Documents.* 2 vols. Norman: University of Oklahoma Press, 1966.

Jenkins, John S. *Daring Deeds of American Generals.* New York: A. A. Kelley, 1857.

Kline, Mary-Jo., ed. *Political Correspondence and Public Papers of Aaron Burr.* 2 vols. Princeton: Princeton University Press, 1983.

*Life of General Jacob Brown: To Which Are Added Memoirs of Generals Ripley and Pike.* New York: Nafis and Cornish, 1847.

Nile, John M. *The Life of Oliver Hazard Perry: With an Appendix, Comprising Biographical Sketches of the Late General Pike and Captain Lawrence, and a View of the Present Condition and Future Prospects of the Navy of the United States.* Hartford, Conn.: W. S. Marsh, 1820.

Pike, Zebulon M. *An Account of Expeditions to the Sources of the Mississippi, and through the Western Parts of Louisiana, to the Sources of the Arkansaw, Kans, La Platte, and Pierre Jaun Rivers; Performed by Order of the United States during the Years 1805, 1806, and 1807; and a Tour of the Interior Parts of New Spain, When Conducted through These Provinces, by Order of the Captain-General, in the Year 1807.* Philadelphia: Cornelius and Andrew Conrad and Co., 1810.

———. *Exploratory Travels through the Western Territories of North America: Comprising a Voyage from St. Louis, on the Mississippi, to the Source of that River, and a Journey through the Interior of Louisiana, and the North-Eastern Provinces of New Spain; Performed in the Years 1805, 1806, 1807, by Order of the Government of the United States.* Philadelphia: C. and A. Conrad and Co., 1810.

Quaife, Milo Milton, ed. *The Southwestern Expedition of Zebulon M. Pike.* Chicago: R. R. Donnelley and Sons, 1925.

Robertson, James A., ed. *Louisiana under the Rule of Spain, France, and the United States, 1785–1807.* 2 vols. 1910. Reprint, Freeport, N.Y.: Books for Libraries Press, 1969.

U.S. House of Representatives. "Report of the Committee Appointed on the Fifteenth Ultimo, to Inquire What Compensation Ought to Be Made to Captain Zebulon M. Pike, and His Companions. December 16, 1808." 10th Congress, 2nd sess., 1808–1809. Washington City: A. and G. Way, 1808.

———. *Report of the Committee Appointed to Inquire into the Conduct of General James Wilkinson, Ezekiel Bacon, Chairman.* Washington City: n.p., 1811.

Wilkinson, James. *Burr's Conspiracy Exposed and General Wilkinson Vindicated against the Slanders of His Enemies on That Important Occasion.* Washington, D.C., 1811.

———. *Memoirs of My Own Times.* 3 vols. Philadelphia: Abraham Small, 1816.

Wright, Nathaniel H. *Monody, on the Death of Brigadier General Zebulon Montgomery Pike; and Other Poems.* Middlebury, Vt.: Slade and Ferguson, 1814.

## SECONDARY SOURCES

### Articles

Allen, John Logan. "The Garden-Desert Continuum: Competing Views of the Great Plains in the Nineteenth Century." *Great Plains Quarterly* 5 (1985): 207–20.

Bierck, Harold A., Jr. "Dr. John Hamilton Robinson." *Louisiana Historical Quarterly* 25 (1942): 644–69.

Bolton, Herbert E. "Papers of Zebulon M. Pike, 1806–1807." *American Historical Review* 13 (July 1908): 798–827.

Boyd, Julian P. "Thomas Jefferson's 'Empire of Liberty.'" *Virginia Quarterly Review* 24 (1948): 538–54.

Carter, Clarence E. "The Burr-Wilkinson Intrigue in St. Louis." *Bulletin of the Missouri Historical Society* 10 (July 1954): 447–64.

Carter, Harvey L. "A Soldier with Pike Tried for Murder." *Colorado Magazine* 33 (1956): 218–34.

Castel, Albert. "Zebulon Pike, Explorer." *American History Illustrated* 7, no. 2 (1972): 4–11, 45–48.

Cox, Isaac J. "General Wilkinson and His Later Intrigues with the Spanish." *American Historical Review* 19 (July 1914): 794–812.

———. "The Louisiana-Texas Frontier." *Texas State Historical Quarterly* 10 (July 1906): 1–57.

———. "Opening the Santa Fe Trail." *Missouri Historical Review* 25 (October 1930): 30–66.

Crichton, Kyle S. "Zeb Pike." *Scribner's Magazine* 82 (October 1927): 462–67.

Foley, William E. "James A. Wilkinson: Territorial Governor." *Bulletin of the Missouri Historical Society* 25 (October 1968): 3–17.

Furstenberg, Francois. "The Significance of the Trans-Appalachian Frontier in Atlantic History." *American Historical Review* 113 (June 2008): 647–77.

Gamble, Judith. "Pike and His Peak." *Colorado Heritage* 3 (1989): 43–47.

Hafen, LeRoy R. "Zebulon Montgomery Pike." *Colorado Magazine* 8 (July 1931): 132–42.

Haggard, J. Villasana. "The Neutral Ground between Louisiana and Texas, 1806–1821." *Louisiana Historical Quarterly* 28 (October 1945): 1001–1028.

Hollon, W. Eugene. "Zebulon Montgomery Pike and the Wilkinson-Burr Conspiracy." *Proceedings of the American Philosophical Society* 91 (1947): 447–56.

———. "Zebulon Montgomery Pike's Lost Papers." *Mississippi Valley Historical Review* 34 (September 1947): 265–73.

Horsman, Reginald. "The Dimensions of an 'Empire for Liberty': Expansionism and Republicanism, 1775–1825." *Journal of the Early Republic* 9 (Spring 1989): 1–20.

Hyslop, Stephen G. "An Explorer or a Spy?" *American History* 37, no. 3 (2002): 58–64.

———. "One Nation among Many: The Origins and Objectives of Pike's Southwest Expedition." *Kansas History: A Journal of the Central Plains* 29, no. 1 (Spring 2006): 2–13.

Jackson, Donald. "The Question Is: How Lost Was Zebulon Pike?" *American Heritage Magazine* 16, no. 2 (February 1965): 11–15, 75–80.

———. "Zebulon Pike: The Poor Man's Lewis and Clark." *We Proceeded On* (October 1978): 6–9.

———. "Zebulon Pike and Nebraska." *Nebraska History* 47, no. 4 (1966): 355–69.

———. "Zebulon Pike's Damned Rascals." In *Thomas Jefferson and the Rocky Mountains: Exploring the West from Monticello,* 242–67. 1981. Reprint, Norman: University of Oklahoma Press, 2002.

———. "Zebulon Pike 'Tours' Mexico." *American West* 3, no. 3 (1966): 67–71, 89–93.

Laugesen, Amanda. "Making a Unique Heritage: Celebrating Pike's Pawnee Village and the Santa Fe Trail, 1900–1918." *Kansas History* 23, no. 3 (2000): 172–85.

Lewis, G. Malcolm. "Early American Exploration and the Cis–Rocky Mountain Desert, 1803–1823." *Great Plains Journal* 5, no. 1 (1965): 1–11.

———. "Three Centuries of Desert Concepts in the Cis–Rocky Mountain West." *Journal of the West* 4, no. 3 (1965): 457–68.

Munday, Frank J. "Pike-Pawnee Village Site: Review and Summary of the Evidence for the Case." *Nebraska History* 10 (1927): 168–92.

Narrett, David E. "Liberation and Conquest: John Hamilton Robinson and U.S. Adventurism toward Mexico, 1806–1819." *Western Historical Quarterly* 40, no. 1 (Spring 2009): 23–50.

Nichols, Roger L. "The Army and Early Perceptions of the Plains." *Nebraska History* 56, no. 1 (1975): 121–35.

Oliva, Leo E. "Enemies and Friends: Zebulon Montgomery Pike and Facundo Melgares in the Competition for the Great Plains, 1806–1807." *Kansas History: A Journal of the Central Plains* 29, no. 1 (Spring 2006): 34–47.

Olsen, Michael L. "Zebulon Pike and American Popular Culture; or, Has Pike Peaked?" *Kansas History: A Journal of the Central Plains* 29, no. 1 (Spring 2006): 48–59.

Orsi, Jared. "Zebulon Pike and His 'Frozen Lads': Bodies, Nationalism, and the West in the Early Republic." *Western Historical Quarterly* 42, no. 1 (Spring 2011): 55–75.

Peterson, William J. "The Zebulon M. Pike Expedition." *Palimpsest* 49, no. 2 (1968): 41–80.

Pike, Donald G. "Reconnoitering the Barrie: Early Spanish and American Exploration of the Rockies." *American West* 9, no. 5 (1972): 28–33, 60.

Platoff, Anne M. "The Pike-Pawnee Flag Incident: Re-examining a Vexillological Legend." *The Raven: A Journal of Vexillology* 6 (1999): 1–8.

Ronda, James P. "The Adventures of Zebulon Montgomery Pike." In *Beyond Lewis and Clark: The Army Explores the West,* 11–16. Tacoma: Washington State Historical Society, 2003.

———. "Dreams and Discoveries: Exploring the American West, 1760–1815." *William and Mary Quarterly* 46, no. 1 (January 1989): 145–62.

———. "A Moment in Time: The West, September 1806." *Montana* 44, no. 4 (1994): 2–15.

Sanborn, Theo A. "The Story of the Pawnee Village in Republican County, Kansas." *Kansas Historical Quarterly* 39, no. 1 (1973): 1–11.

Scheffer, Theodore H. "Following Pike's Expedition from the Smoky Hill to the Solomon." *Kansas Historical Quarterly* 15 (1947): 240–47.

Shepherd, William R. "Papers Bearing on James Wilkinson's Relations with Spain, 1787–1816." *American Historical Review* 9 (July 1904): 748–66.

———. "Wilkinson and the Beginnings of the Spanish Conspiracy." *American Historical Review* 9 (April 1904): 490–506.

Warner, Robert M. "The Death of Zebulon Pike." *Colorado Magazine* 32 (April 1955): 105–109.

Whiting, Henry. "Life of Zebulon Montgomery Pike." In *Lives of County Rumford, Zebulon Montgomery Pike, and Samuel Gorton,* by James Renwick, Henry Whiting, and John M. Mackie, 217–314. Boston: Charles C. Little and James Brown, 1845.

Wood, Gordon S. "The Real Treason of Aaron Burr." *Proceedings of the American Philosophical Society* 143 (June 1999): 280–95.

## Books

Abernethy, Thomas P. *The Burr Conspiracy.* New York: Oxford University Press, 1954.

Adams, Henry. *History of the United States of America during the Administrations of Thomas Jefferson.* Reprint, New York: Library Classics, 1986.

Allen, John Logan. *Passage through the Garden: Lewis and Clark and the Image of the American Northwest.* Urbana: University of Illinois Press, 1975.

Baker, Nina Brown. *Pike of Pike's Peak.* New York: Harcourt, Brace, 1953.

Beers, Henry P. *French and Spanish Records of Louisiana: A Bibliographic Guide to Archive and Manuscript Sources.* Baton Rouge: Louisiana State University Press, 1989.

Beirne, Francis F. *Shout Treason: The Trials of Aaron Burr.* New York: Hastings House, 1959.

Benn, Carl. *The Battle of York.* Belleville, Ont.: Mika Publishing, 1984.

———. *Historic Fort York, 1793–1993.* Toronto: Natural Heritage/Natural History, 1993.

Bennet, Robert Ames. *A Volunteer with Pike.* Chicago: A. C. McClurg and Co., 1909.

Bernstein, R. B. *Thomas Jefferson.* New York: Oxford University Press, 2003.

Blevins, Tim, Matt Mayberry, Chris Nicholl, Calvin P. Otto, and Nancy Thaler, eds. *To Spare No Pains: Zebulon Montgomery Pike and His 1806–1807 Southwest Expedition.* Colorado Springs, Colo.: Clausen Books, 2007.

Buckley, Jay H. *William Clark: Indian Diplomat.* Norman: University of Oklahoma Press, 2008.

Calloway, Colin. *One Vast Winter Count: The Native American West before Lewis and Clark.* Lincoln: University of Nebraska Press, 2003.

Carter, Carrol Joe. *Pike in Colorado.* Fort Collins, Colo.: Old Army Press, 1978.

Carter, Harvey L. *Zebulon Montgomery Pike: Pathfinder and Patriot.* Colorado Springs, Colo.: Dentan Print Co., 1956.

Cohen, I. Bernard. *Science and the Founding Fathers: Science in the Political Thought of Thomas Jefferson, Benjamin Franklin, John Adams, and James Madison.* New York: W. W. Norton, 1997.

Conrad, Glenn R., and Carl A. Brasseaux. *A Selected Bibliography of Scholarly Literature on Colonial Louisiana and New France.* Lafayette: University of Southwestern Louisiana, 1982.

Cook, Warren L. *Flood Tide of Empire: Spain and the Pacific Northwest, 1543–1819.* New Haven, Conn.: Yale University Press, 1973.

Cox, Isaac J. *The Early Exploration of Louisiana.* Cincinnati: University of Cincinnati Press, 1906.

Cumberland, Barlow. *The Battle of York: An Account of the Eight Hours' Battle from the Humber Bay to the Old Fort in the Defense of York on 27th April, 1813.* Toronto: W. Briggs, 1913.

DeConde, Alexander. *This Affair of Louisiana.* New York: Charles Scribner's Sons, 1976.

DeWitt, Donald. *Pike and Pike's Peak.* Colorado Springs, Colo.: Gowdy-Simmons Press, 1906.

DuVal, Kathleen. *The Native Ground: Indians and Colonists in the Heart of the Continent.* Philadelphia: University of Pennsylvania, 2006.

Glazier, Willard. *Headwaters of the Mississippi: Biographical Sketches of Early and Recent Explorers of the Great River, and a Full Account of the Discovery and Location of Its True Sources in a Lake beyond Itasca.* New York: Rand, McNally, 1893.

Goetzmann, William H. *Army Exploration in the American West, 1803–1863.* New Haven, Conn.: Yale University Press, 1959.

———. *Exploration and Empire: The Explorer and the Scientist in the Winning of the American West.* New York: Alfred Knopf, 1966.

Greely, A. W. *Men of Achievement: Explorers and Travelers.* New York: Charles Scribner's Sons, 1893.

Hämäläinen, Pekka. *The Comanche Empire.* New Haven, Conn.: Yale University Press, 2008.

Hay, Thomas R., and M. R. Werner. *The Admirable Trumpeter: A Biography of General James Wilkinson.* Garden City, N.Y.: Doubleday, Doran and Co., 1941.

Heitman, Francis B. *Historical Register and Dictionary of the United States Army from Its Organization, September 29, 1789, to March 2, 1903.* 2 vols. Washington, D.C.: Government Printing Office, 1903. Reprint, Urbana: University of Illinois Press, 1965.

Helferich, Gerard. *Humboldt's Cosmos: Alexander von Humboldt and the Latin American Journey Changed the Way We See the World.* New York: Gotham Books, 2004.

Hickey, Donald R. *The War of 1812: A Forgotten Conflict.* Urbana: University of Illinois Press, 1989.

Hill, Roscoe R. *Descriptive Catalogue of the Documents Relating to the History of the United States in the Papeles Procedentes de Cuba Deposited in the Archivo General de Indias at Seville.* Washington, D.C.: Carnegie Institution of Washington, 1916.

Hoffer, Peter Charles. *The Treason Trials of Aaron Burr.* Lawrence: University Press of Kansas, 2008.

Hollon, W. Eugene. *The Lost Pathfinder: Zebulon Montgomery Pike.* Norman: University of Oklahoma Press, 1949.

Hutchins, John M. *Lieutenant Zebulon M. Pike Climbs His First Peak: The U.S. Army Expedition to the Sources of the Mississippi, 1805–1806.* Lakewood, Colo.: Avrooman-Apfelwald Press, 2006.

Hyslop, Stephen G. *Bound for Santa Fe: The Road to New Mexico and the American Conquest, 1806–1848.* Norman: University of Oklahoma Press, 2002.

Isenberg, Nancy. *Fallen Founder: The Life of Aaron Burr.* New York: Viking, 2007.

Jackson, Donald. *Thomas Jefferson and the Rocky Mountains: Exploring West from Monticello.* 1981. Reprint, Norman: University of Oklahoma Press, 2002.

Jacobs, James R. *Tarnished Warrior: Major-General James Wilkinson.* New York: Macmillan, 1938.

Kastor, Peter J. *The Nation's Crucible: The Louisiana Purchase and the Creation of America.* New Haven, Conn.: Yale University Press, 2004.

Kennedy, Roger G. *Mr. Jefferson's Lost Cause: Land, Farmers, Slavery, and the Louisiana Purchase.* New York: Oxford University Press, 2003.

Kessell, John L. *Spain in the Southwest: A Narrative History of Colonial New Mexico, Arizona, Texas, and California.* Norman: University of Oklahoma Press, 2002.

Kukla, Jon. *A Wilderness So Immense: The Louisiana Purchase and the Destiny of America.* New York: Alfred A. Knopf, 2003.

Lewis, James E., Jr. *The American Union and the Problem of Neighborhood: The United States and the Collapse of the Spanish Empire, 1783–1829.* Chapel Hill: University of North Carolina Press, 1998.

Linklater, Andro. *An Artist in Treason: The Extraordinary Double Life of General James Wilkinson.* New York: Walker Publishing, 2009.

Lomask, Milton. *Aaron Burr.* 2 vols. New York: Farrar, Strauss and Giroux, 1979, 1982.

McCaleb, Walter F. *The Aaron Burr Conspiracy and a New Light on Aaron Burr.* 1903. Reprint, New York: Argosy-Antiquarian, 1966.

Melton, Buckner F., Jr. *Aaron Burr: Conspiracy to Treason.* New York: John Wiley and Sons, 2002.

Montgomery, M. R. *Jefferson and the Gun Men: How the West Was Almost Lost.* New York: Crown Publishers, 2000.

Onuf, Peter S. *Jefferson's Empire: The Language of Nationhood.* Charlottesville: University of Virginia Press, 2000.

———. *The Mind of Thomas Jefferson.* Charlottesville: University of Virginia Press, 2007.

Pasley, Jeffrey, Andrew W. Robertson, and David Waldstreicher, eds. *Beyond the Founders: New Approaches to the Political History of the Early Republic.* Chapel Hill: University of North Carolina Press, 2004.

Pike, Allen R. *The Family of "John Pike of Newbury, Massachusetts, 1635–1995."* Carmel, N.Y.: Penobscot Press, 1995.

Renwick, James, Henry Whiting, and John M. Mackie. *Lives of Count Rumford, Zebulon Montgomery Pike, and Samuel Gorton.* Boston: C. C. Little and J. Brown, 1845.

Sabin, Edwin L. *With Lieutenant Pike.* Philadelphia: J. B. Lippincott, 1919.

Sadosky, Leonard J. *Revolutionary Negotiations: Indians, Empires, and Diplomats in the Founding of America.* Charlottesville: University of Virginia Press, 2010.

Schachner, Nathan. *Aaron Burr.* New York: A. S. Barnes, 1961.

Severin, Timothy. *Explorers of the Mississippi.* Minneapolis: University of Minnesota Press, 2002.

Sharp, James Roger. *The Deadlocked Election of 1800: Jefferson, Burr, and the Union in the Balance.* Lawrence: University Press of Kansas, 2010.

Sheehan, Bernard W. *Seeds of Extinction: Jeffersonian Philanthropy and the American Indian.* Chapel Hill: University of North Carolina Press, 1973.

Smelser, Marshall. *The Democratic Republic, 1801–1815.* New York: Harper and Row, 1968.

Stagg, J. C. A. *Borderlines and Borderlands: James Madison and the Spanish-American Frontier, 1776–1821.* New Haven, Conn.: Yale University Press, 2009.

———. *Mr. Madison's War: Politics, Diplomacy, and Warfare in the Early American Republic, 1783–1830.* Princeton: Princeton University Press, 1983.

Taylor, Alan. *The Civil War of 1812: American Citizens, British Subjects, Irish Rebels and Indian Allies.* New York: Alfred A. Knopf, 2010.

Terrell, John Upton. *Zebulon Pike: The Life and Times of an Adventurer.* New York: Weybright and Talley, 1968.

Tucker, Robert W., and David C. Hendrickson. *Empire of Liberty: The Statecraft of Thomas Jefferson.* New York: Oxford University Press, 1990.

Wallace, Anthony F. C. *Jefferson and the Indians: The Tragic Fate of the First Americans.* Cambridge, Mass.: Harvard University Press, 1999.

Weber, David J. *The Spanish Frontier in North America.* New Haven, Conn.: Yale University Press, 1992.

Wheat, Carl I., ed. *Mapping the Trans-Mississippi West, 1540–1861.* 5 vols. San Francisco: Institute of Historical Cartography, 1957–63.

Wheelan, Joseph. *Jefferson's Vendetta: The Pursuit of Aaron Burr and the Judiciary.* New York: Carroll and Graf, 2005.

White, Richard. *The Middle Ground: Indians, Empires, and Republics in the Great Lakes Region, 1650–1815.* Cambridge: Cambridge University Press, 1991.

Wood, Gordon S. *Empire of Liberty: A History of the Early Republic, 1789–1815.* New York: Oxford University Press, 2009.

# Contributors

**John Logan Allen**, professor emeritus of geography at the University of Wyoming, is the author of several books, including *Passage through the Garden: Lewis and Clark and the Image of the American West,* and editor of the three-volume *North American Exploration.*

**Jay H. Buckley**, associate professor of history at Brigham Young University, is the author of *William Clark: Indian Diplomat* and coauthor of *By His Own Hand? The Mysterious Death of Meriwether Lewis.*

**William E. Foley** is professor emeritus of history at the University of Central Missouri. He is the general editor of the Missouri Biography Series and author or editor of numerous books, including *Wilderness Journey: The Life of William Clark* and *The Genesis of Missouri: From Wilderness Outpost to Statehood.*

**Matthew L. Harris**, associate professor of history at Colorado State University–Pueblo, is the coauthor of the forthcoming book *The Founding Fathers and the Debate over Religion in Revolutionary America* and numerous essays and articles on the founding era and early republic.

**Leo E. Oliva** taught history at Fort Hays State University and is the author of numerous books on the American West, including *Soldiers on the Santa Fe Trail* and *Fort Union and the Frontier Army in the Southwest.*

**Jared Orsi**, associate professor of history at Colorado State University, Fort Collins, is the author of *Hazardous Metropolis: Flooding and Urban Ecology in Los Angeles* and other works on American environmental history and the American West.

**James P. Ronda** held the H. G. Barnard Chair in Western History at the University of Tulsa, where he is a professor emeritus of history. He is the author of numerous works, including *Astoria and Empire* and *Lewis and Clark among the Indians.*

# Index